Xmas 2003

Hello,

We were going to write something cool and christmassy, but then we realised...

ALL CITY

THE BOOK ABOUT TAKING SPACE

COMPILED BY PAUL 107

WRITING IN THIS BOOK IS ILLEGAL.
DEFACING OF PROPERTY IS NOT, AND NEVER
COULD BE, COOL.

So we did it!

JRD + SD.

ECW PRESS
ecwpress.com

Published by ECW PRESS
2120 Queen Street East, Suite 200, Toronto, Ontario, Canada M4E 1E2

NATIONAL LIBRARY OF CANADA CATALOGUING IN PUBLICATION DATA

Paul 107
All-city: the book about taking space / Paul 107.
ISBN 1-55022-568-5
1. Graffiti. I. Title.
GT3912.P39 2003 302.2'22 C2002-905428-1

Editor: Emma Jane
Art direction: Sekondhand Projects
Design and illustrations: Dyske and Turf
Production: Emma McKay
Printing: Imago
Cover design: Sekondhand Projects
Front cover photo: Paul 107

This book is set in Univers and Hardcore

The publication of *All-City: The Book about Taking Space* has been generously supported by the Canada Council, the Ontario Arts Council, and the Government of Canada through the Book Publishing Industry Development Program.

Canadä

DISTRIBUTION

Canada: Jaguar Book Group, 100 Armstrong Avenue, Georgetown, ON L7G 5S4

United States: Independent Publishers Group, 814 North Franklin Street, Chicago, Illinois 60610

Europe: Turnaround Publisher Services, Unit 3, Olympia Trading Estate, Coburg Road, Wood Green, London N2Z 6T2

Australia and New Zealand: Wakefield Press, 1 The Parade West (Box 2266), Kent Town, South Australia 5071

PRINTED AND BOUND IN SINGAPORE

ECW PRESS
ecwpress.com

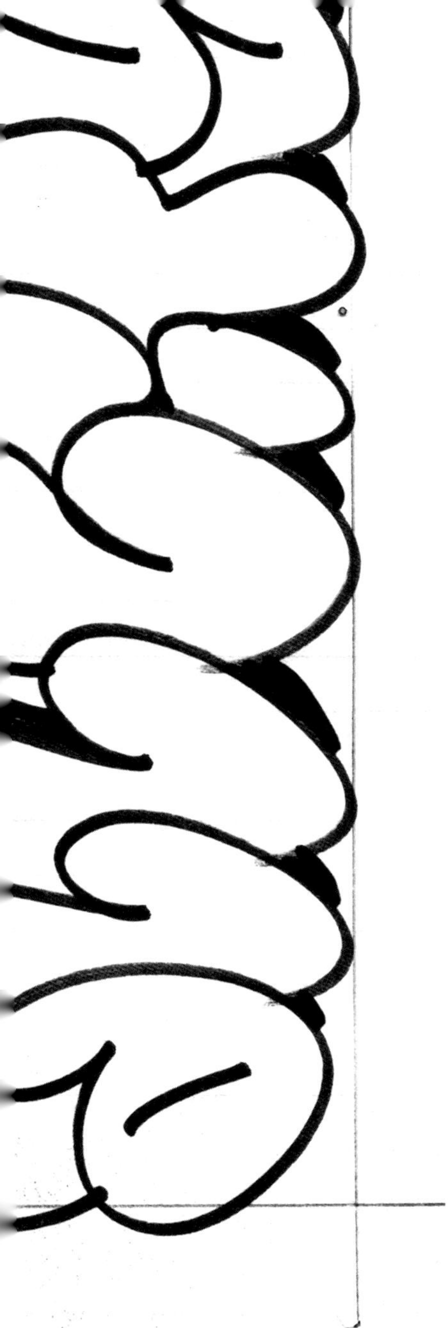

CONTENTS

CONTRIBUTORS

(Photos, Time, or Patience):

Shok One, Silvio Magaglio, Turf One, Dyske, Emma Jane, Rebel, Amaze, Desa, Grey, Min One, Chino, Colorz, Creez, Earl, Céline Cabrolier, Gutch, Legz, Flow, Mersh JKRew, Vivian Host, Hazel Bell-Koski, Desa, Auto, Neeks, Kaves, Raudia Kepper, KR

THANKS: Mom (the Bo Jackson of parenthood), Emma Jane (what more can I say), Ian Alexander, Jean Labourdette, Scott Clyke, Osea One, Tim Ring, *Pound* magazine, Flow, Dyske, Kas, and Seaz, The whole GYP, Simahlak, David Macklovitch, A-Trak, Mersh, Shok, Silvio Magaglio, Tommy (Ehh?), Chino, Ket, Sake, Cose, Jennifer Elliott, PF Guay, S.O.C., *Under Pressure* magazine, PSC/Verdun, Malakoff, Longeuil, and the ECW gang.

DISCLAIMER

Graffiti is vandalism. Vandalism is against the law. No one involved in this book is encouraging you to do any of this. This is one of those "if he jumps off a bridge it doesn't mean I have to" scenarios....

DEDICATED TO BABIES THAT CAME FEET FIRST.

INTRO

I was never really into art. I grew up on rap, so by association, I thought graffiti was alright. I didn't really like the pieces, though. I mean, I thought they looked hot on trains and rooftops, but seeing a wall done up nice in the neighborhood really wasn't my high. I liked tags and throwups because they were stamped all over the city, everywhere you went. I couldn't understand why and how people were doing this. I think my fascination had something to do with the degree of difficulty involved in the act, and the risks these guys were taking. That, and I guess growing up in the '80s, I was used to marketers plastering my surroundings with product propaganda. Bombing the streets was kind of like those marketing campaigns, except without the possibility of financial gain. I wanted to understand why people write like that, and what motivates them to keep doing it, because the guys that were really up had to be treating it like a job. Their only goal was to go all-city; to take all the space.

All I wanted to know was why.

All I ever figured out was how.

This book contains photos, interviews with bombers from different parts of the world, and some of the things I picked up along the way (mostly things writers complained that toys didn't know). Writing is something that's handed down from generation to generation. There are no set rules, so trying to make a textbook or a "how to" on the subject would be retarded. Besides, how can you make rules for something that's already illegal?

All you can really do is go out and do it. It's pure. This is the side of graffiti they don't talk about in art galleries. This graffiti locks down your neighborhood with fill-ins, holding it hostage with tags etched into windows. It's an addiction for some—an all-consuming addiction—one that ruins lives. It's about never leaving your home without paint or a marker and feeling the need to scribble on everything you see. It's about testing paint on your bedroom walls and ruining your clothes. It's about missions at four in the morning, stealing paint, hitting rooftops, subway stations, and getting chased by the police. It's about getting famous, catching wreck, and going all-city, and it almost always ends with court dates.

Anyone with the ambition to get up should remember something: a whole bunch of people did this before you, so don't expect to be an innovator. All you can do is more, then eventually more with style, and for longer. There are a million kids who paint for six months and think they're on top of the world, only to fade away shortly thereafter. Graffiti isn't a sprint. It's more like a marathon.

– Paul 107

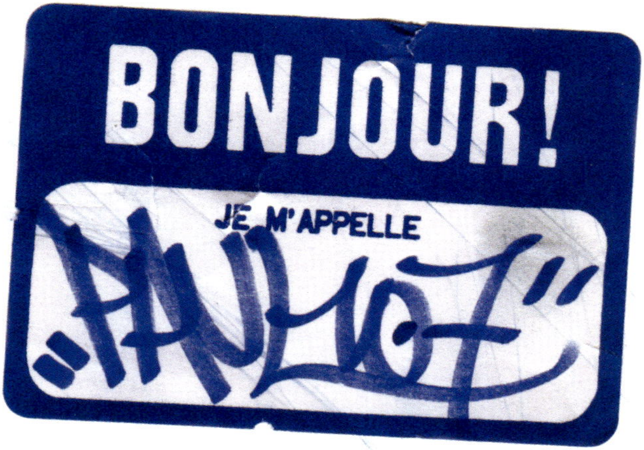

CHOOSING A NAME

When you are picking a name, you must take a few things into consideration. As cool as writing your real name sounds, it's dumb—that's right up there on the "when I get busted I want them to have no doubt who I am" list. Writing the name that you already see up in your hood is also not the flavor. As brilliant as names like Best, King, Ace, Devil, Snake, Gunman, and Badboy sound at the time, they should be reserved for the 12-year-old demographic. The best way to go about it is to choose a name that means something to you, that sounds good, and that has good letters. Don't worry too much about someone already having written it. Odds are somebody is writing the same name in three other cities anyway. It's what you do with the name that matters: get it up.

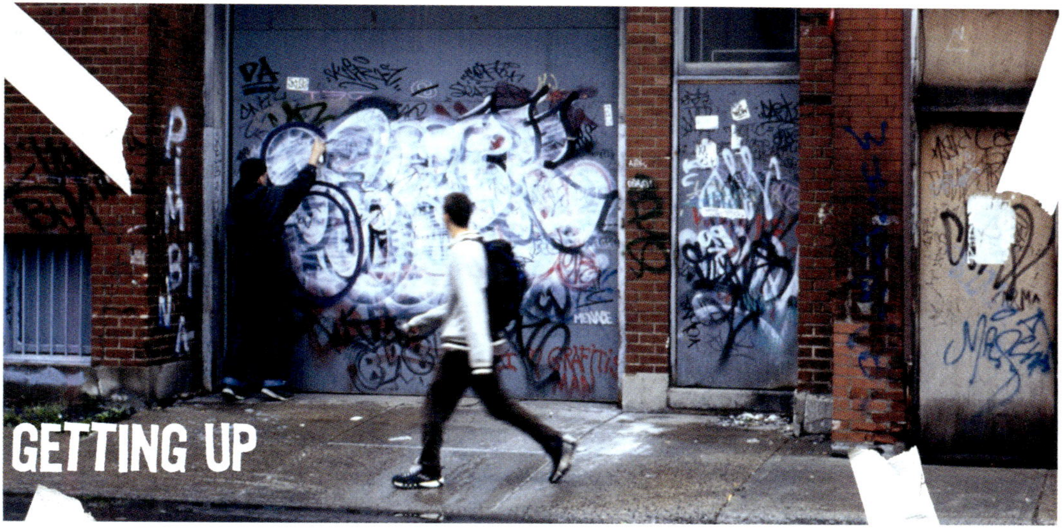

GETTING UP

No one's going to tell you what you can and can't hit. After all, the idea is to paint as much as you can, right? You should, however, avoid hitting places of worship, art installations, cars, small businesses (they have little to no dough), and statues. Basically, stay away from anything that strikes a chord with the "little people." It will save you a lot of grief in the future.

In the beginning, tag everything. Go all out.

Once you've saturated your immediate surroundings, it will be time to hit other neighborhoods. A good way to do that is to choose a different subway station every night and hit a four- to six-block radius around the station. Painting things that move is a good idea. Find out where the city keeps its garbage trucks, buses, and subway cars. They go all-city all day, but it's one of those risk-versus-reward scenarios. Yeah, it will make a nice flick, but will it run? And if so, for how long? Some companies have all-white trucks. Those are the best to get. They rarely get buffed and can be anywhere on any given Sunday.

Once the city is locked down, think of the motorists. Many people commute into the city by car. Lock down the highways and the bridges. People are usually in bumper-to-bumper traffic and mad pissed. Give them a little eye candy; rock rooftops along the highways, go big. If it's a virgin rooftop, hit it with a blockbuster and a few fill-ins—don't leave any room. Make it yours.

CREWS

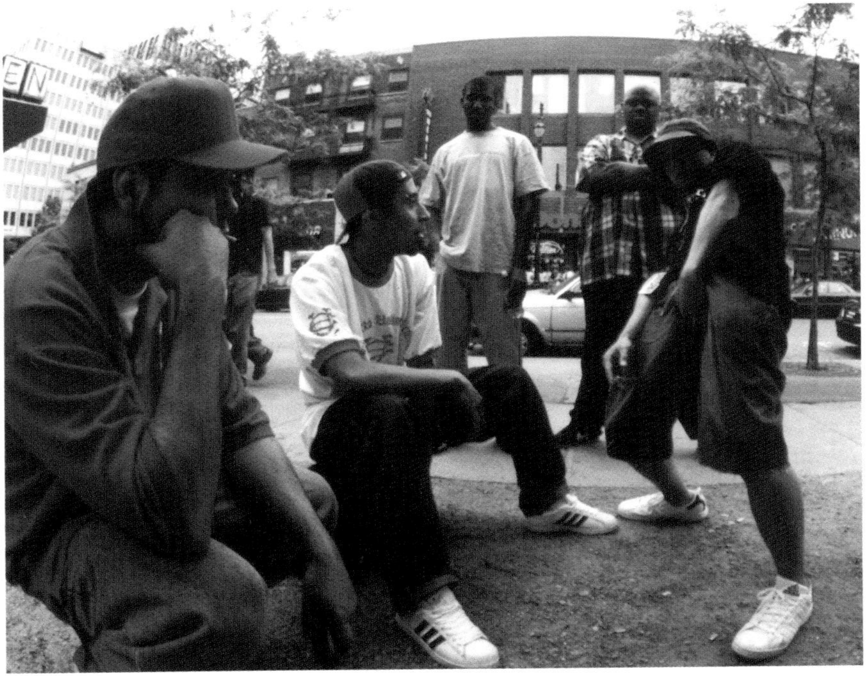

Being in a crew is way overrated. Yes, it's nice to have a support system, a bunch of guys you can depend on. But fact of the matter is that nine times out of ten those same dudes you paint with will jet when there's beef, rat on you when it's convenient, and even set you up. They're also the same dudes that will hate on you when you get more ups than them. Your best bet, if you don't want to paint alone, is to find one dude that you really trust and paint with him.

PAINTING WITH PEOPLE

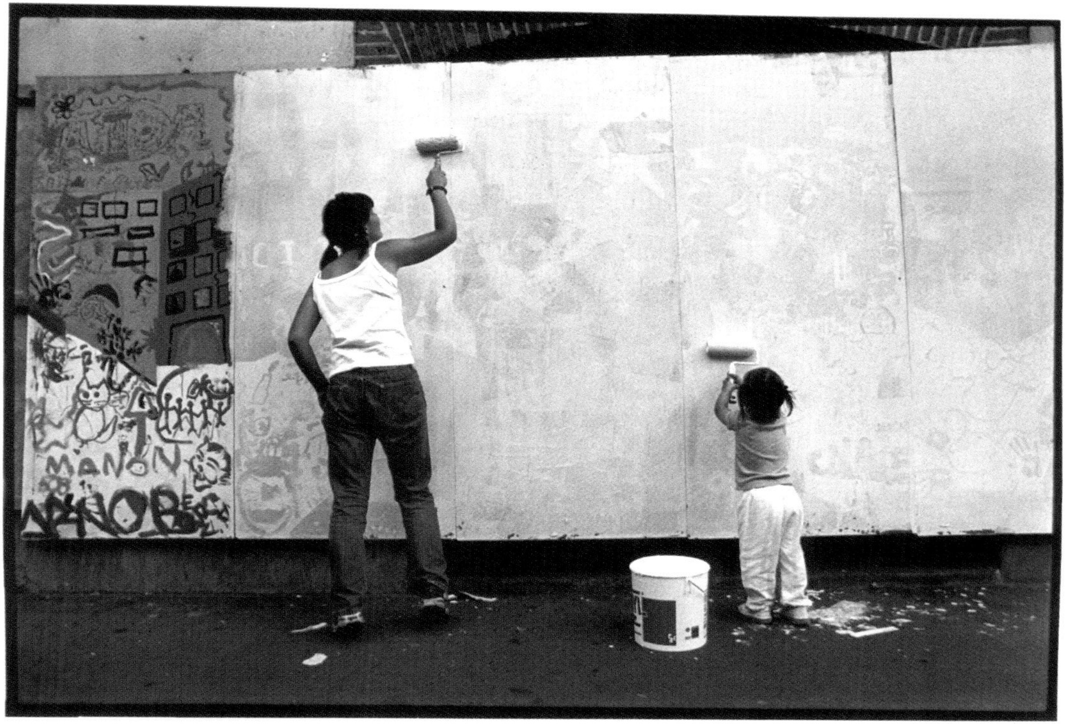

Painting with someone is cool. You got company, plus someone to look out for you. It's like having eyes behind your back, except you don't control those eyes and you can't be sure if they're really looking out. It's a false sense of security, plus you have to share spots, so you end up beefing over who gets the prime real estate and who gets to paint first. If you go first, you will start getting sketched out at the amount of time it takes the person to finish. After all, it does double the time you spend in any given spot. Then there are the paint moochers. "I don't have any paint left, lemme catch a tag," they say. "Well fuck you, you shoulda brought more," is how you should respond.

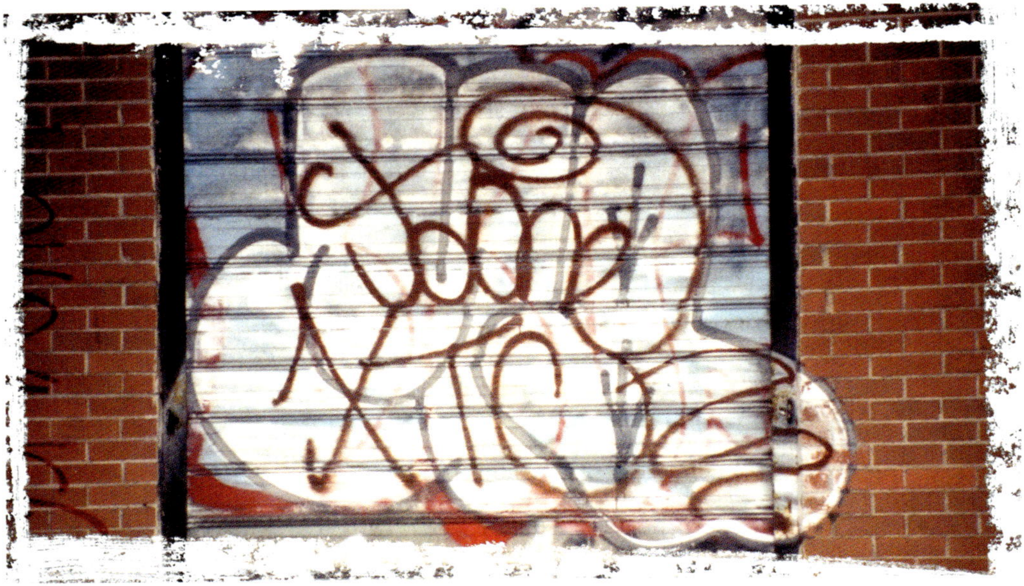

CROSS OUTS

If someone crosses you out, take the spot back. If someone goes over one of your spots and doesn't completely cover it up, take the spot back. If he crosses you out again, find out who he is and give him an eye jammy. Then tell him what you write and why you hit him. Tell him that if he does it again you'll take all his spots, and tell him to expect the same kind of treatment every time he sees you. The idea is to stay away from the politics of graffiti as much as possible. Confronting somebody and discussing problems will only suck you into the graff soap opera. The punch in the face will put everybody in line. It will get around that you don't play.

Another way to play the situation is to find a burner of his, rock a fill-in right in the middle of it, and rub petroleum jelly (Vaseline) all over your throwup. This way he can never come back and fix the burner. Paint can't cover Vaseline. You should write something really obnoxious in your fill-in as well.

EXCUSES

At some point, family members and friends will take notice of your habit. They won't understand why you do it. You will be questioned about it frequently. Here are few of the excuses that will spew from your lips:

1. It's a political statement. Property is bullshit; no one really owns anything. Besides, it was the natives' land first (the last part works best in North America).

2. Just because (insert corporation's name here) has the money to put all these bill-boards up and I'm broke doesn't mean I shouldn't be allowed to do the same thing.

3. It's freedom of expression.

4. It's my art.

5. Everybody's doing it.

6. It's your building? Fuck it, who told you to build it there?

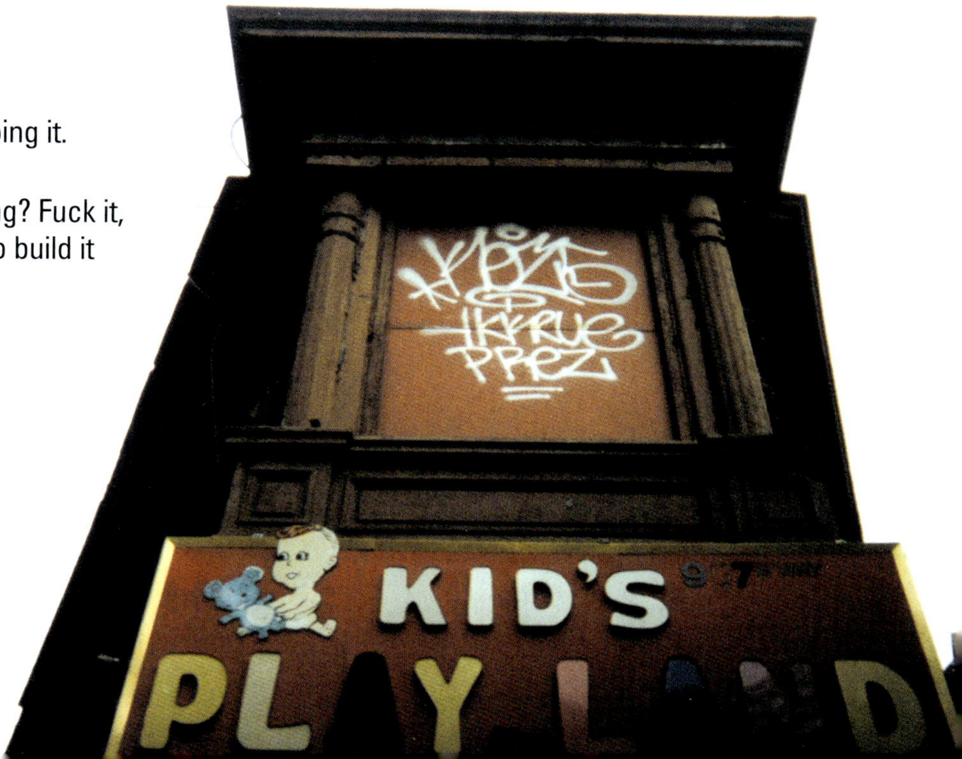

GETTING BUSTED

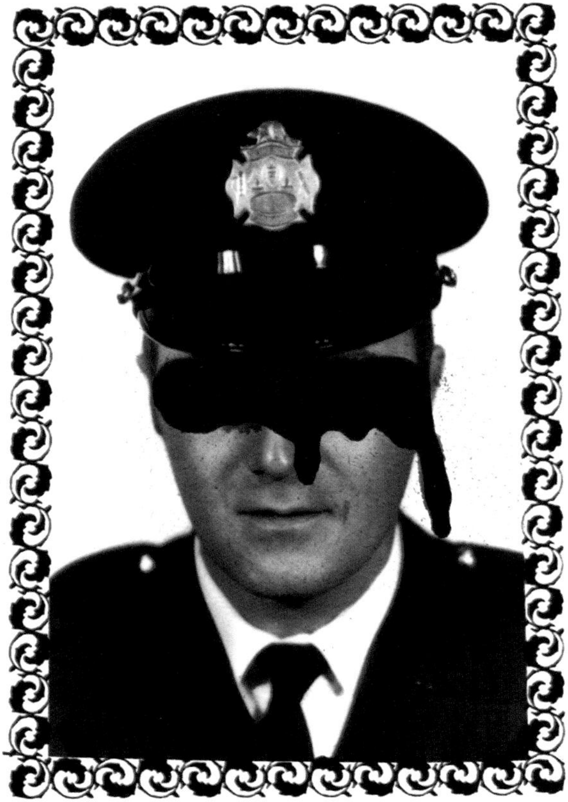

If you get stopped by building security or anyone who isn't a cop, run. Odds are they can't chase you off the property they are paid to protect. Plus they're probably fat. If you're in a crowd and a civilian catches you in the act and grabs you, start yelling: "He grabbed my dick faggot faggot." This may not be the PC thing to do, but it will embarrass the hero. When he loosens his grip, bust a Carl Lewis. Carrying mace or bear spray can also be handy in these situations.

If the real police have you in custody, don't fall for the good cop bad cop routine. No one in the cop car is your friend.

1. Be polite, cooperate. Being a ball-buster only agitates the boys in blue. Plus, they love having their egos stroked—compliments go a long way.
2. Don't speak. Anything you say can and will be used against you. That's real.
3. Don't rat on anyone.
4. Get a lawyer. If you can't afford one, go to Legal Aid. You didn't go to law school, and watching *Law & Order* doesn't make you an expert.
5. Don't admit to anything at all. If no one saw you in action, it's their word against yours.
6. Sometimes, instead of taking you in, cops will make you empty whatever paint you have on yourself. If the option is offered, take it. I don't care how much your jacket cost—court is a bitch.

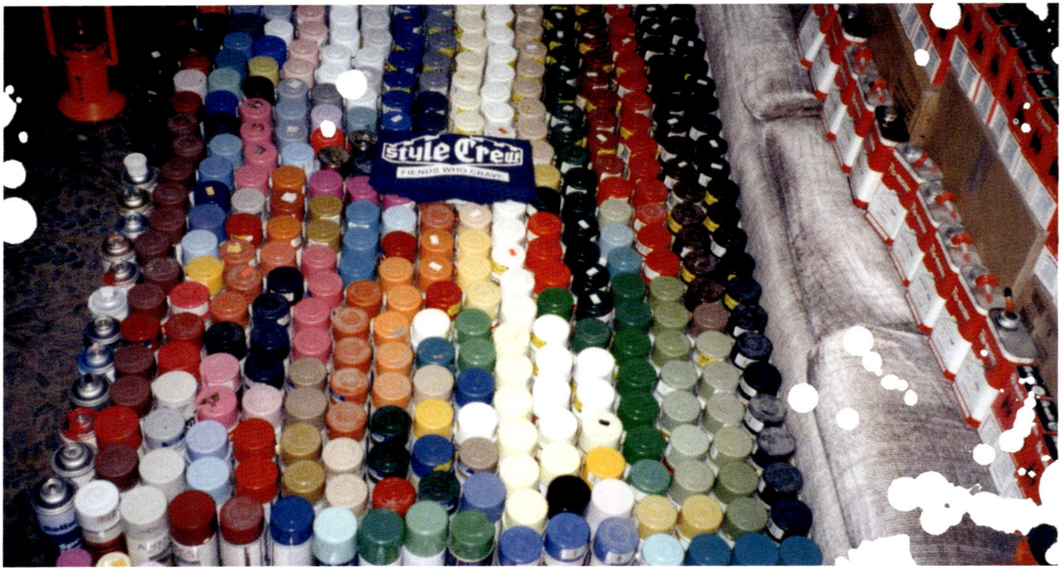

HOME

Your house is where you rest at, where you keep your stuff, and where you probably did most of your research and development. Don't "test" the paint on your bedroom walls, and don't keep pictures of your work, black books, home videos of you rocking the local bread-delivery truck, or any papers or stickers that you've tagged there. When your house gets raided, all these things will be seized and become evidence. Rebel said it best: "Don't shit where you sleep."

GLOVES

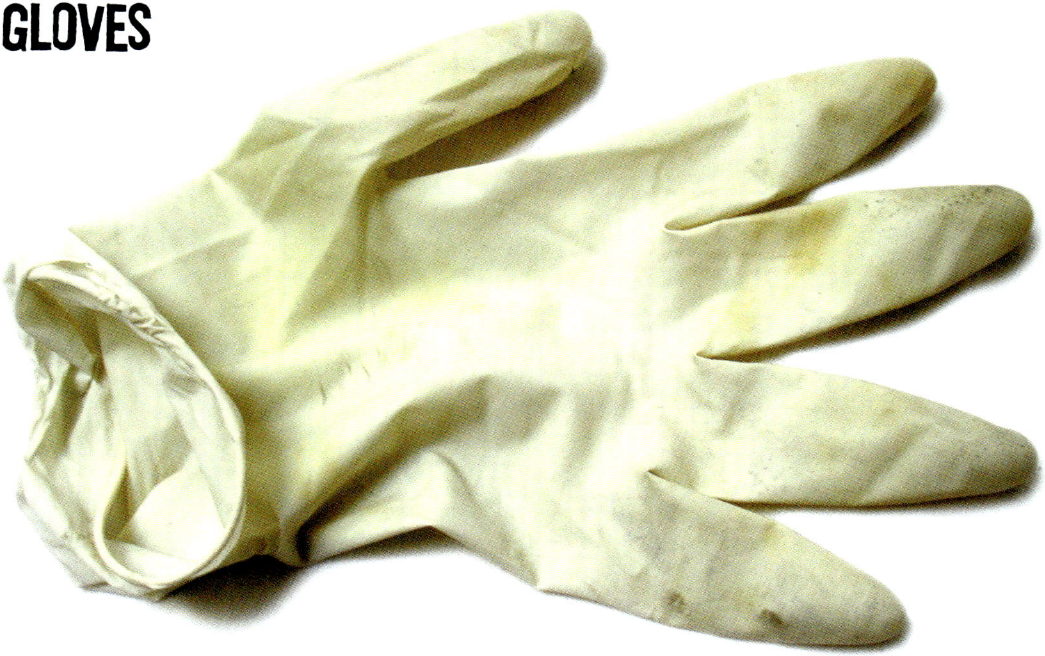

Next time you go to the doctor, bring a backpack. When you get into the exam room, scope it out. Look for a box with latex gloves in it. The box usually looks like the kind that dispenses Kleenex. Put it in your bag right after the nurse leaves, just before the doctor comes in. The gloves are great because they're disposable. Oftentimes, tagging leads to dirty hands, and dirty hands are incriminating.

TAGS

Paint, a marker, your finger in dust—it doesn't matter on what or with what you do it—it's just your signature. It's funny to me, because it's the thing that probably bothers people the most, and in the end, it's the thing a writer probably practiced the most on paper over the years.

MARKERS

Depending on where you live, there are different brands of markers. Pilots are the best investment, in my opinion, because when they run out you can always use the carcass to make a new marker.

MOPS

These are the containers that liquid shoe polish comes in. They're good because they're refillable and easy to come by. They work real nice with KRink and homemade-style inks. Some homemade inks eat through plastic, though, so don't expect it to last long.

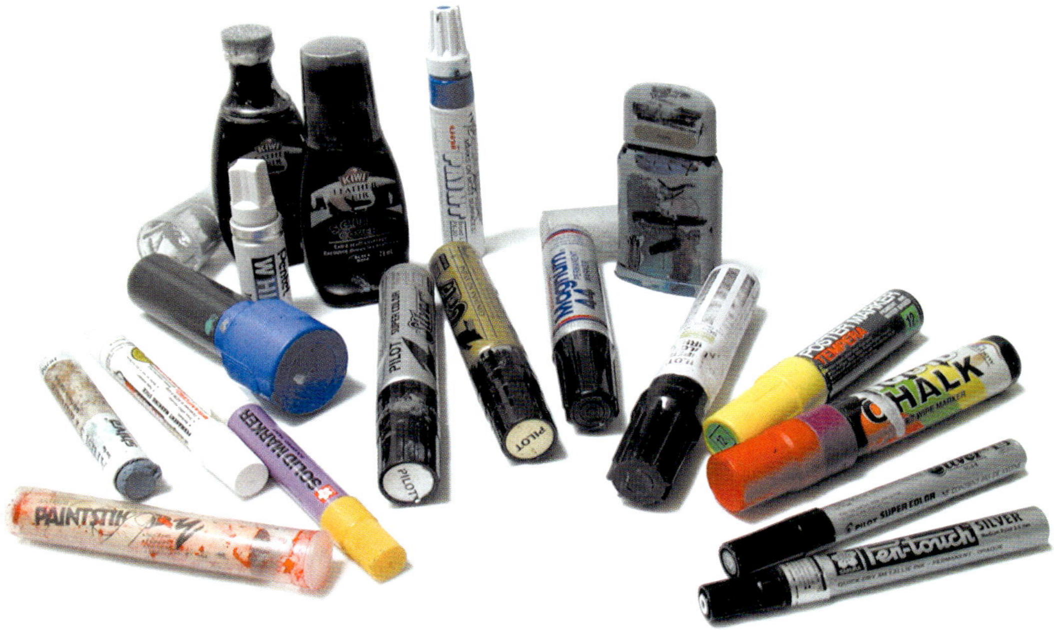
PAINTSTIK
SOLID MARKER
PILOT
SUPER COLOR
PILOT
Magnum 44
PILOT
POSTER MARKER
TEMPERA
CHALK
PILOT SUPER COLOR
Pen-touch
SILVER

BEGINNER MARKER

What you need: a Pilot marker, a mélange of your favorite inks, the felt from a chalkboard eraser, some electrical tape, and a 35 mm film canister.

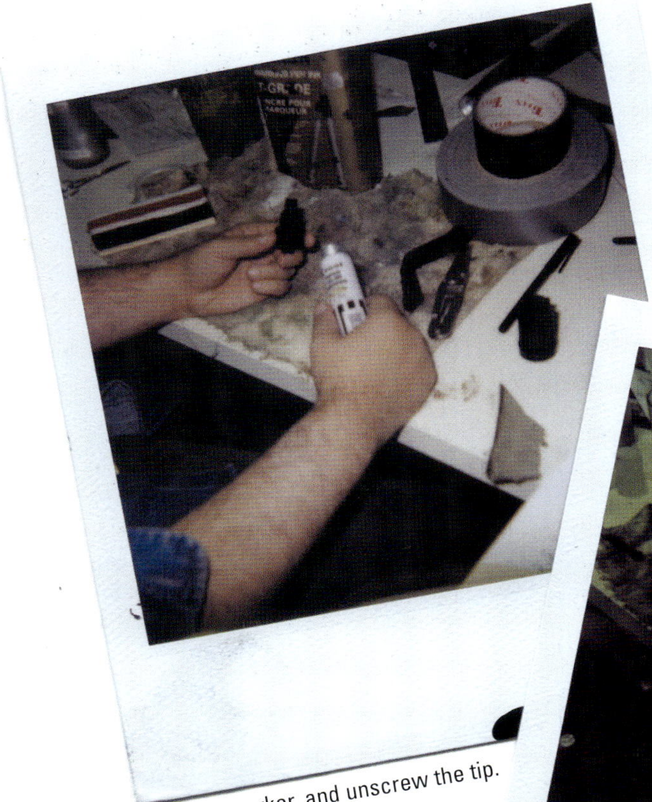

1. Take a Pilot marker, and unscrew the tip.

2. Throw out the tip, the filter, and the cap. All you should be left with is a metal carcass.

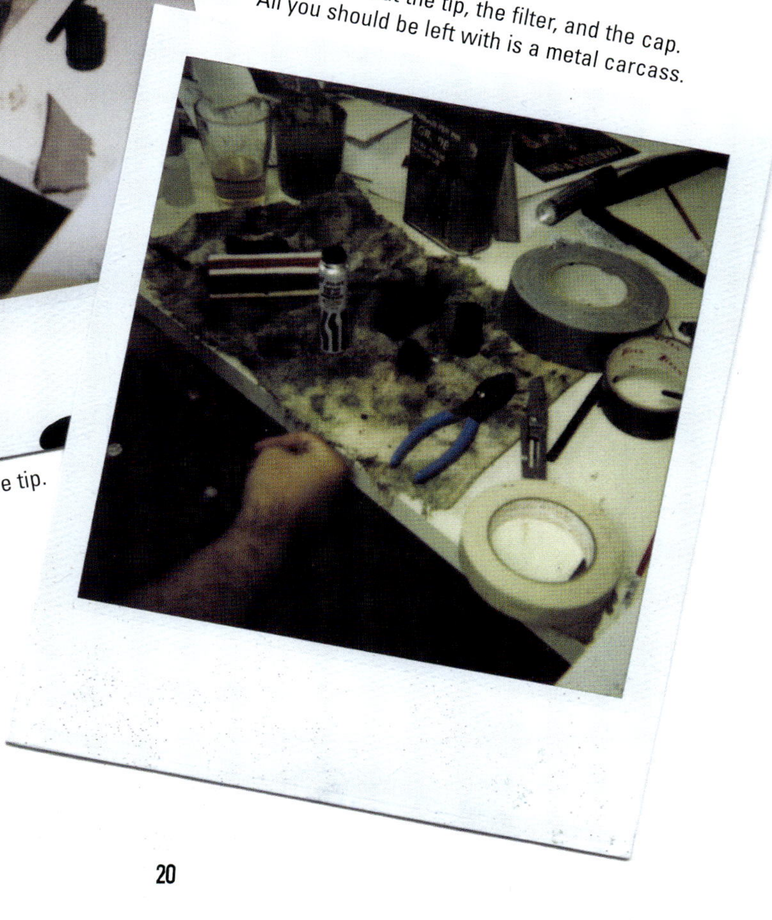

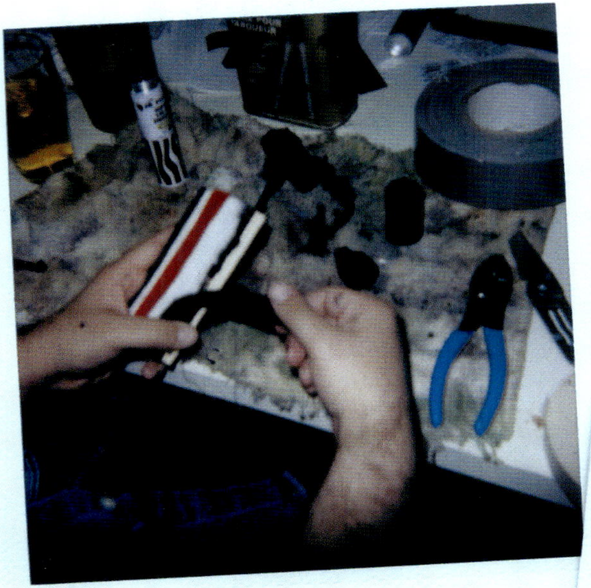

3. Rip a section of the eraser off, and cut it in half. Fold one of the halved eraser pieaces in two. It should be big enough to plug the Pilot carcass.

4. Wrap electrical tape around the opening of the carcass like a hockey player wraps the end of his stick. It should create a knob that will hold the film canister on the Pilot like a cap.

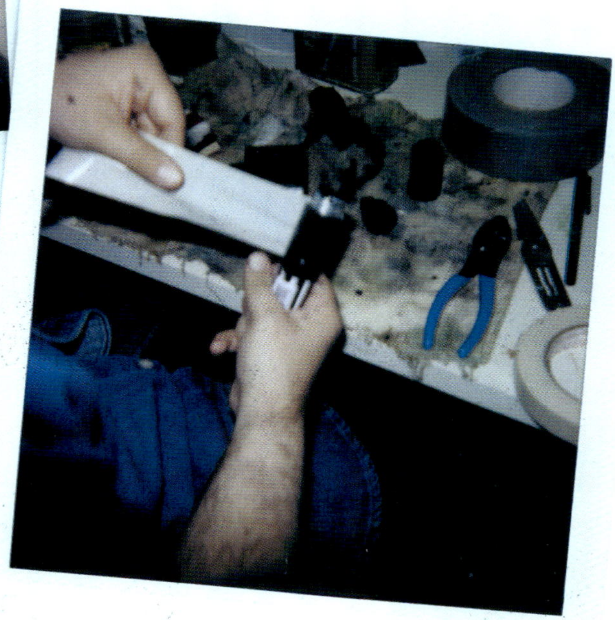

5. Fill the empty carcass with the ink mélange.

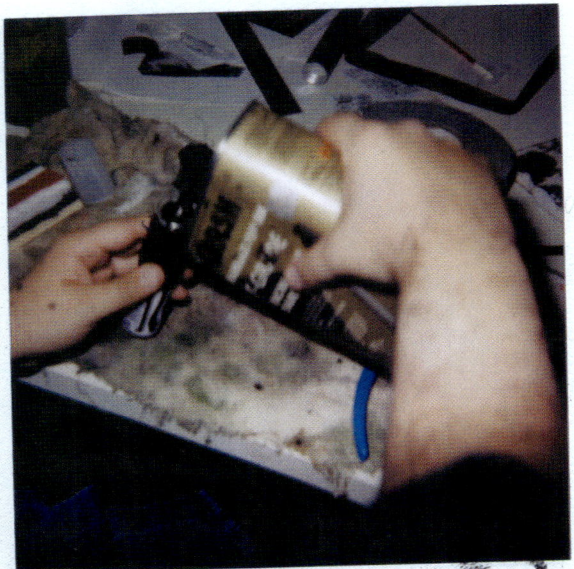

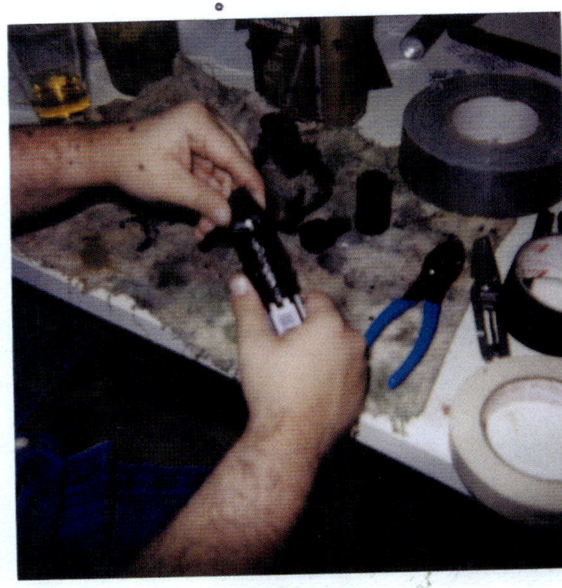

6. Plug the carcass with eraser felt.

7. Cap the tip of the marker with the canister.

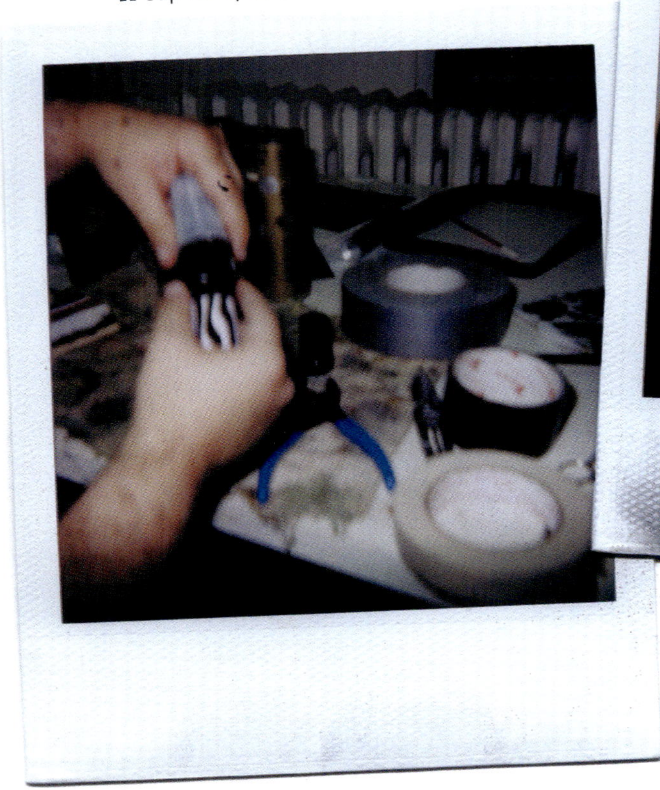

8. Bug out.

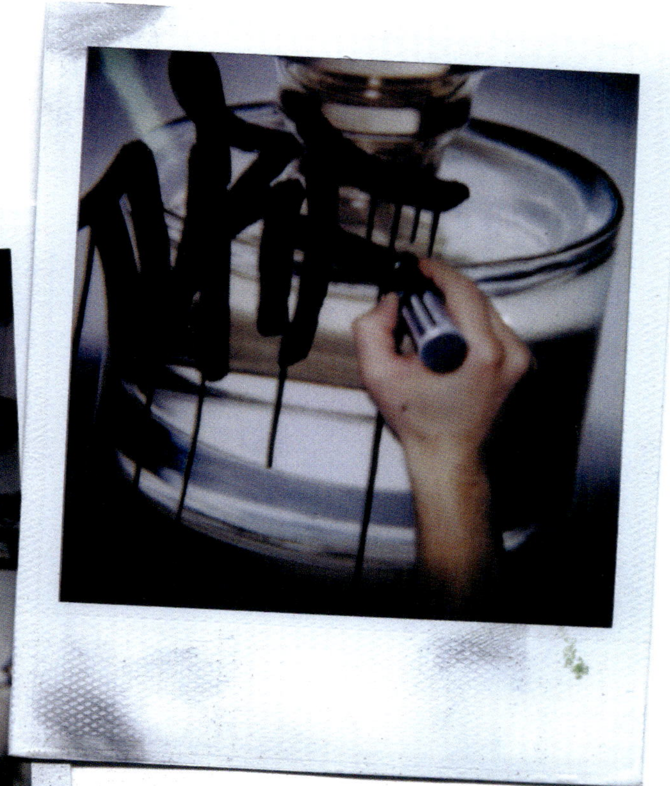

Remember to keep the marker in a plastic bag, and do not turn it over until it's time to use it. This marker is pretty basic, so if you've got a little time on your hands, you'll be able to make drastic improvements to its design.

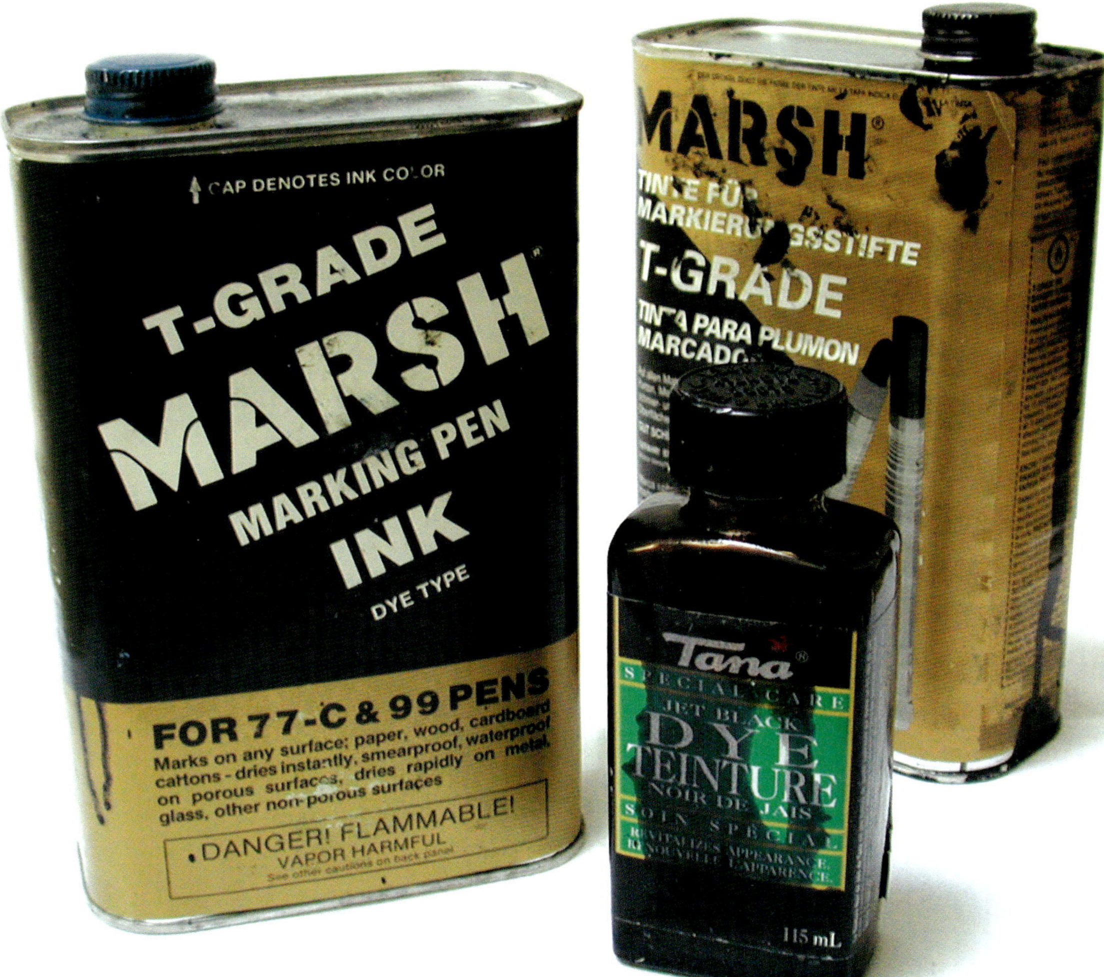
CAP DENOTES INK COLOR
T-GRADE
MARSH
MARKING PEN
INK
DYE TYPE
FOR 77-C & 99 PENS
Marks on any surface; paper, wood, cardboard cartons - dries instantly, smearproof, waterproof on porous surfaces, dries rapidly on metal, glass, other non-porous surfaces
DANGER! FLAMMABLE!
VAPOR HARMFUL
MARSH
T-GRADE
Tana
SPECIAL CARE
JET BLACK
DYE
TEINTURE
NOIR DE JAIS
115 mL

A MÉLANGE OF YOUR FAVORITE INKS

What you need: Marsh, Garvey, Flo-Master, leather dye, whatever else you can find lying around, and a bowl.

1. Fill bowl with equal parts of all the inks you have.

2. Stir it up.

3. Pour into a marker (See "Beginner Marker," above).

LEATHER DYE

Leather dye is really permanent, and the dabber applicator it comes with is just real messy. It's best to carry the container in a sturdy plastic bag. The dye will seep into the pores of most surfaces, including metal and plastics. This means that no matter how hard they scrub, traces will always remain.

EARL'S KITCHEN:
Building a Better Ink

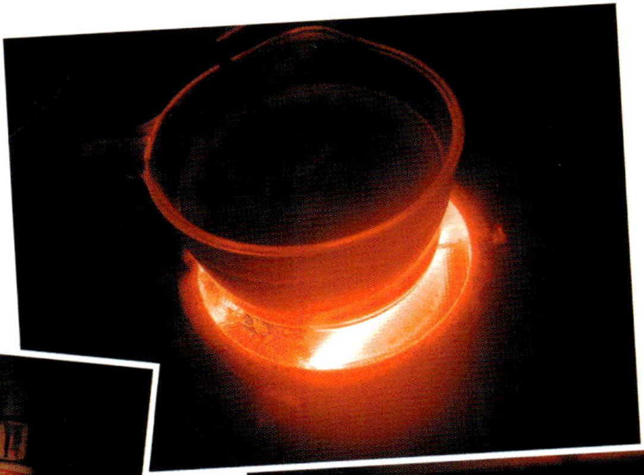

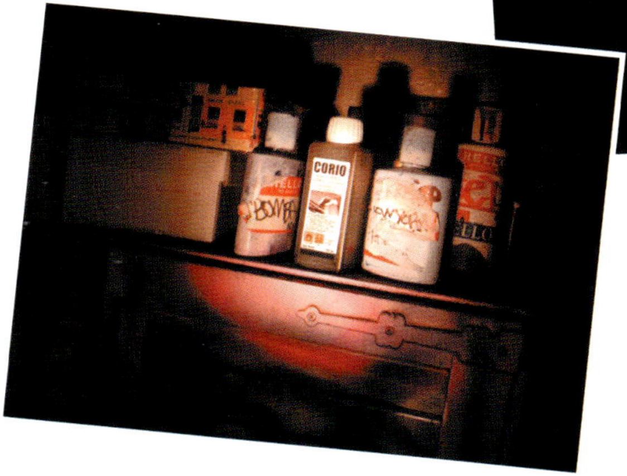

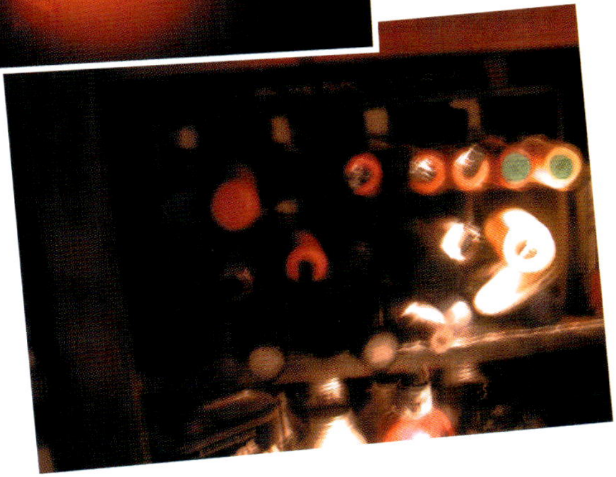

1. Choose a mix of your favorite inks.

2. Put it in the pan.

3. Boil to hell.

4. Add a bit of gentian violet (pigment).

5. Stir well. If the mix turns into a paste, take away from heat and add mo' ink.

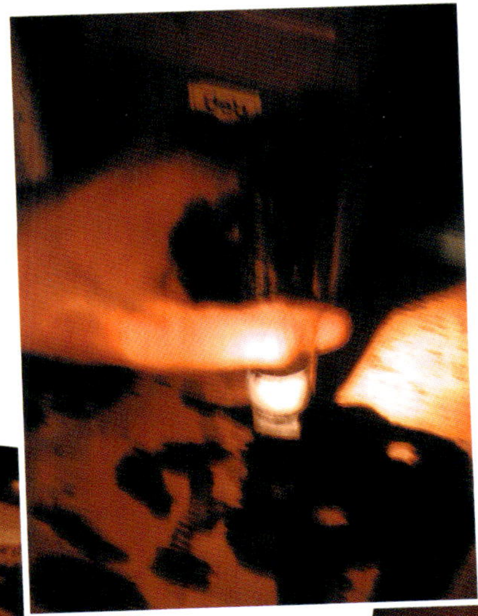

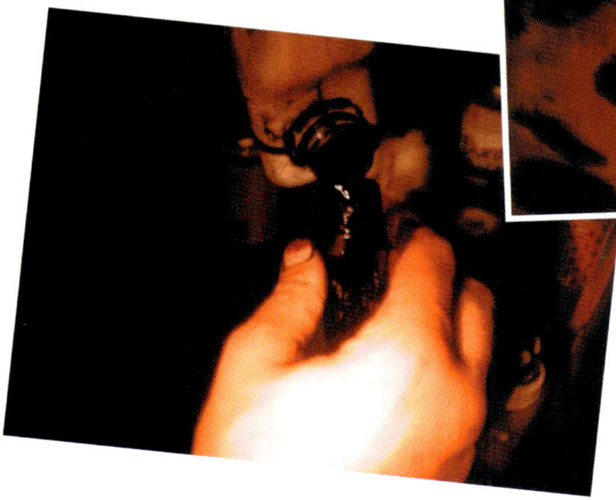

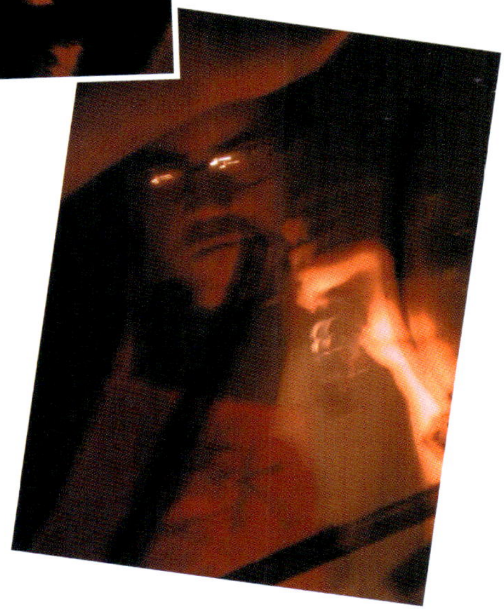

6. Put it in a bottle.

7. Take a good marker.

8. Fill it up!

9. Let the ink flow.

10. Share recipe with friends, and apply to surfaces worldwide.

KR ON KRINK

How long has KRink been around? How did you come up with it?

I first made KRink around 1993, maybe '94. I came up with it kind of by accident. I was working with certain materials, and I noticed that they had certain properties that would be good for an ink. I tested different formulas, and over time I came up with what is now KRink.

Word is you spent years killing San Fran with the ink or "prototypes" of it. Is that true?

I first came up with KRink while living in SF, so that's where the initial field research was done. KRink was an easy way to get up. KRink worked well, had style, and no one else had anything like it. It was a recipe for success. The materials I needed to make KRink were easy to get, and I got them all for free.

How long 'til you got it perfect?

Not long. I knew what I wanted in an ink. I grew up riding bombed trains in the '80s. The insides were all destroyed. There was this guy, Roaches, he had shit on lock. Roaches had tags so drippy they were almost illegible, but you always knew it was him. His shit stood out. To me, that was style.

Also, the insides of trains were exactly that—inside. The tags on the inside of a train rarely, if ever, saw sunlight. The inks that were commonly used on the insides of trains faded when used outdoors.

I didn't bomb trains in the '80s; I came up on streets. I wanted to bring that whole look of the mop tags that I grew up looking at to the streets, and have the tags be perm.

What the best applicator for it? What other applicators will do?

I've tried KRink in a lot of different applicators. I've found that it works best, for me, in the KRink applicators that are available in stores now. Now that KRink is available to the public, it can be so many things to so many people. If you want to use a brush, or a pen, it doesn't matter. Whatever works for you.

Why is it better than any other ink?

KRink is permanent outdoors. That is a quality that you don't find in many inks.

Besides KRink, what other types of markers/inks/paint/etching creams do you fuck with?

I think bucket paint is the next big thing.

How permanent is KRink?

KRink is permanent. Period.

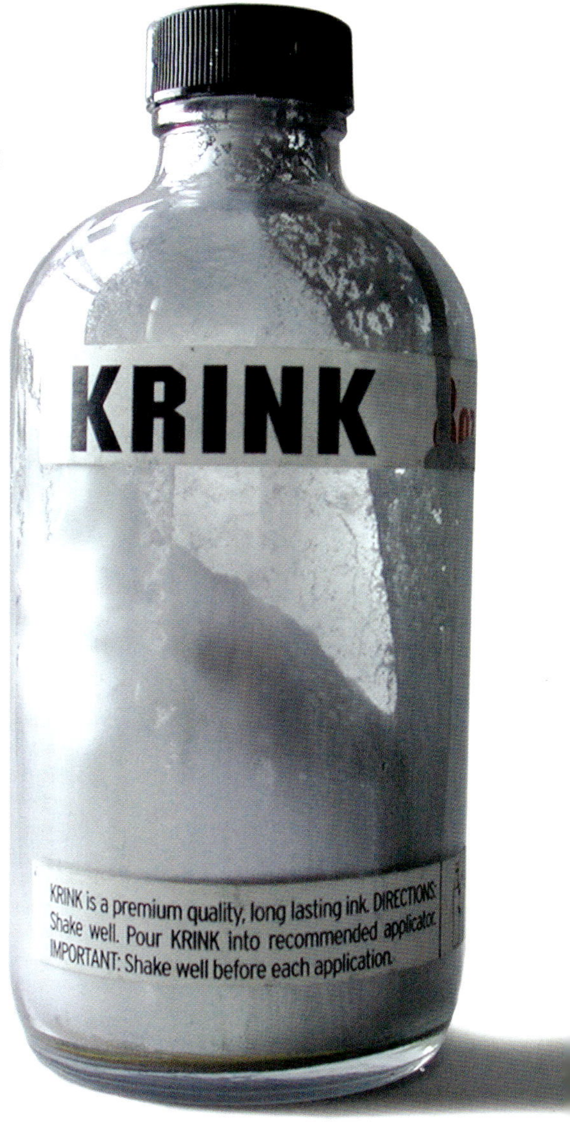

STICKERS

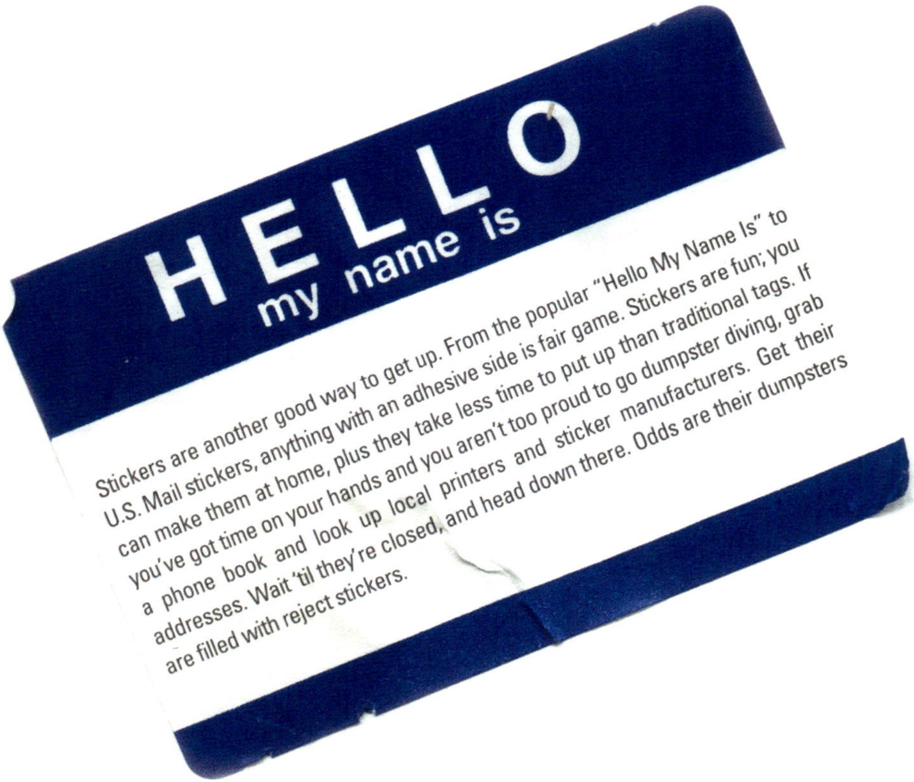

Stickers are another good way to get up. From the popular "Hello My Name Is" to U.S. Mail stickers, anything with an adhesive side is fair game. Stickers are fun; you can make them at home, plus they take less time to put up than traditional tags. If you've got time on your hands and you aren't too proud to go dumpster diving, grab a phone book and look up local printers and sticker manufacturers. Get their addresses. Wait 'til they're closed, and head down there. Odds are their dumpsters are filled with reject stickers.

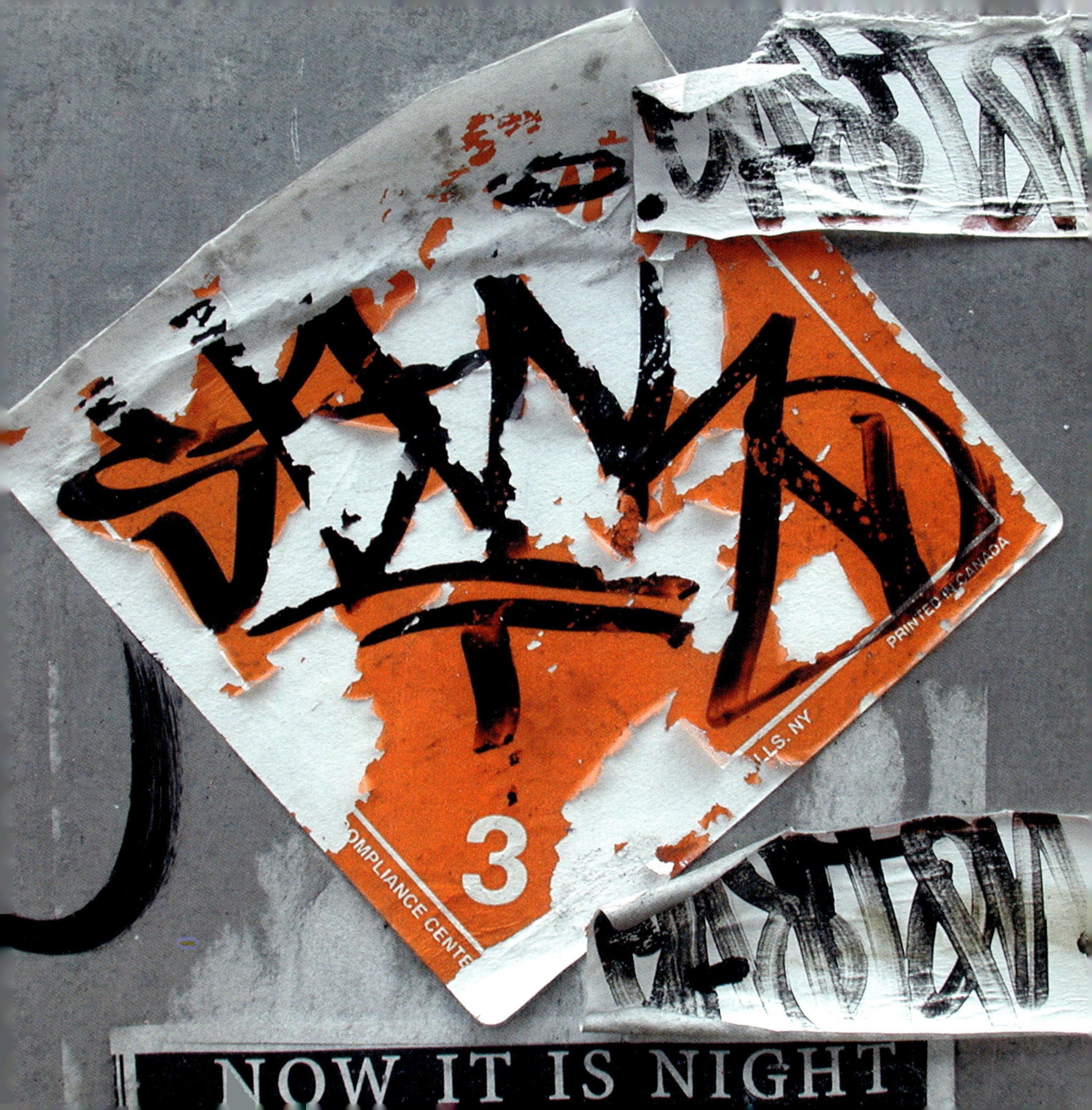
3
OMPLIANCE CENTE
PRINTED IN CANADA
LLS, NY
NOW IT IS NIGHT

SCRATCHIES

Scratchies have been around forever. I remember first seeing them on picnic tables and on trees, usually with someone's initials followed by "wuz here." When the Transit Authority rid New York City subways of tags on the insides, people started scratching their tags into the train windows. It's an efficient way to stay up, but it makes proprietors of said windows pretty angry. It's best to do them on bus and subway windows—places where you're gonna be hanging out for a bit.

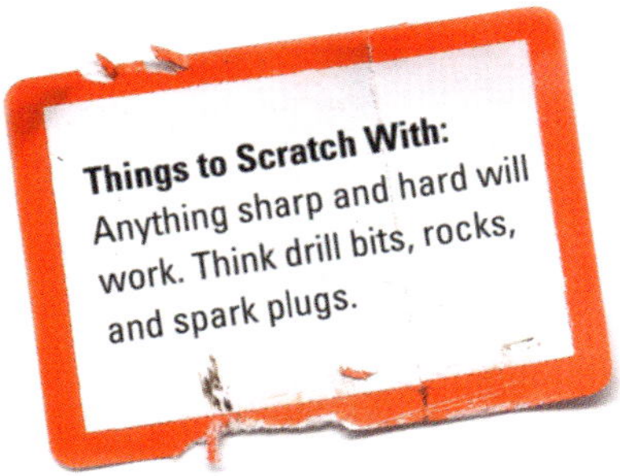

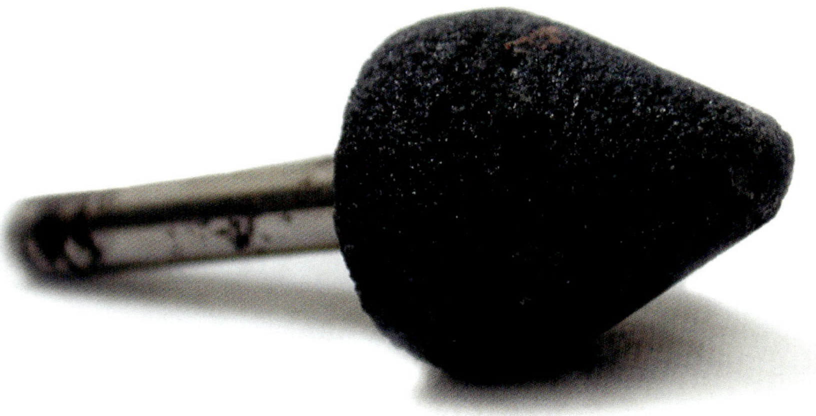

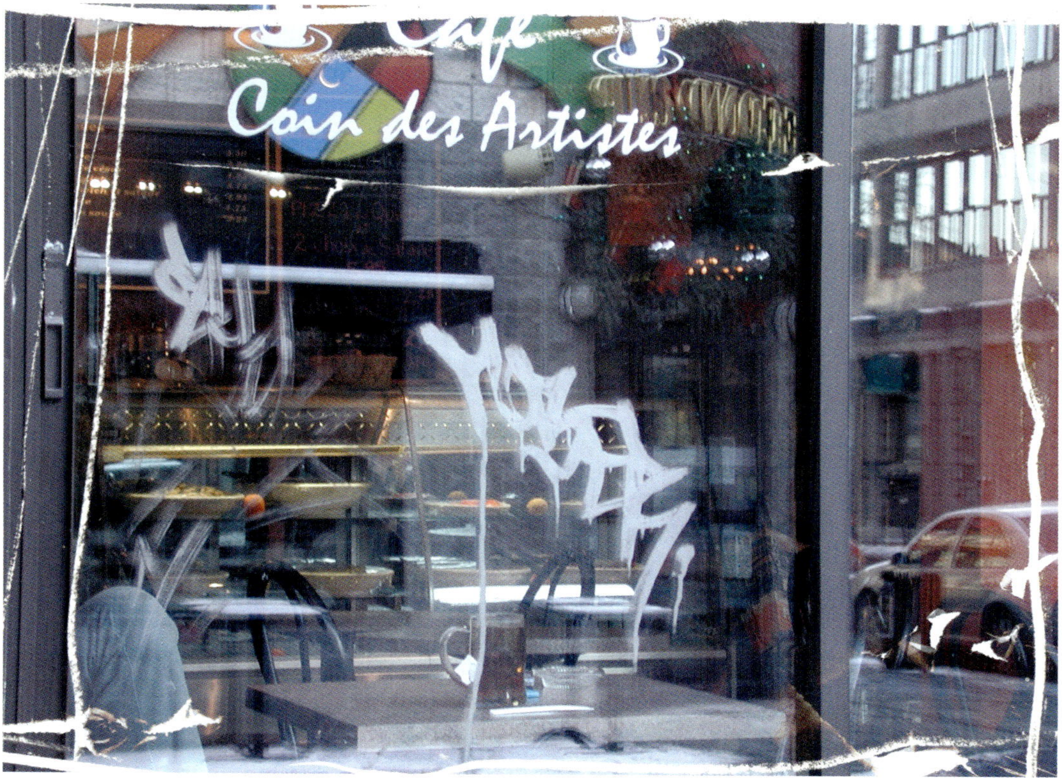

ETCH TAGS

There's a saying, "It's no fun unless you're ruining someone's day." Well, etch tags are a sure shot. Etch bath burns through glass, making your tags permanent. There's no way to buff them out; all that's left to do is change the whole windowpane. Tagging with this is a risk-versus-reward decision: if you know the spot gets buffed out a lot but it's high-traffic, then yes, the tag will stay up a little longer and it will get you shine. However, people tend to remember tags that really inconvenience their lives, so whoever owns or takes care of the property you hit will be real anxious to meet you, and that's unnecessary attention.

THROWUPS

When a tag just doesn't say enough.

At first, your best bet is to stay proportional. Make sure the letters are consistent. Bubble letters are always timeless and are pretty fast to do.

1. **Do your first outline in the color you plan to fill in.**

2. **Fill in the letters with a smooth back-and-forth motion.**

3. **Outline the letters in another color.**

4. **Add drop shadow.**

5. **If you've got time on your hands, hang out and throw an additional outline around the whole thing in a third color to make it punch out. Example: my favorite is always a silver fill, black outline, followed by a St. Patrick's Day green or hot pink outline around the whole thing.**

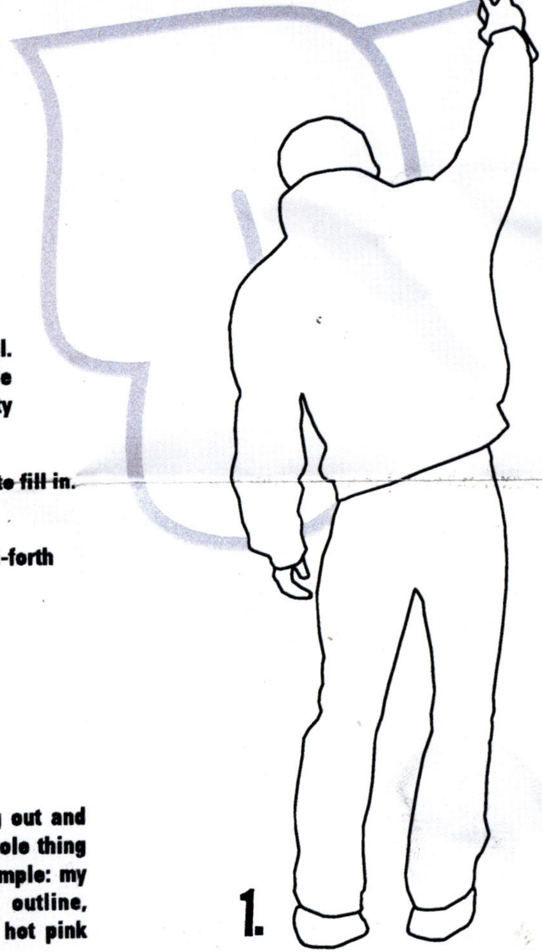

1.

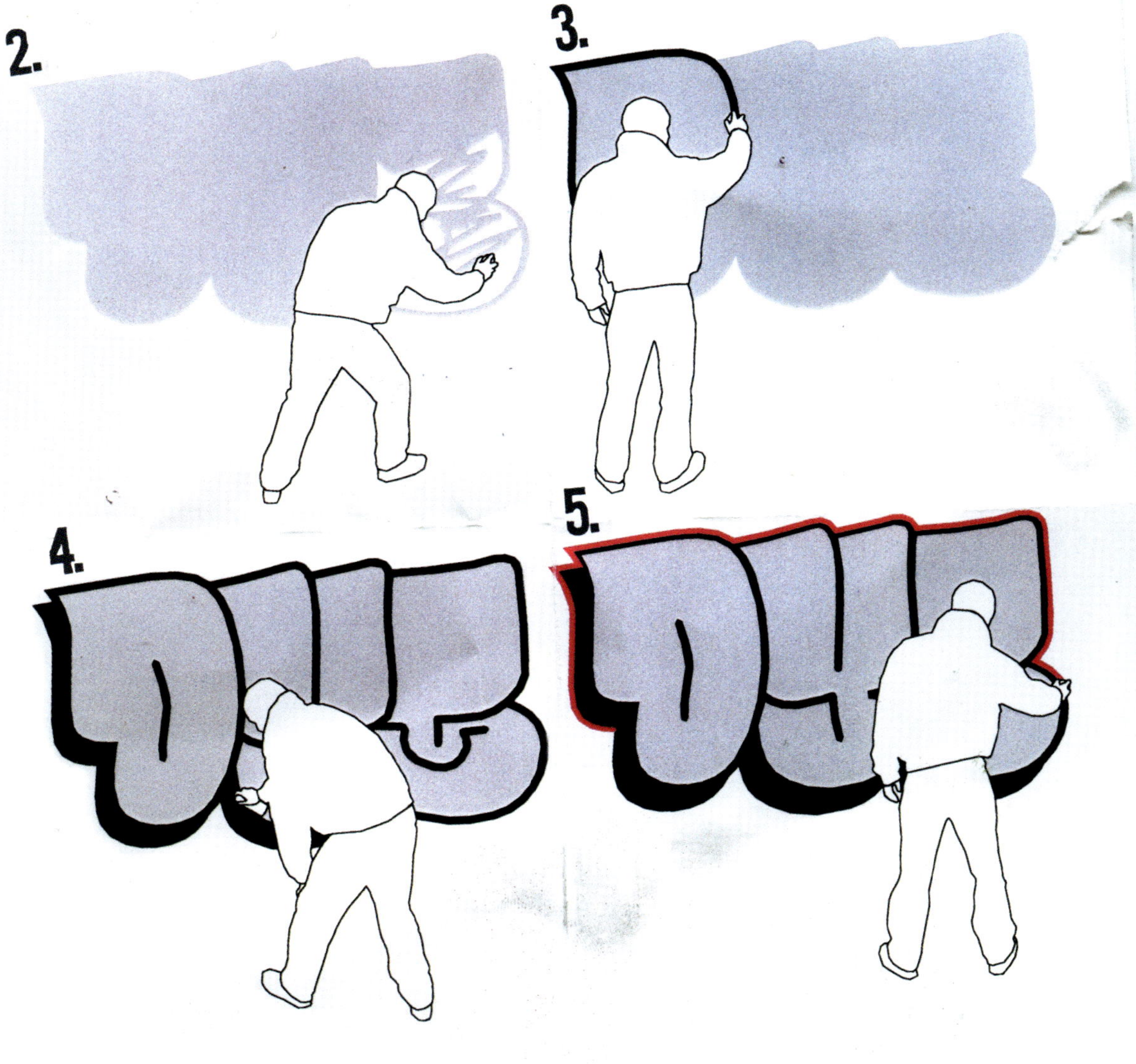
2.
3.
4.
5.

ROLLERS (A.K.A. LEAN-OVERS)

Rollers are usually high up on walls, where they can't be touched. When you can't get to them from the ground, it's best to lean over from the top of the roof.

What you need: bucket paint, a roller, maybe a paint pan.

1. Count out with your feet how much space you have from end to end. If that's not working for you and it's a brick wall, count bricks.
2. Break out your calculator. Divide space by amount of letters in name.
3. Mark out where letters begin and end along the top of the wall.
4. Lean over. The end of your reach with the roller stick should be the bottom of your letters. Again, count the amount of bricks and stick to that distance.
5. Apply paint.

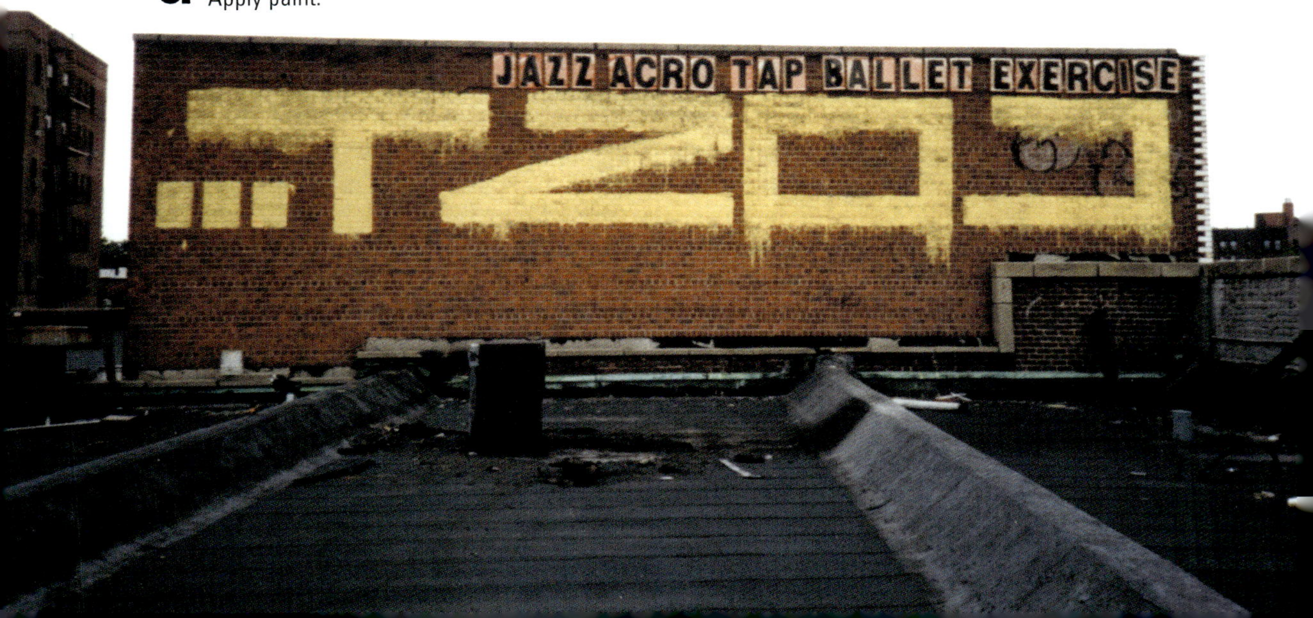

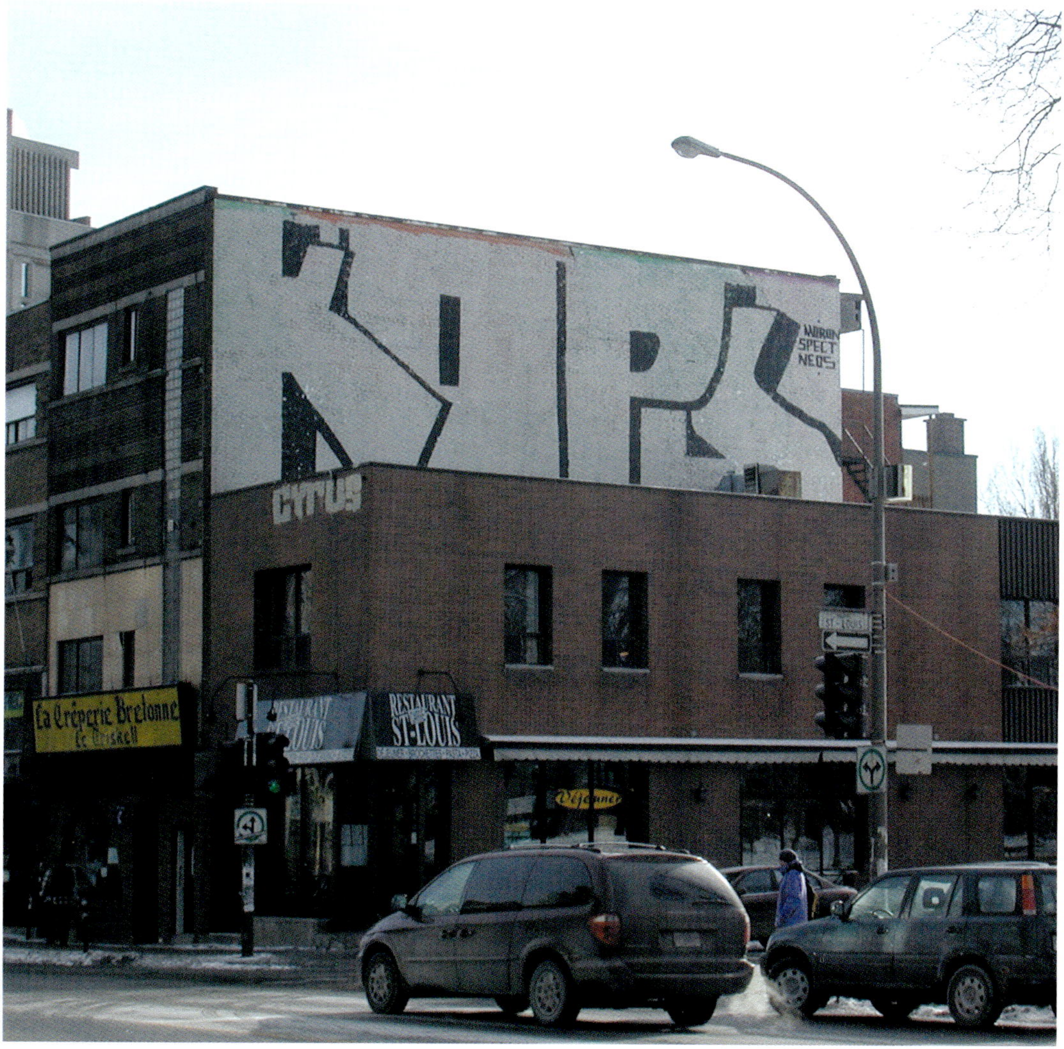
La Crêperie Bretonne
RESTAURANT
ST-LOUIS
CYRUS

PAINT

Krylon
Krylon is like an abusive spouse: it's the brand of paint that turns against its most loyal customers, but it's familiar and available everywhere. It doesn't cover well, and it doesn't come in great colors. You should check out their website—they're all about creating programs to rid cities of graffiti. "Keep America Beautiful." Read up on it: www.krylon.com.

Rust-Oleum
Everyone I have met who paints in the eastern United States loves Rust-Oleum. They say it covers better than anything, and is great for bombing. Everyone I have heard speak on the brand outside of the United States has no love for it. You should check for their silver paint. It's long-lasting.

Montana
Covers well, has good pigmentation, and has just the right amount of pressure to it. It comes with a German cap, which, according to the Europeans, is great for tagging. Add a fat cap, and it's great for filling in.

Auto K
Covers well, works best with a fat cap, but also works with True Colorz caps. It's an all-around good brand for bombing.

The Shit Brands
If you don't have the balls to steal paint and you have no budget, it's best to pick up the in-house brands at your local hardware chain or Wal-Mart. Stick to colors like silver, flat black, and white. They should cost at least fifty percent less than the other cans. I can't guarantee quality, but the savings are worth it.

True Colorz
Has low pressure, generally covers well (depending on the color), and is great for when your lines have to be clean.

Belton
Has good pressure, comes out matte, and covers well. It's a well-rounded paint that's great for tags, throwups, and burners.

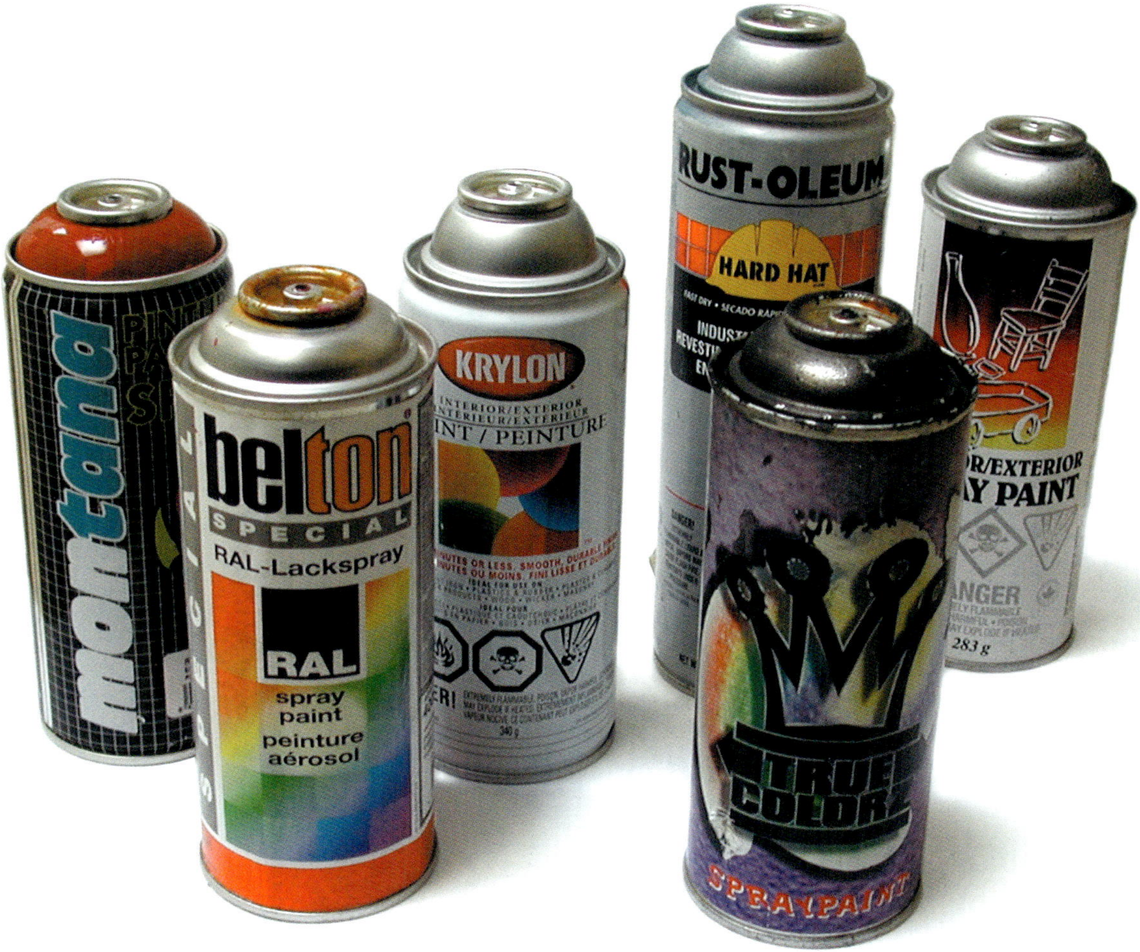
montana
belton
SPECIAL
RAL-Lackspray
RAL
spray paint
peinture aérosol
KRYLON
INTERIOR/EXTERIOR
RUST-OLEUM
HARD HAT
TRUE COLOR
SPRAYPAINT
283 g

CAPS

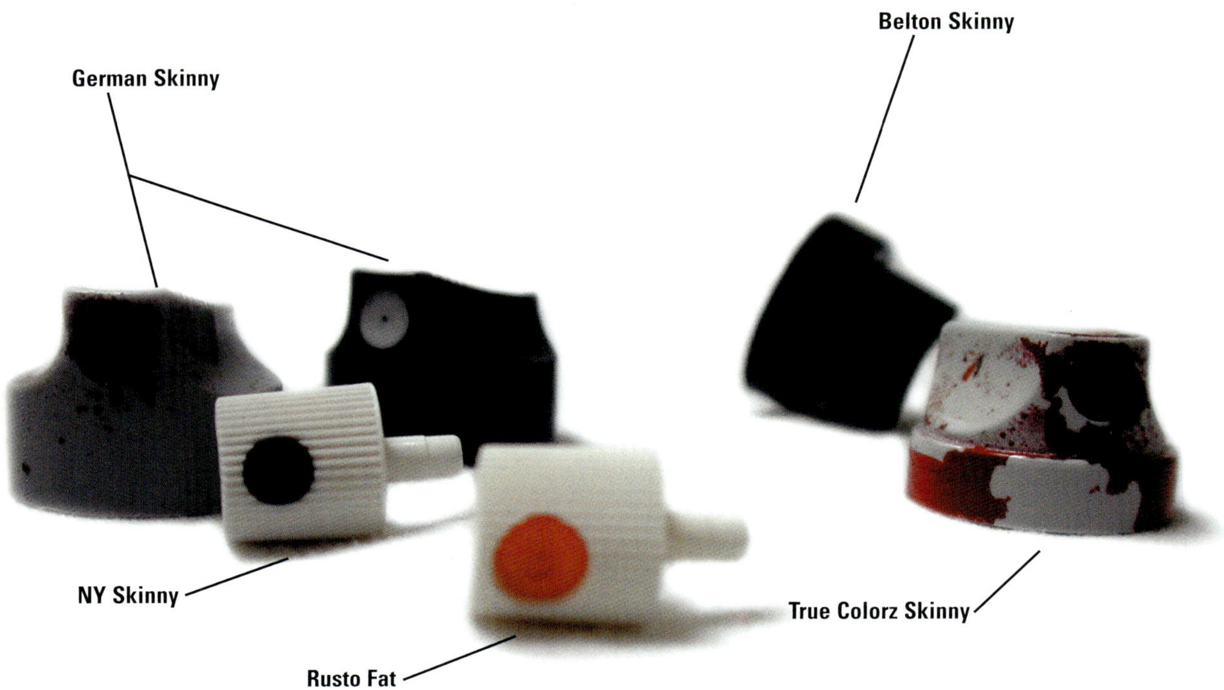
Belton Skinny
German Skinny
NY Skinny
True Colorz Skinny
Rusto Fat

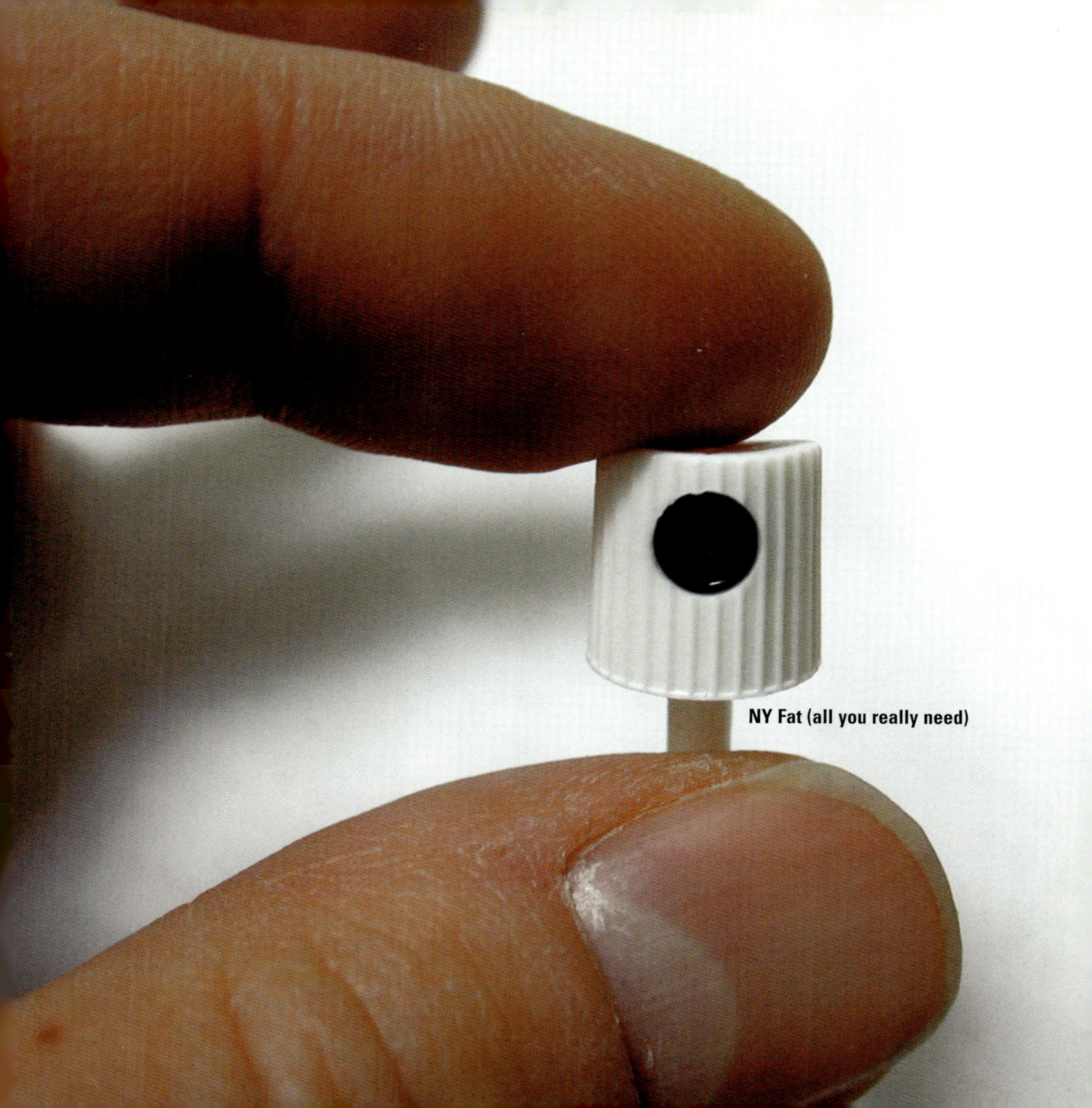

NY Fat (all you really need)

TIPS FOR TAKING FLICKS

Soon after getting into graffiti, you will, out of necessity, get into photography. You will feel the need to document what you do. In the end, this is pointless, because everything you did has already been done.

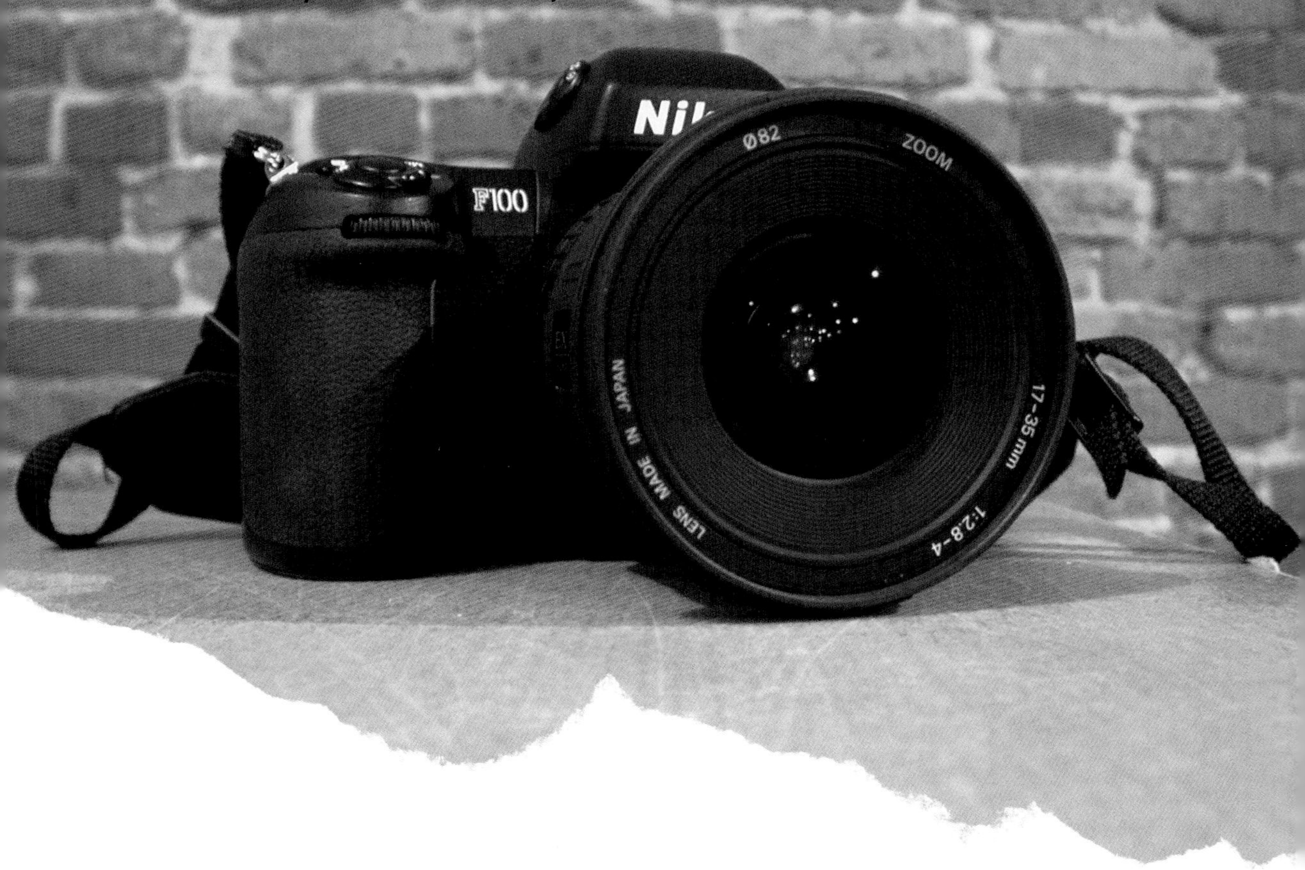

1. Detail is important: get as close as possible without cutting anything out of the frame.

2. If you're in a tunnel and you can't see it, chances are the camera can't see it either.

3. If you're piecing trains, wait 'til the morning to get the pic. A flash, nighttime, and metal don't mix—it's a recipe for flash burn. If you can't risk going back and you have to get out, shoot on an angle so you won't get the reflection. Remember to leave the yard immediately: flashes, like fireworks, attract attention. Railway police are horny for thieves, writers, and pretty much anyone trespassing. This, of course, doesn't apply to all you cats in the suburbs who paint in fields, smoke some pot and "make an afternoon of it" . . . come to the city and get in the yard.

4. If the sun is shining on half the piece, wait 'til the sun shifts to take the pic.

5. Yeah sure, the camera has a zoom—so what? You have feet; you're allowed to move closer or further away . . . perspectives change like sneakers.

6. Photography isn't rocket science—you can pick it up through trial and error. Don't get frustrated. Keep at it, and it will work out in the end.

7. There is no such thing as a bad camera. You're the one that sucks. Just because you're flossin' with your mom's SLR doesn't mean you know how to use it. If you're not going to invest the time, stick to the automatic point-and-shoot.

8. If you're going to take connectors of production walls:
   a) Move your feet but keep the exact same distance from the wall at all times.
   b) Make sure to overlap the images (it's better to have too much than not enough).
   c) The art is on the wall. Don't get creative with your photo. Shoot dead on, straight ahead. You're documenting something, not expressing yourself.
   d) When possible, step back after you've taken your shots and take another photo that encompasses the whole production.
   e) There's no shame in carrying or using a tripod.

9. If you had any heart at all, you would be taking pics of live bombing.

10. If cats are still at the wall, ask to take pics before you start shooting. Often, writers don't like to have their pictures taken. You could catch a bad one . . . .

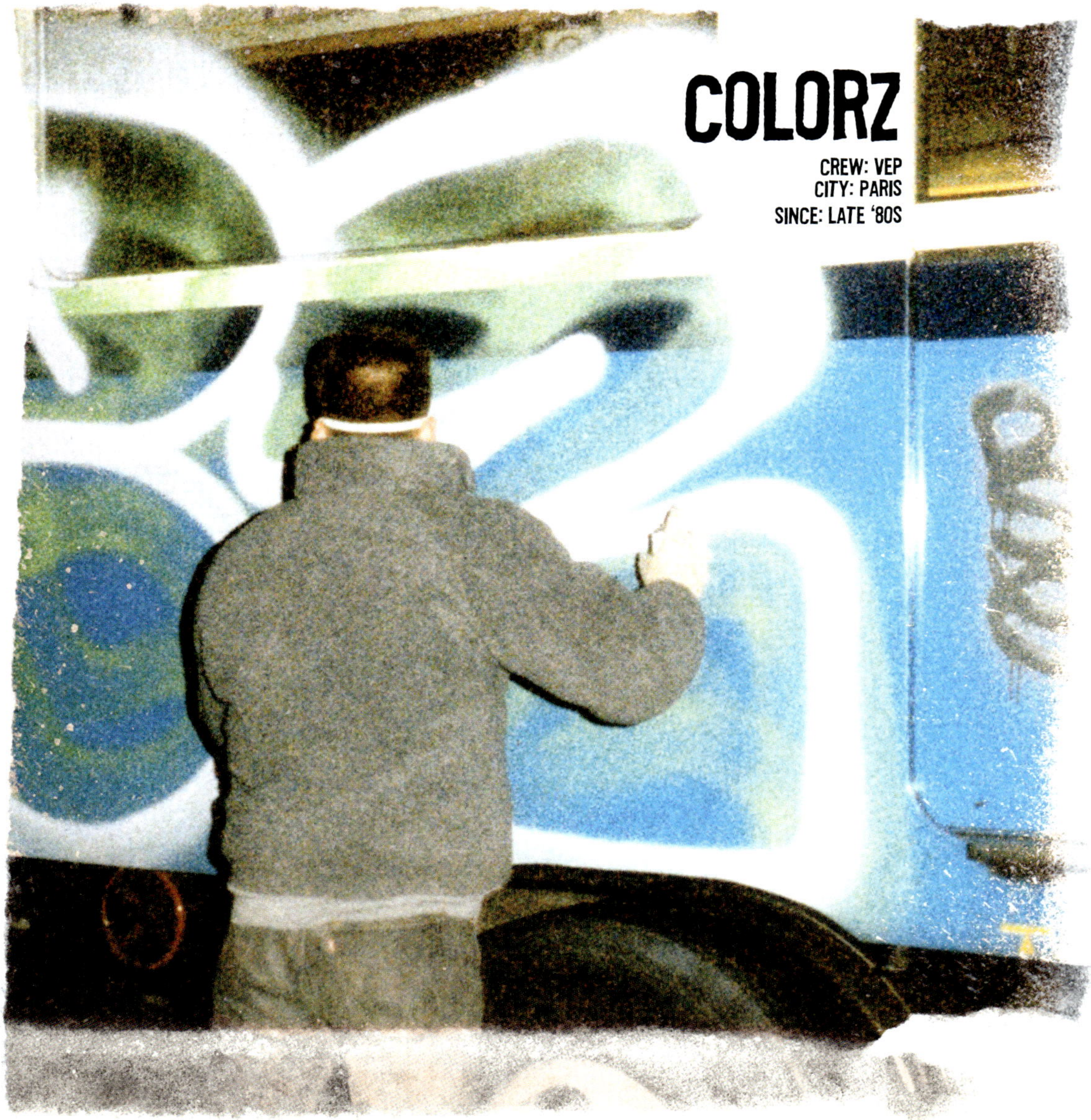

COLORZ

CREW: VEP
CITY: PARIS
SINCE: LATE '80S

What do you write, and when did you start writing?

I write Colorz VEP, 156, MV, GT, UK. I started writing in 1987 in Sartrouville (a suburb of Paris). My first tag was Isaac. I had discovered hip-hop just before that, watching a French hip-hop show that was hosted by this guy Sydney. We used to bring cardboard to school and breakdance at recess, and from that I started writing nonsense on walls—random stuff, like "Public Enemy." At that point in my life we didn't really know about writing, but then we started noticing tags on the way to Paris, names like Boxer, Sign, and Sheek. On our way home, we started dropping tags in my city, on bus shelters and things like that. I was with Shest and Stak. During that era, not many people were into hip-hop. Most of the people our age didn't understand what we were doing, the way we dressed, or the music we listened to. The kids around us were more into funk [music], being in gangs, and beefing with other gangs—basically getting into trouble.

What's your favorite tool?

A can or marker. It doesn't really matter, but I guess I prefer paint.

Were you fuckin' with different kinds of inks or building markers?

When we started we were using really basic stuff: Onyx, Edding. We would take out the felt and fill it with magic marker ink, but it would leak and we would get it everywhere, so we didn't do that a lot. We didn't really have to, anyway; the inks back then were all fairly potent. Then the Posca markers came out and the buffing intensified. One day Oeno found Corio, this leather dye, and we would add blue methylene [available at drugstores worldwide] to it. But by 1989, everybody was tagging with markers and walls were saturated, so I started doing tags and throwups with paint instead.

Which writers, past or present, stand out in your mind?

Boxer, San, Squat, Dozer, Muck, the TCG Crew . . .

The notion of style—is it important to you? Your thoughts?

Style comes with time; it's something that's developed. No one just starts with pure style. Back in the day there were no mags to "inspire" you. Each crew was just trying to stand out from the others, but I also think that there was a Parisian style. Paris was pretty much influenced by Bando, who was directly inspired by Dondi CIA. There were also the CAS guys on the A line—guys like Yank influenced me a lot.

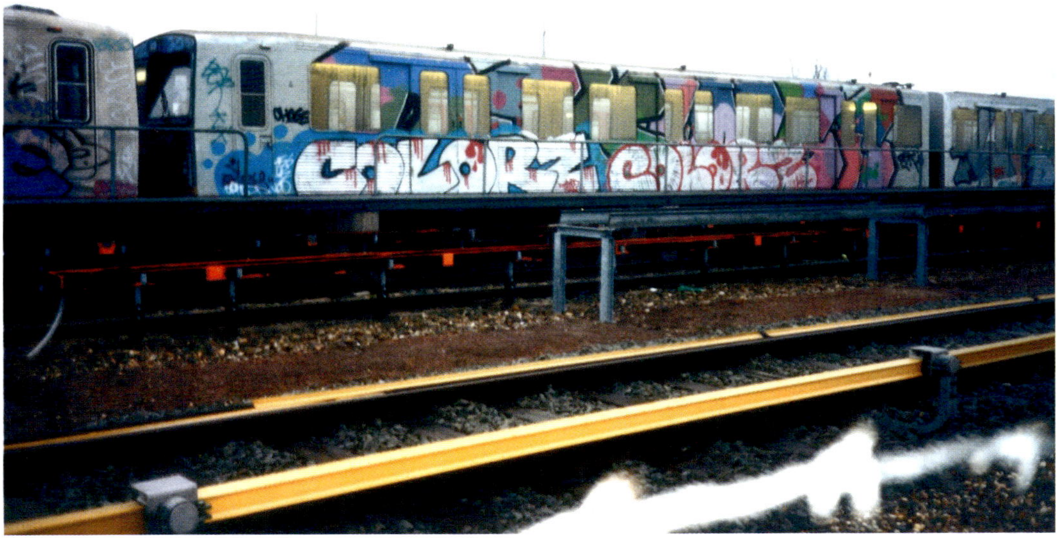

Were guys robbing paint in France? Was it like that?

Yeah, we would hit, like, supermarkets and art supply stores at, like, recess or after school. We would go fill up our backpacks, or we would send someone with a stolen check and get boxes of paint . . . those were good times.

What kind of paint do you like?

It's always been Auto K, Krylon, and Buntlack. I need paint with good pressure and strong pigment so I can go fast.

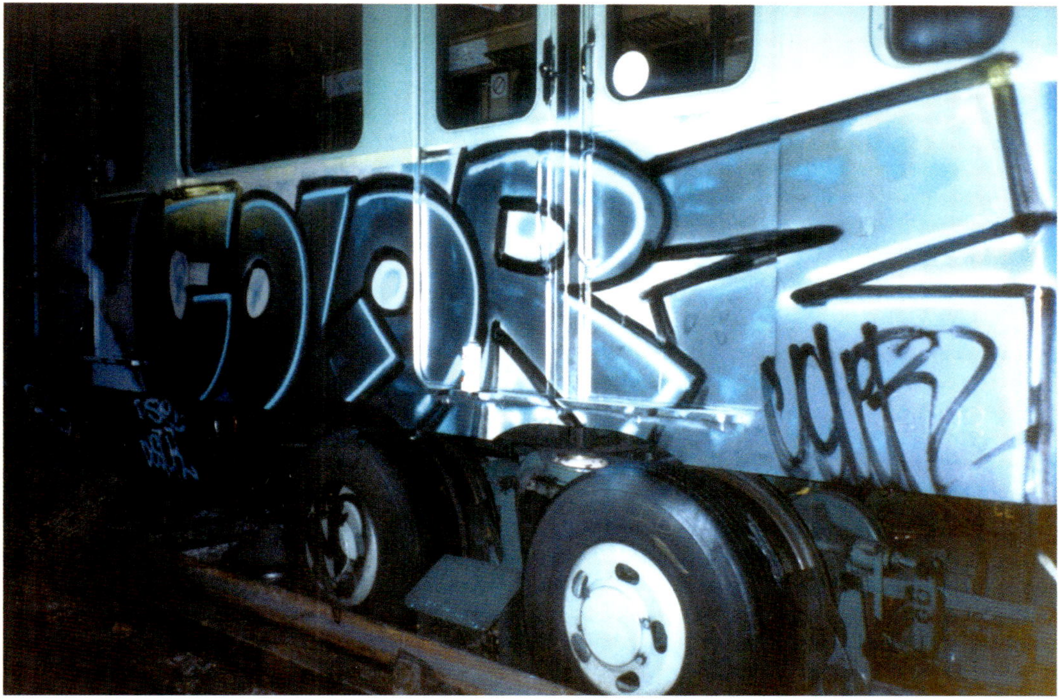

Would you plan bombing missions or just carry paint?

I always tucked a marker to tag up where I went. But when I started chilling with the VEP guys, I went on strategically planned missions to hit up different subway lines and commuter trains. There were always workers at the depots, so we had nights of just waiting around. We acted like terrorists.

Did you bomb outside of Paris?

It's clear that I tagged a lot in Paris, 'cause at one point I ended up living there, but basically, my favorite spots were all of the outer regions, the suburbs, without exception. I always wanted to take spots that no one had before. I can't imagine how many kilometers I walked along train tracks.

Did you get crossed out a lot? Is it like that in France?

I got crossed out a few times by jealous guys when I started killing the A line. But the few dudes that did cross me out always ended getting fucked up. I never really got crossed out a lot, though, 'cause I always have respected others.

What do you think about getting paid for murals and stuff like that?

I was never really thrilled with the idea, or, how do you say . . . fascinated by it. I have done some for spare cash and extra paint, but I couldn't even tell you when. It happened rarely and it didn't really fit into my vandal rebellion. It wasn't what I took to heart. I never really wanted to commercialize graffiti or encourage others to do it. It's true that the general public prefers to see elaborate murals with lots of color, but I enjoy taking three tags on a subway train way more than painting a production over two weeks.

What's a complete writer to you?

For me, it's somebody like O'Clock; someone who has had his hand in everything—trains, streets, abandoned buildings, just all around. I don't think people should make rules or disciplines, though. Graffiti has been way too institutionalized these past few years. Graffiti is rebellion; it's about standing out from the bunch. It's easy now to get drowned in this phenomenon that the media has created, and the way marketing companies use graffiti tactics, it makes for less authentic people in graffiti today.

What has writing done for your life?

To a certain extent, it channeled my destructive energy. I can't really say bombing brought me anything, but then again, I wasn't expecting anything from it.

Shout outs: my family (Katia, Anastasia, Come, Lucien), Oeno, Sacha, Goze, Psy, Cap, Orel, Smoker, Aro, Mode 2, Peuto, Creez, Kongo, Madly et les enfants, Jonone, O'Clock, Pro, Sari, Dize, Chari, Satur, Legz, Stak, C4, TW, TCS, TKC, VEP, GT, Metro Veterans, C4, Boxer (RIP), all the vandalz, big up, live long . . .

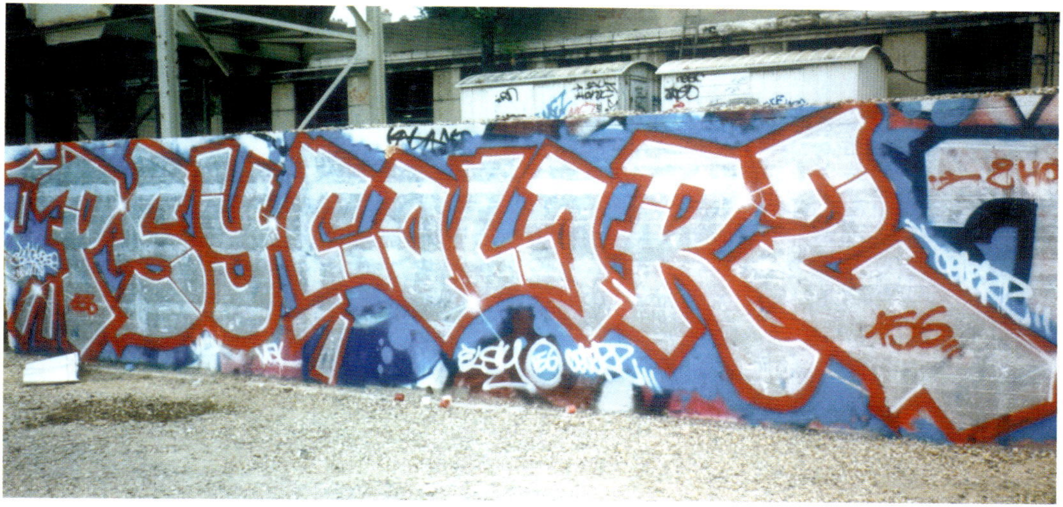

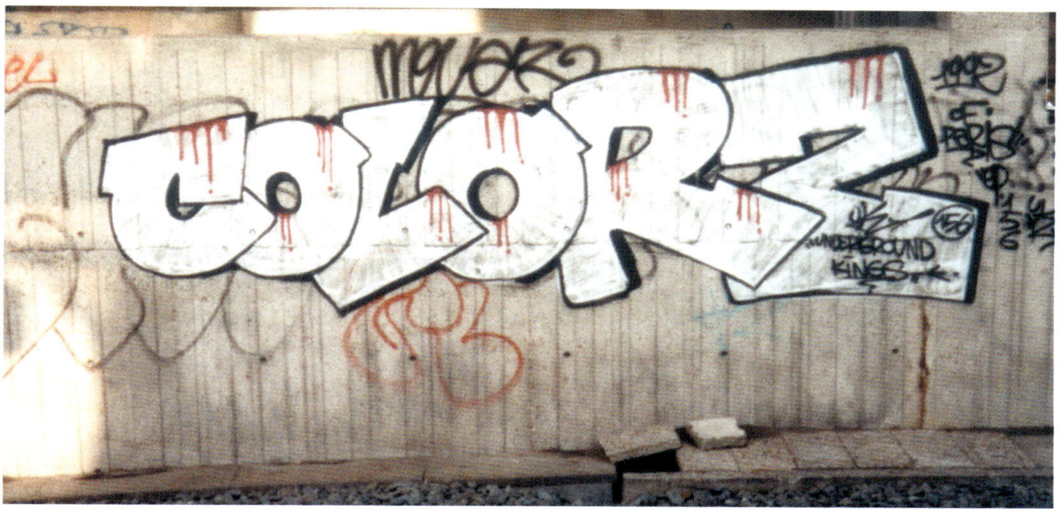
UNDERGROUND
KINGS

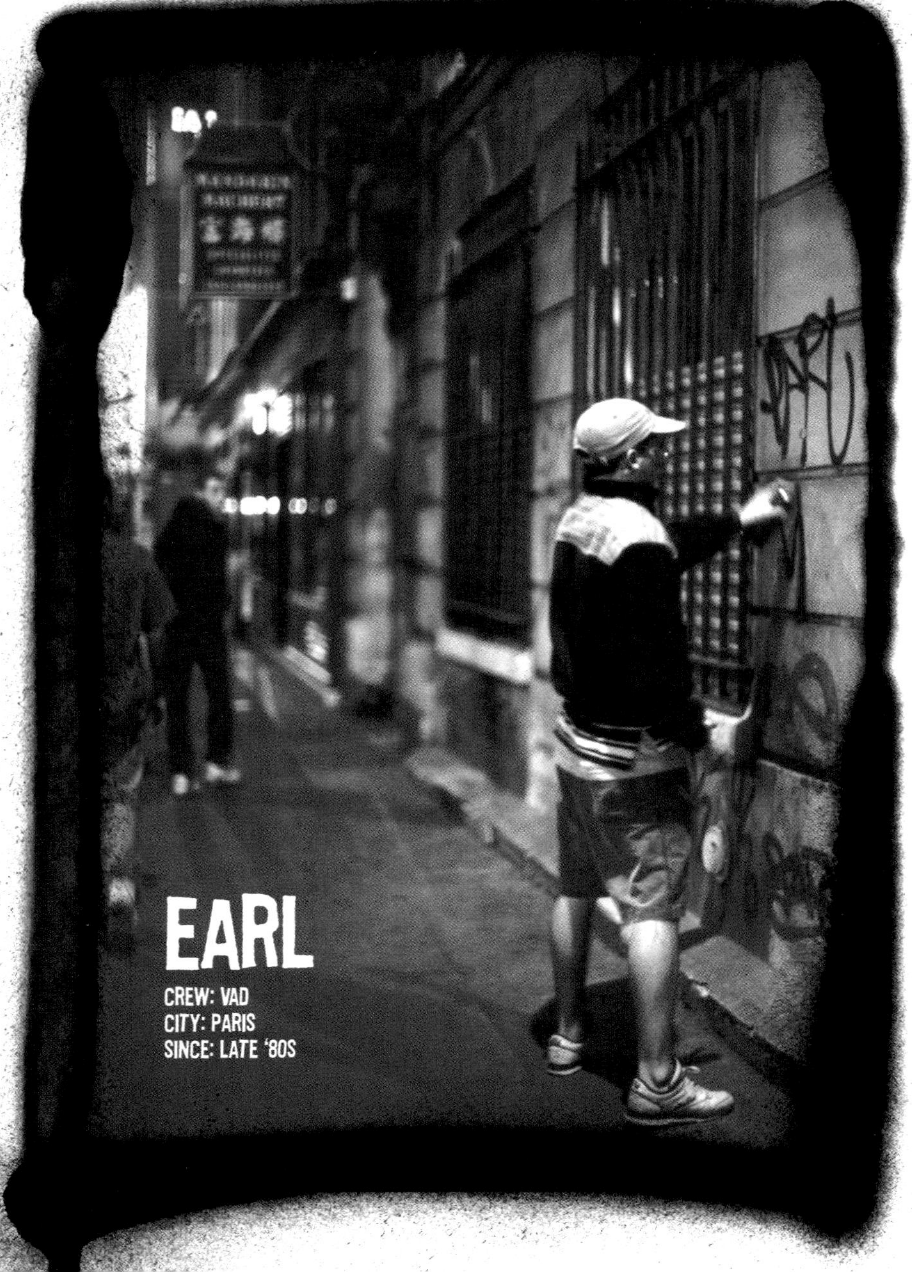
EARL
CREW: VAD
CITY: PARIS
SINCE: LATE '80S

"Mister Earl is, was, and always will be a tagger. Not a graffiti artist, but a constant, untamed, and uncontrollable vandal. He takes tags as consistently and as regularly as others brush their teeth. His hand styles stink like feet, and it's too late to try to change them. His tags are to the city of Paris what a pimple is to the ass of a syphilis-infected whore: try to get rid of one, and two come back in its place. Any attempt to get rid of them is futile, and after all, their presence adds to the old bitch's charm. I like that." —Turf One, 2002

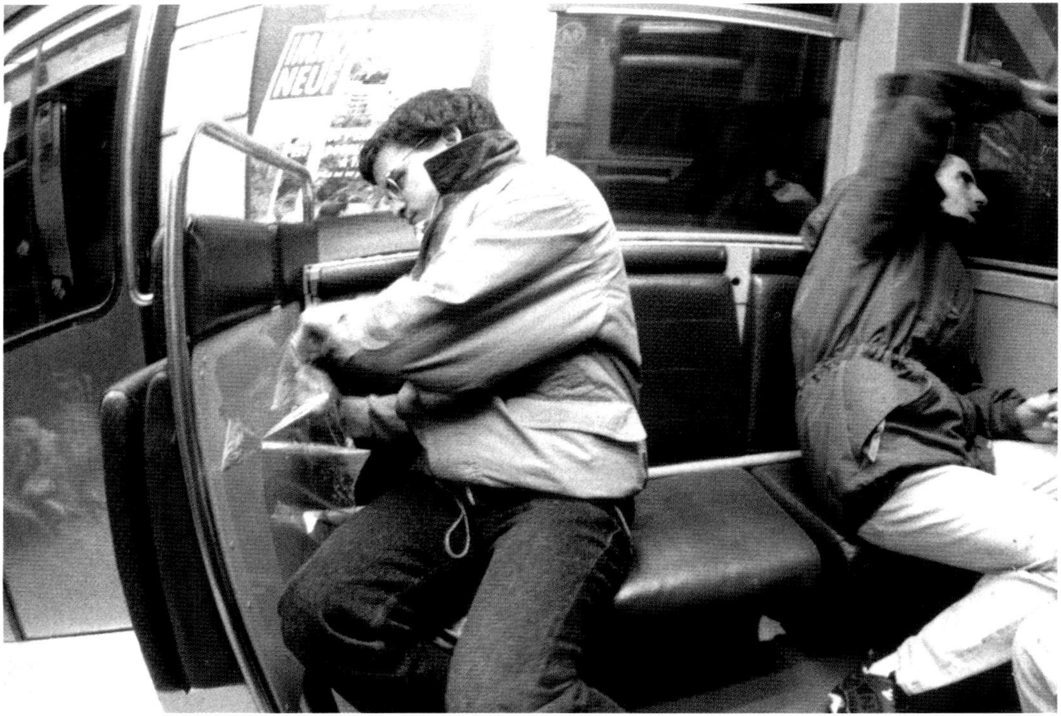
NEUF

Break it down for me. What do you write?

I've had a few tags, but the one that I got up the most is Earl VAD [translated, VAD stands for "Go To Hell"] . . . TW, 666, DKA. VAD is the crew that I created in 1989, when I was fifteen. I started tagging in 1989 in Paris all by myself, then little by little, I met more people who painted, like the guys in TW and in DKA. So at that point I started going to paint with those guys, but not too much. I definitely prefer to paint alone. It's more of an adrenaline rush, fewer problems, plus you don't have to share the fame that way.

Did you ever get caught?

I've been arrested a bunch of times for shoplifting, a whole bunch of times for tagging, and for being drunk in public.

Is graffiti an addiction?

Yeah, it's an addiction—maybe more of a mental illness. What else would drive an individual to write his name sixty times in a row on a wall? Either a huge mental problem, or an even bigger ego problem.

Do you have a favorite writing instrument, or tool?

My favorite tool is in my pants, but I haven't figured how to write with it. Seriously, I like markers and paint sticks. My favorite kind of paint is Blackson, but it's for cars.

Do you guys make markers over there?

I personally don't build them much, but I like to make ink. Nowadays, kids scratch up windows with screwdrivers and stuff.

What advice would you give to someone who just started painting?

The more you drink alcohol, the more you will get a sensation of being invincible, the more you will tag.

Really? That's your advice?

Actually, no: Stop right now and go home to mama. The market is already flooded. Go to school, and if you're gonna write, strive to be the best . . . and remember to do unto to others as . . . .

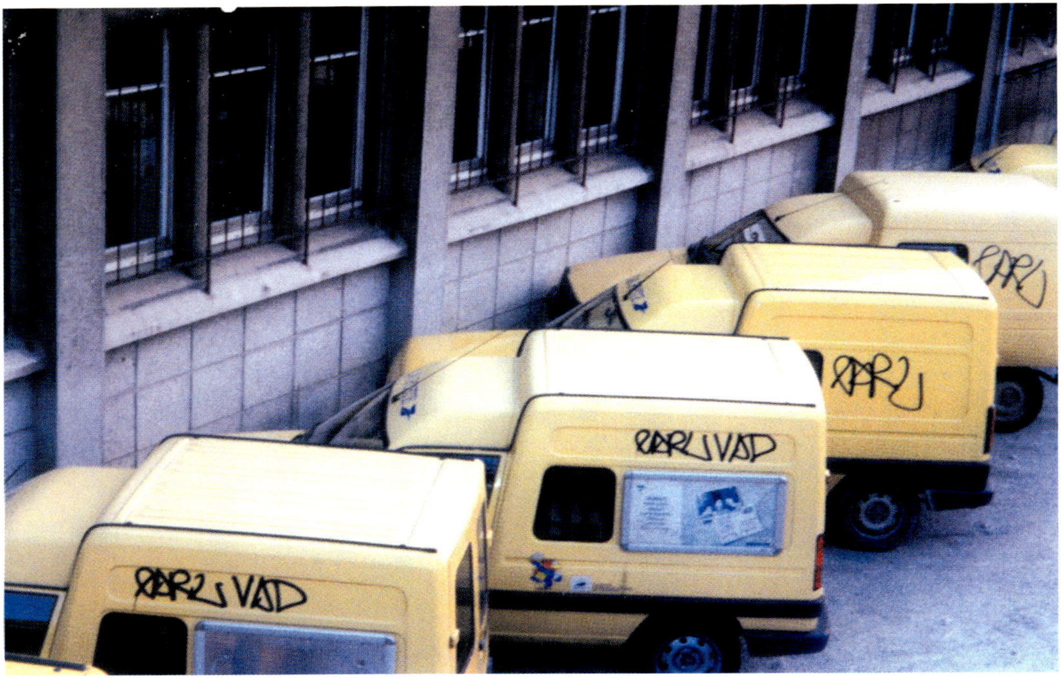

Do you have any regrets?

I guess my only regret is stepping on the third rail [750 volts]. I tripped on it and ended up in the hospital for too long. It left me with a magnificent scar on my face . . . besides that, I don't really have any regrets.

What do you think of getting paid to paint murals? Is that still graffiti?

If someone does that sort of thing and is paid for it and does it well, in my opinion, that's still graffiti. It just doesn't interest me. I'm a tagger. I'm a vandal.

What's writing done for you?

Well, I run a lot faster than I used to. I have a sick scar. I made great friends, and I have a great girlfriend (Fancie SDK).

What's your ultimate goal in this?

Stock up on memories, avoid boredom, and express my megalomaniac tendencies.

What do you think of cross outs?

Paris is big enough for everyone to leave my stuff alone. Fuck all the jealous cats.

When do you see yourself stopping?

I see myself in twenty years being fifty, getting drunk and taking tags, then coming home and getting yelled at by the wife and kids.

Do you steal paint?

I used to steal everything, but I stopped three years ago. My girl owns a graffiti boutique . . . I get hooked up.

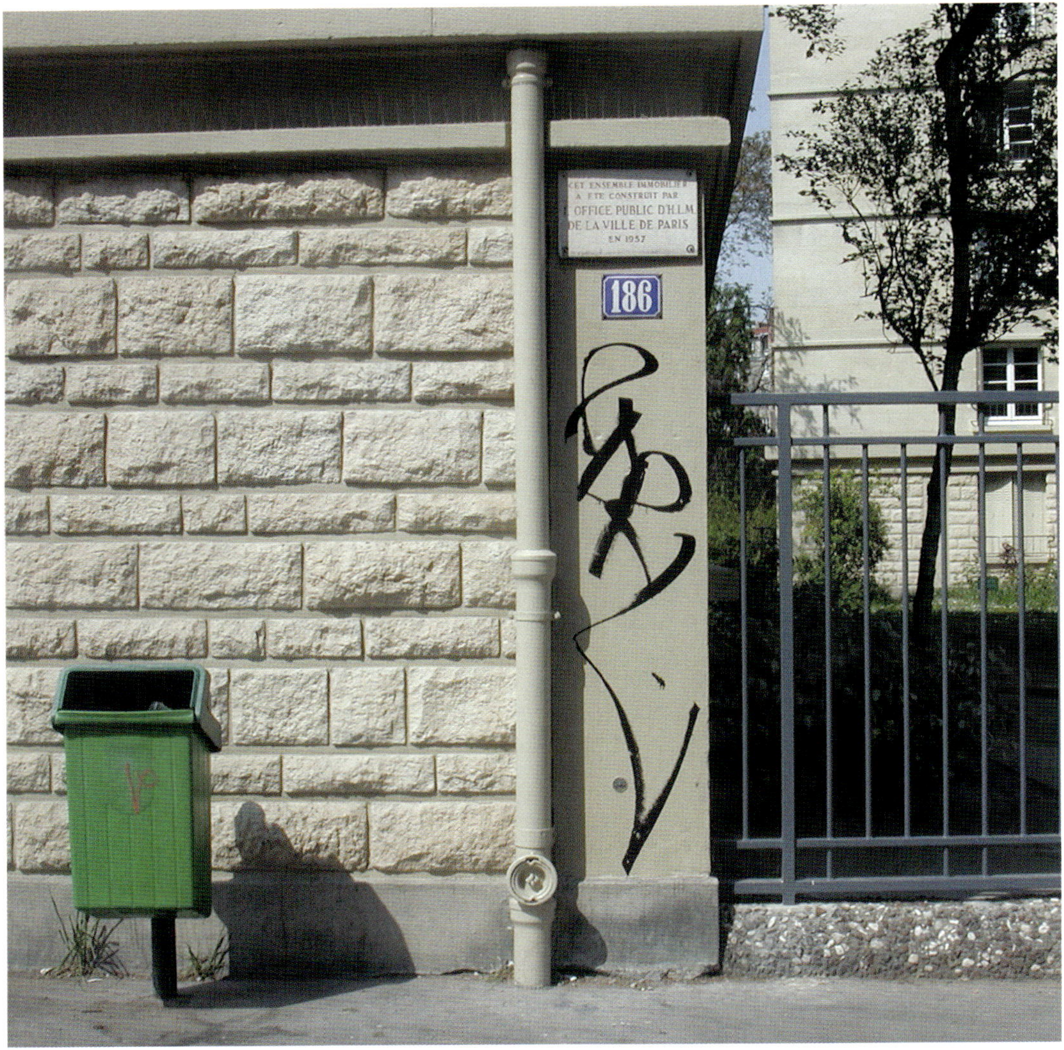
CET ENSEMBLE IMMOBILIER
A ETE CONSTRUIT PAR
OFFICE PUBLIC D'H.L.M
DE LA VILLE DE PARIS
EN 1957
186

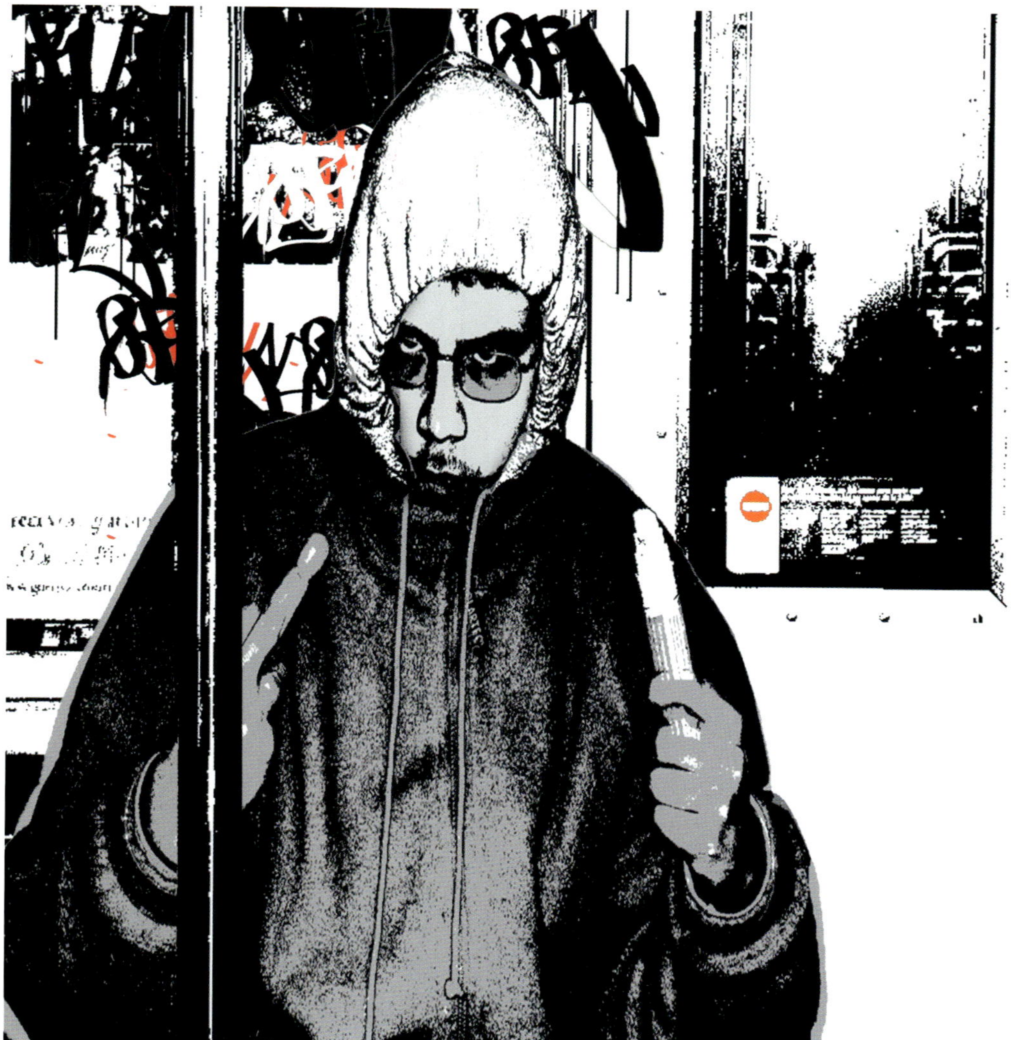

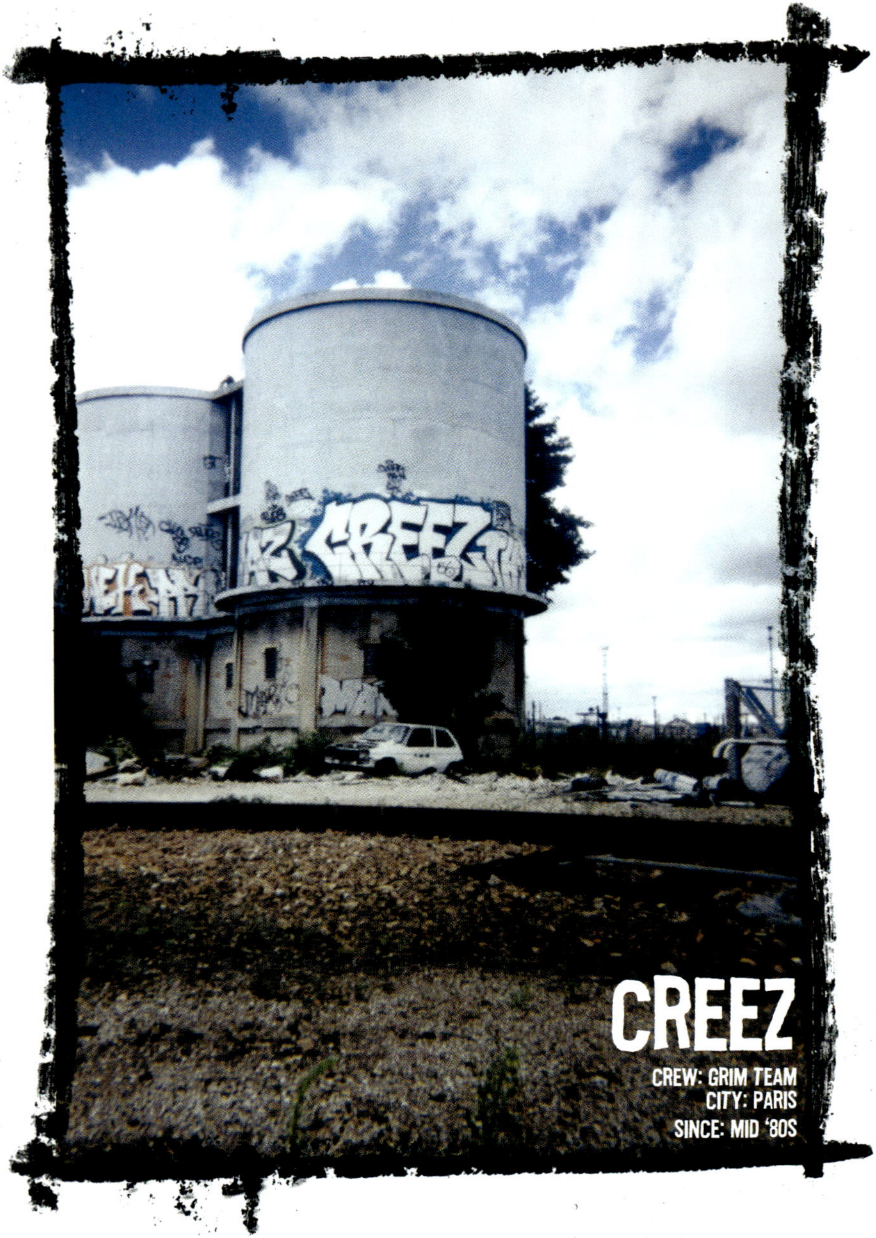

CREEZ

CREW: GRIM TEAM
CITY: PARIS
SINCE: MID '80S

What do you write?

I write Creez, a.k.a. Iceberg Slim. I'm in GT, 156, TOP, Wrung Division, and Jungle Orchestra. My first tag was Freez. When I met Echo a little later, I found out his brother was DJ Freez the Cat. At that time, having the same tag as someone just wasn't cool, so I picked up a book and I wrote my tag, took the F away and replaced it with a C. That's how I came up with Creez.

When did you start writing?

One day I was chillin' with these skater kids, and I found a purple marker on the ground. I started writing shit on the walls of my apartment and on my street. I started looking at tags. At the time there weren't many writers aside from Muck and Majesty, and TCG had barely just started. Near my crib there was a home hardware store, and I went there every day to rack three or four cans. It was usually red Krylon. I started a crew with my boy Mercure, and we called it NCS (New Criminal Subway). There was also Dezign (a.k.a. Venus). In time, I met Ose (a.k.a. Skeed) and Stef, who were already into graff. Then I met Psyckoze. He would come down from the Catacombs, and we soon became friends. That was the beginning of the 156 in France. Meo and Jon had just moved to Paris, and there was also Colt, Squat, Sign, and the BBC Crew. I started chilling with TCG (Kaze, Dozer, Sheek, etc.). Alcohol, fights, and tagging provided the ambiance at that time . . . we were the obnoxious guys in Stalingrad for a few years. Then me and Aro put TOP together with East (RIP), Sarko, Shest (RIP), and a few other guys. At that point, I was really getting into graffiti. For seven years I only tagged, then my first piece was with Jon, Meo, and Psyckoze—guys that had been around for quite a while. We all hung out quite a bit, and they put me down with their crew. Then with Oeno, Chase, and Smoker, we put together a new crew, called Underground Kingz. Later on we integrated the PCP guys (Cap, Smoker, Number 6), and eventually that turned into the Grim Team.

What do you like to write with the most?

At first it was red Krylon, but since we stole from a couple of different stores, we wrote with different things. I always liked tagging with markers best, but I think my tags come out doper with cans. Besides, one paint tag is worth five marker tags.

What about markers and ink?

In the beginning we heard about Marsh, but it was hard to find in France, so we would steal bottled Magic Marker ink. We would steal it from the Graphigro [an art supply store], but at a certain point that got sketchy. At the end of the '80s, the VEP guys found Corio. They would mix it with blue methylene and other products to make it more permanent. Me and Colorz were down in that era, so he always made sure I was taken care of.

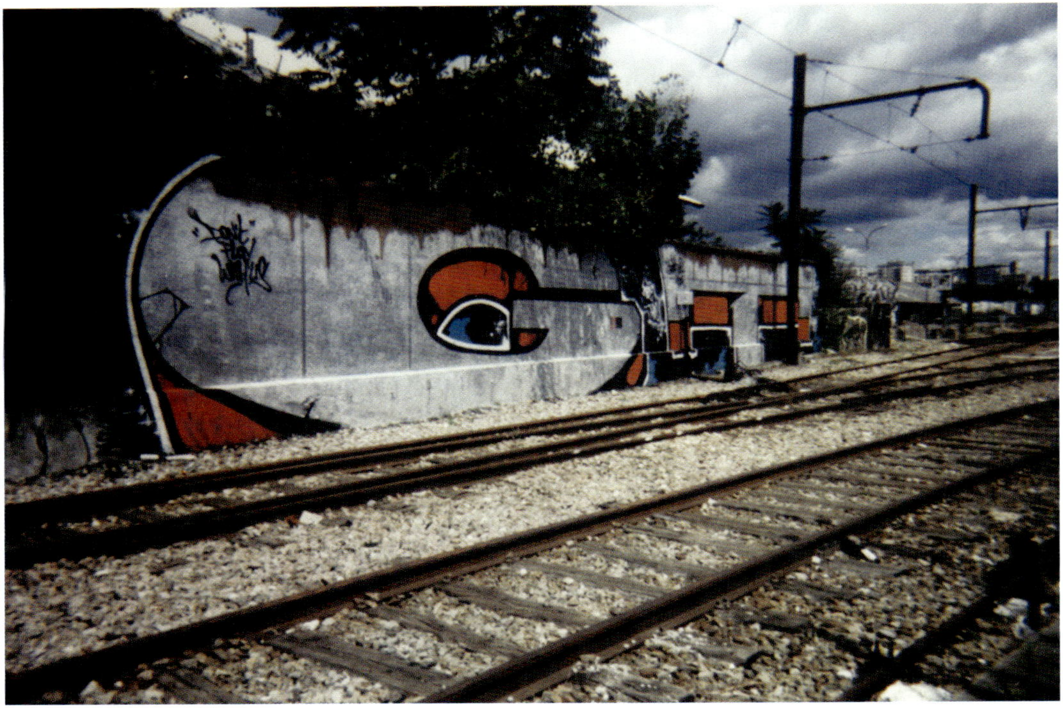

Do taggers get props from you? Which ones do you like most?

Back in the days it was Majesty, Muck, Colt, and the BBC Crew for piecing. TCG gets props from me though, 'cause they put style in their tags. Guys like Kaze, Aro, Dozer . . . the tags they did fifteen years ago are hotter than most of the new ones today. Sometimes they had so much style that you couldn't read them. For me, it's TCG for tags and BBC for pieces.

There's something that irks me these days. It's that writers, and even rappers, deny they ever wrote. It's like they're denying their roots, their background. But you can't deny your past. Colt was four years older than us. He was one of the best writers. He and Mode 2 killed shit. Colt never denied his past; he kept it real, and that's something I've got to give him props for. I saw him get caught tagging in the train when he was thirty years old. He's a father and a husband, and he has his life together, but that's just how graff is. It's always in your blood.

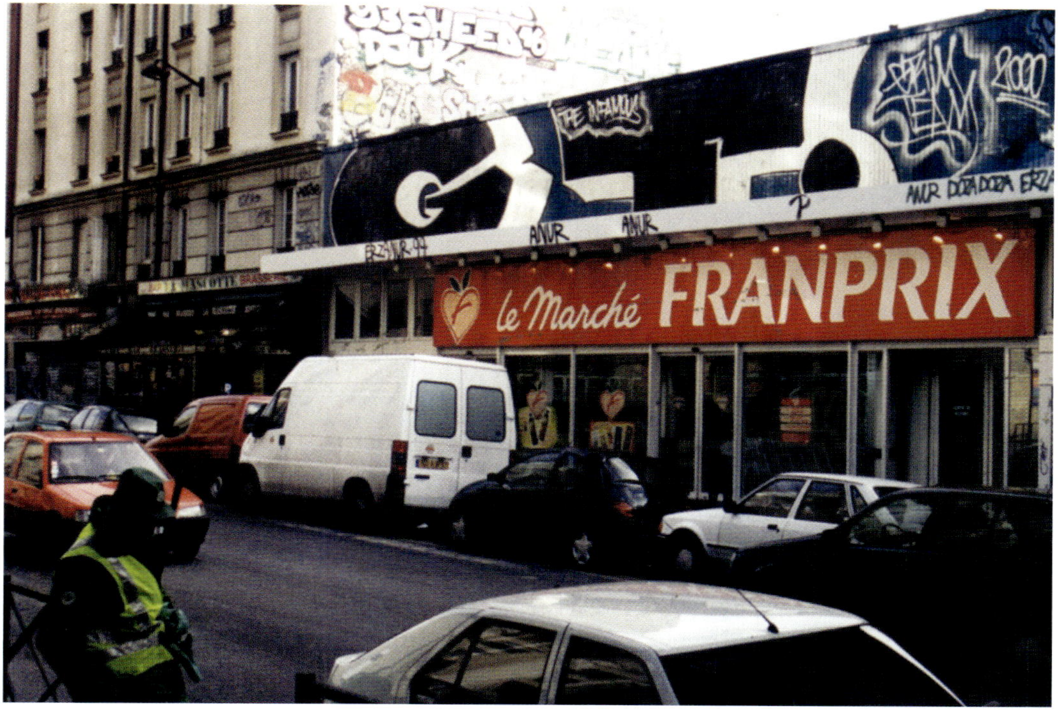

Do you rack paint?

Back in the day, you had to steal your paint. Even if you could afford it, you stole it. There wasn't a choice, 'cause around '92, people started importing paint from Holland. It was Sparvar. For a while, me, Aro, and the gang would just rob other writers in Stalingrad and Mouton-Duvernet. Those were good times . . . these days, though, I'm thirty-two. I'm not about to spend my days lifting paint.

Were you going on planned missions, or would you just always carry paint?

I never did mission like the VEP or the TKV; they would go out specifically for a spot. When we would go out (TCG Crew), we would always carry paint and markers, so we would always end up painting. We weren't going out to tag; we would just be going out, you know, here or there, and we would just tag along the way. I can't say I was running around with forty cans on me and that the sole objective of the night was to empty them.

What's your favorite brand of paint, and why?

At first it was Krylon. Buntlack is killer, you know, but it was harder to steal than Krylon. Then I got into Sparvar, and now I like Montana Hardcore.

Did you blow up anywhere other than Paris? Where?

I bombed on my way to places. If I was going St. Denis, I'd bomb St. Denis, but I never chose where I bombed. That's why I killed more areas than most people. Boxer (RIP) was more strategic. He was older than us. He had dogs, and he'd use them as a cover. He'd walk them when he was bombing. He had a truck, too, which is useful for changing neighbourhoods fast when you've been busted. I killed the neighbourhoods I went to a lot, like around les Halles and Place d'Italie. At first, I was killing subway cars and subway walls.

Did you ever get caught? If so, how many times?

I got caught at least fifteen times. In the beginning it was easy; I never ran away. My attitude was that if I didn't put up a fuss, I'd get locked up and released in the morning. That didn't really bother me too much. I tagged in broad daylight in front of mad people, 'cause I just didn't have any fear. One day this cop tried to catch me, but I pushed him down and ran away. Ever since that day, I haven't spent too many nights at the police station.

If you had to give advice to kids that are starting out, what would it be?

Stay true to yourself. Bomb everything while you can, and while you're young, and stay real. O'Clock bombed a lot and began to get crossed out by a bunch of jealous toys. He never gave up, though, and he continued to smash everything. He repped shit, and in the end he's the one everyone will remember, not the toys that crossed him out.

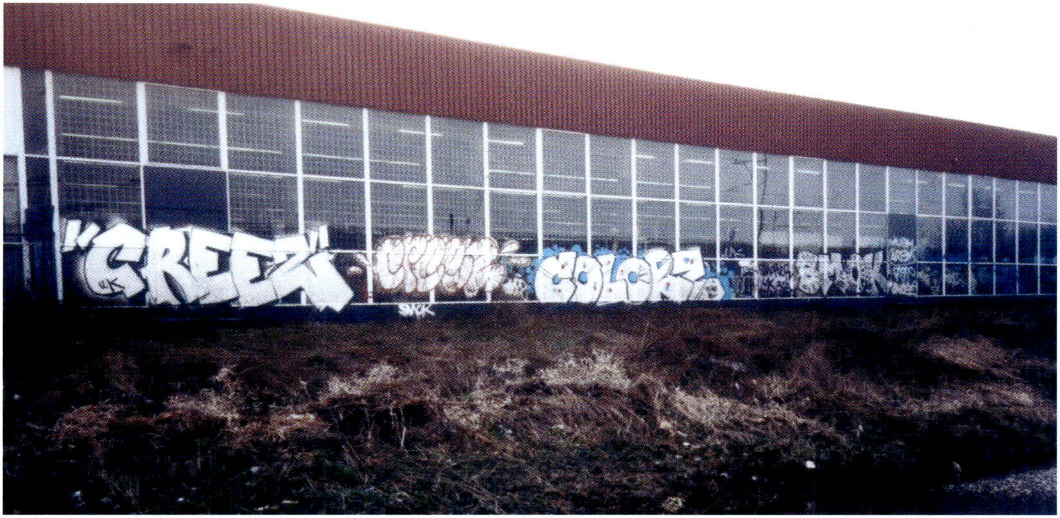

How do you feel about crossing people out? Some don't do it, others are all about it—what's your take on it?

The old school writers get tons of respect here. Back in the day, we did cross people out a lot. We didn't have beef with anyone in particular, but we did it to get talked about. There wasn't really anyone to respect back then. The dope writers were all my boys, so I didn't cross them out. We didn't give a shit about those that came after us. These days, I don't bother with that too much. Kids cross me out in yards, but it goes back and forth. In the streets though, I show people respect and I get it back in return.

Do legal walls count as graffiti?

I don't hate on legal walls, but I'd rather do illegal shit than a paid mural. There are guys that only do legal walls and contracts, but for me that's not graffiti. Graffiti is part of street culture. When you see kids from MAC that rep France for the world in mags and do tons of legal walls, it's wack to me that they don't have a single writer who wrecks shit on the street. When you cover bombing with legal walls I don't hate on it, but it's not what graff is about for me.

Who's an all-out King, in your opinion?

One I can think of is Oeno. He tagged, he bombed, he pieced, and he ripped in all those categories. Tons of kids killed Paris with tags like Aro or Boxer, but they don't piece. Mode 2 is a dope piecer, but he never bombed. There aren't many Kings out there.

What did graffiti bring to your life?

With PCP, 156, and TW, I was able to start up a company, Wrung Division. We started by putting our pieces on T-shirts, and it was successful. From there we became interested in graphic art and computers, and it led to the creation of our company. All my life today is built around graffiti.

What do you hope to accomplish with all this?

Keep doing what I do. I'd like to bomb a little more. Lately, I've been working in sound. I've got some boys in the music industry. In fact, the connections are the same as in the graff scene. Rap is linked closely to graff, since it's one aspect of hip-hop. It's a sort of evolution for me, but in the same domain. I started a crew of music producers with Gallegos and Chase (Grimuzik & Jungle Orchestra). For the moment, everything's running smoothly.

How much longer do you plan on writing for?

For now and forever . . . .

Any shout outs?

To all my crews: 156 All Starz, Grim Team, TOP, PCP, Wrung, Jungle Orchestra. To all my boys (they know who they are), 'nuff love to my wife and daughter (Caro & Emma), Miguel P4 (RIP), East (RIP), Boxer (RIP), and Shest (RIP).

Any last words?

The better I get to know men, the more I like my dog, Faya.

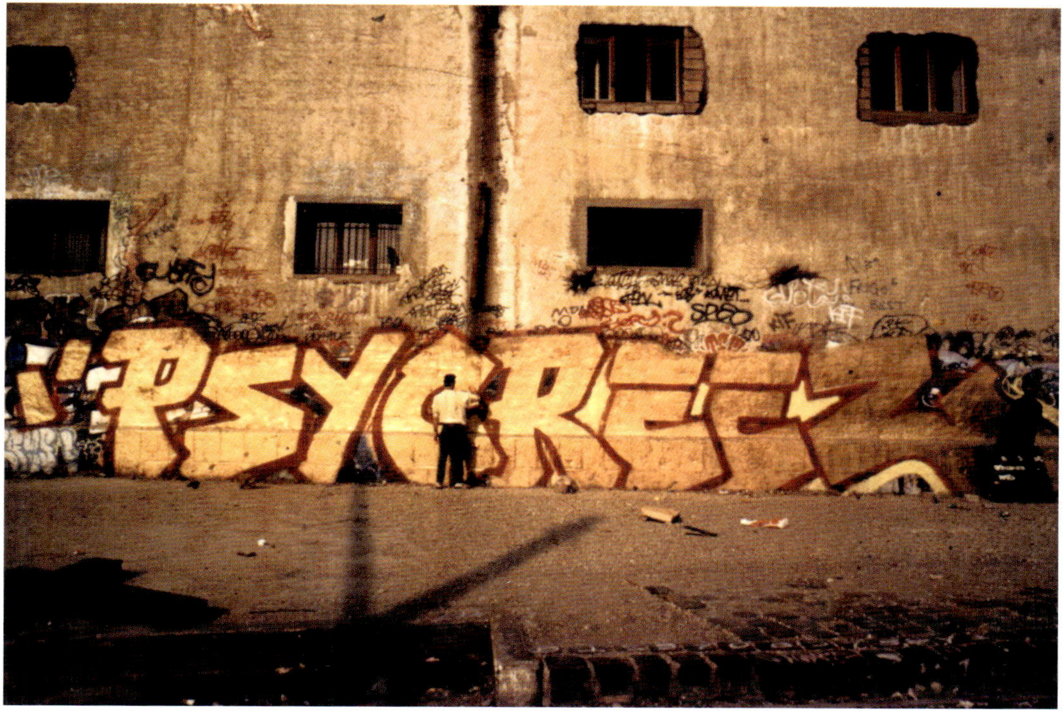

FLOW

CREW: SAT
CITY: MONTREAL
SINCE: EARLY '90S

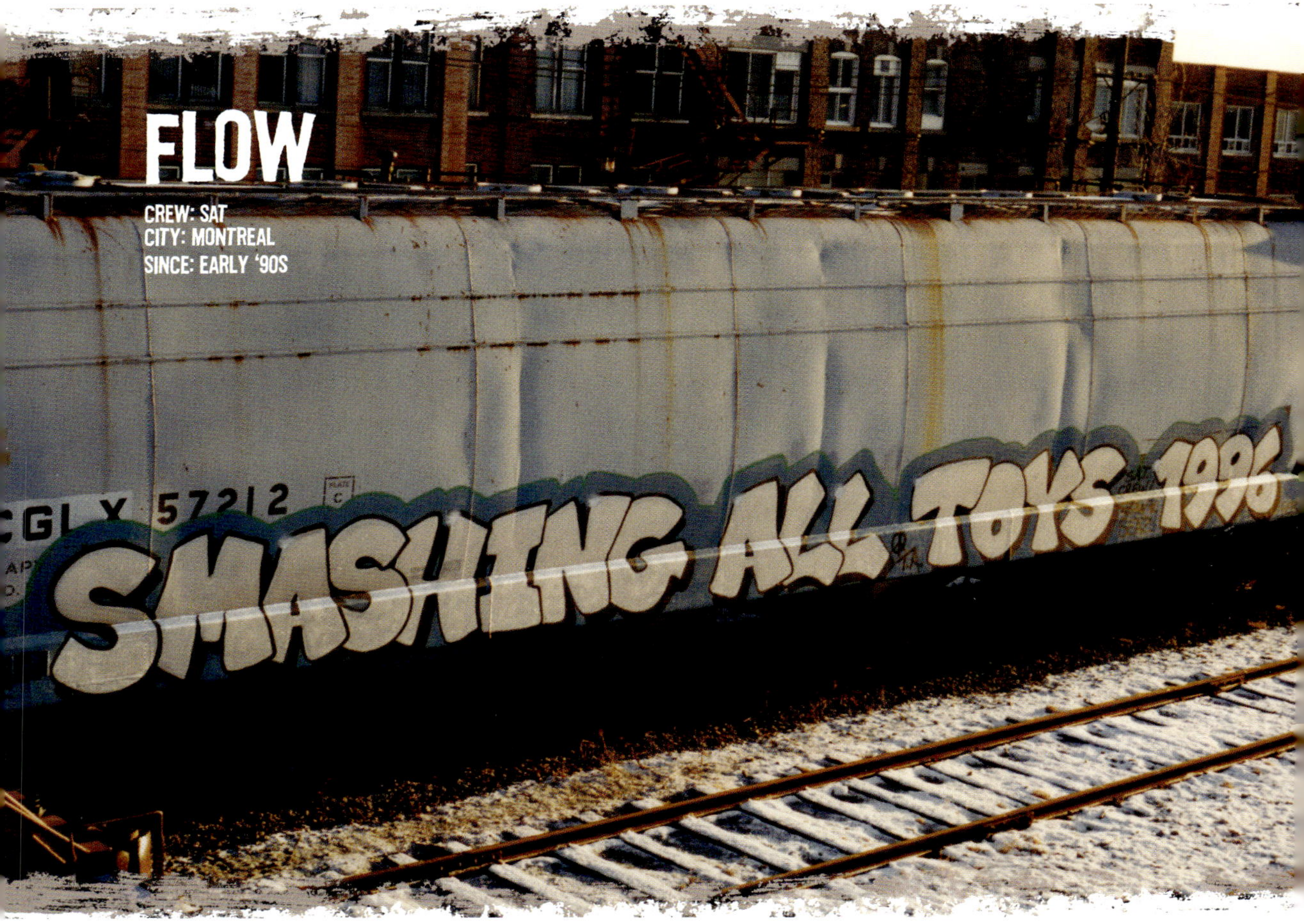

Growing up in Montreal, I saw a lot of graffiti. It wasn't dudes' names, though; it was political stuff. I grew up in a bilingual neighborhood on the English side of the city, and I saw mostly anti-English or anti-French stuff. For me, Flow changed the game. I remember seeing his big readable spots everywhere—highways, downtown rooftops, subway tunnels, bridges—all kinds of different things.

A few years later we ended up meeting, and his house became a library for me. Whether it was his photo albums or his collection of magazines, books, and movies, he had at it all. This is pre-Internet, when info wasn't so readily available. His story isn't really like those of traditional bombers; his impact was different. People may say that he didn't kill the city with tags and throwups the way others did after him, but what they forget is that he was, and is, the only guy I know of who'd hang out in the shadows on a high-traffic street corner for three hours to rock a multicolor burner.

When did you start painting?

The first thing I did was in March of '93. I did a tag under the Jacques Cartier Bridge, along the bike path. And then . . . I'm trying to remember if I did a throwup . . . and then I did a piece, my first piece.

Montreal didn't have much graffiti at that time, right?

At the time, Montreal was just basically political graffiti—Sike, Soak, Santi, Jest, Jam, Mersh, Maink, and East—but normally just political graffiti.

Can you give me an example of political graffiti?

101. Well, must be '93, not too close to the referendum, but still it's always been prevalent, the 101 stuff, the Quebec separation, "Anglos Go Home."

So "Anglos Go Home" was getting up then.

Yeah, and "No Parking."

"No Parking?"

Yeah, "No Parking" was up.

How did you get into it?

I started breakdancing in 1982. I was eleven and got into the whole hip-hop, breakdancing, write-your-name-with-marker-around-the-neighborhood—strictly just neighborhood stuff. Stole a can of spraypaint, spraypainted my shoes, wrote on the wall, and that was basically it for my career in graffiti back then. Once breakdancing got too popular, I left that, and then got back into hip-hop around '88.

I went down to New York in '91, and saw all the graffiti down there, around Lower Manhattan. Took the bus down, so I came in through New Jersey, then across through a tunnel into the port, so I didn't really see too much highways that time. That was later. That was like two trips after. But anyways, came back to Montreal, and started thinking about doing graffiti, because I had always wanted to get back into it when I got back into hip-hop, and it was prevalent in the videos. Not too too prevalent—it wasn't everywhere—but it was in videos. I'm trying to remember if it was in some advertising, or album covers, and so forth. But definitely videos, like Naughty by Nature, it was in their video, and some other stuff.

So thinkin' about it, thinkin' about it, thinkin' about it, talking to my best friend about it—he said I should get into it, and he was kind of there back at the end of my breakdancing in '84. So, spoke to him about it, he said I should get back into it, and then in December of '92 he died. He was a musician, a writer, so he wanted to do stuff, get his name out there. At the time, I was almost put in a mental hospital, because I wasn't talking to anybody. I was introverted, didn't want to talk to anybody. In school, they got annoyed because I wouldn't participate in anything.

You were introverted even when you were with him, or was it because he passed away that you stopped talking?

No, before. I was never social. I was pretty much shy my whole life. And then, they say, about Grade 8, I started to really close off from everybody. Grade 7, I started to close off. I was going to private school, and I got kicked out of there, and I went to a special school.

Why did you get kicked out?

Thieving from people's lockers, loan sharking, and just not participating in class. The teachers, at a certain point, they just knew not to ask me anything, or for my homework or anything. And at the private school, you're paying, so I was gone. Then, Grade 8 and Grade 9, I went to school in a mental hospital. I wasn't in the mental hospital. But they wanted to put me in the mental hospital 'cause I was too shy and closed-off from everybody, and I robbed, and I drew skulls or something, I'm not too sure. So my friend passed away, and he didn't get a chance to do what he wanted to do, so it kind of made me figure I should try to put my name out there. I started a little bit of drawing—not too much, some little bit of drawing—and then I brought one tag to the wall after that. I'm not too sure if I did a throwup, and then one piece—a multi-colored piece—nothing special, but it was a piece.

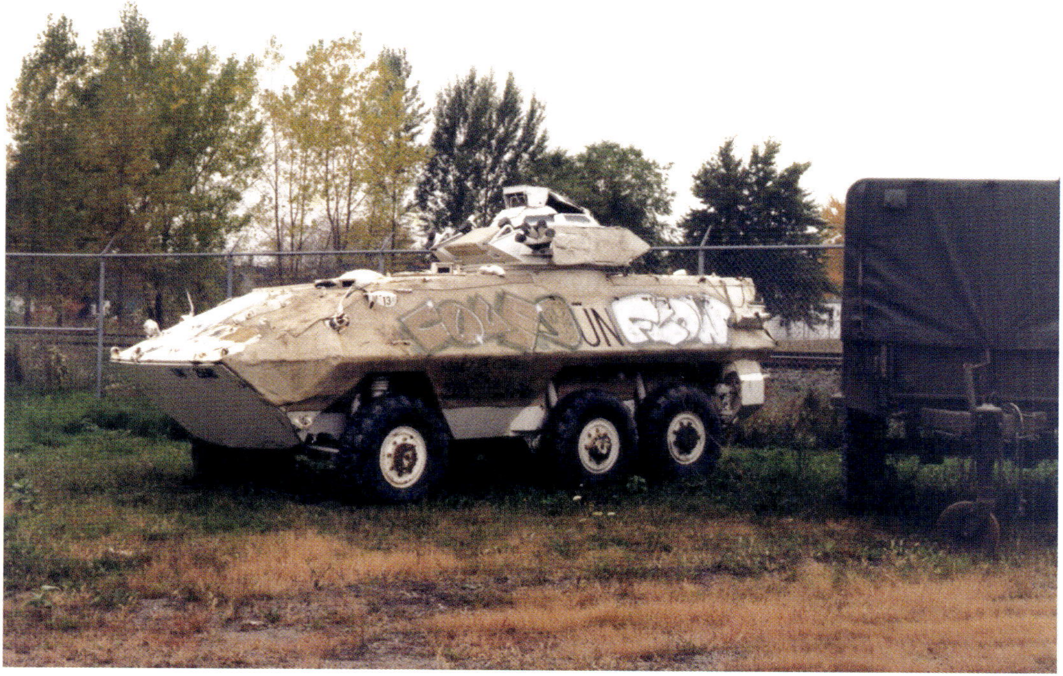

So at the time, besides the political stuff, you mentioned that there were a few other writers up. What were they doing? They basically had tags and throwups, and it was more like what was going on in New York, right?

Yeah, they were basically strictly Plateau and DTC Crew, who lived near St. Laurent and St. Catherine, at Jeanne-Mance projects. That was basically the border of graffiti, was like St. Catherine, up into the Plateau, and maybe a couple of things downtown.

So pretty much the red-light district.

Kind of. I can't speak for NDG, because I never experienced NDG. I know they had some there; I don't know who was up, though. From what I saw, it was the Plateau.

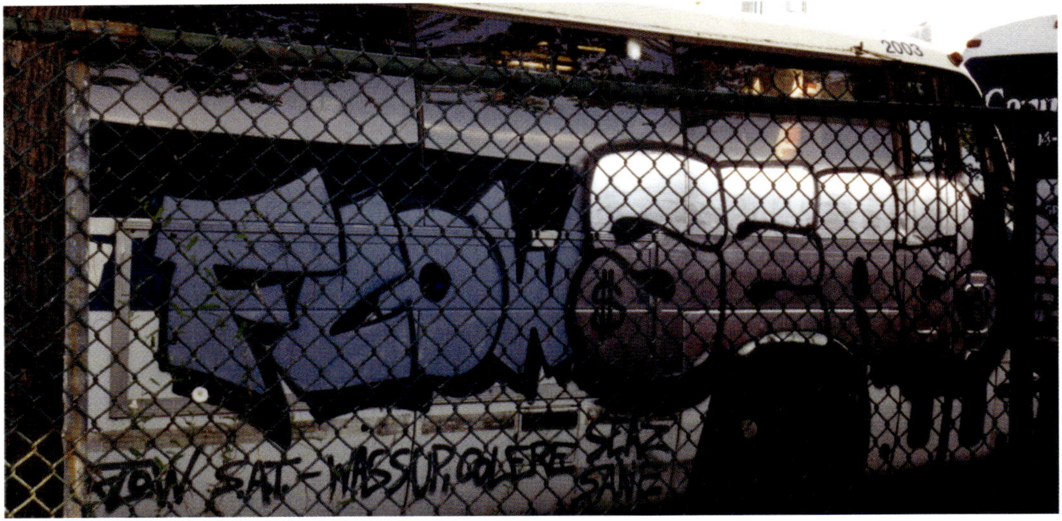

You got way more famous than anyone from your era. Anyone who grew up in Montreal at the time knows you, A) because your style is readable, and B) because if you didn't live on the Plateau or on the corner of St. Laurent and St. Catherine, there was no other graffiti in the city besides you.

As far as I know . . .

Basically, you started, you did a couple of tags, you think you did a throwup, and then you rocked a piece.

One tag, maybe a throwup—I don't think so—and then a piece. Just straight like that. I wanted to do something more than just a tag. I wanted to do something that would flash a little bit more, and get attention.

This is early '93?

March of '93. I did a tag, and I did a piece in March of 1993.

When do you think you got famous?

When I got the front page of *The Gazette*. That was October 11, 1994.

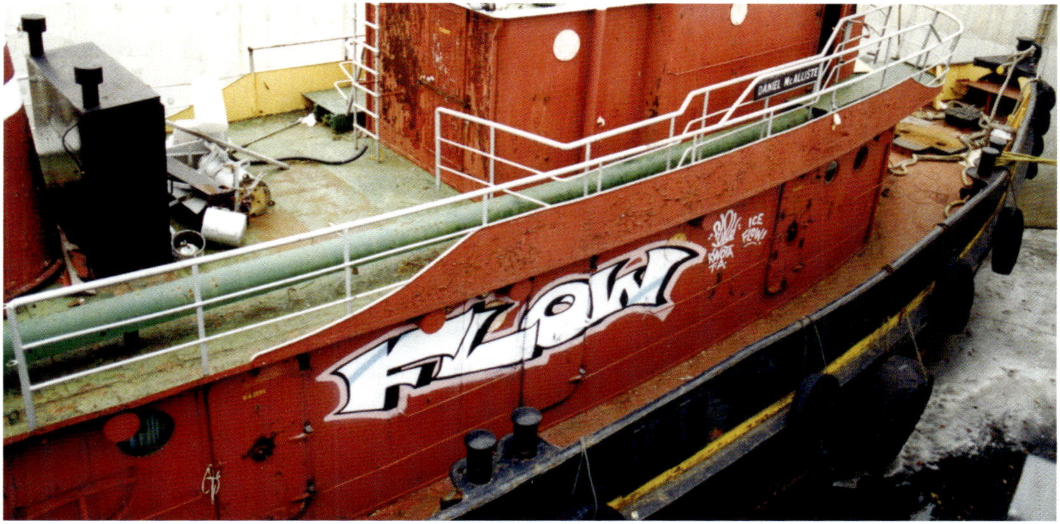

That's like a year and six months after you started painting. How many pieces do you think you did before that cover?

I have no idea how many pieces I did, but I guess I did enough to get the public to notice me.

But it wasn't one particular thing?

No. It was just the culmination of everything up until that point, I guess.

What was the process that made you famous?

The way I caught fame was doing stuff in visible spots, and not straight-letter, but very readable stuff. Very legible for the masses. You didn't have to be a graffiti artist to read anything into it. It was just for the masses. Going around, I'm not sure exactly where, but just spreading out, not just the Plateau. Spreading out across a little bit, downtown, highways, and other areas. That's basically it.

Did you have a plan? This was before magazines and stuff were available in this city.

No. I picked up my first magazine in New York. I think it was just after I started painting. At the time, caps, magazines, and all that stuff didn't exist up here.

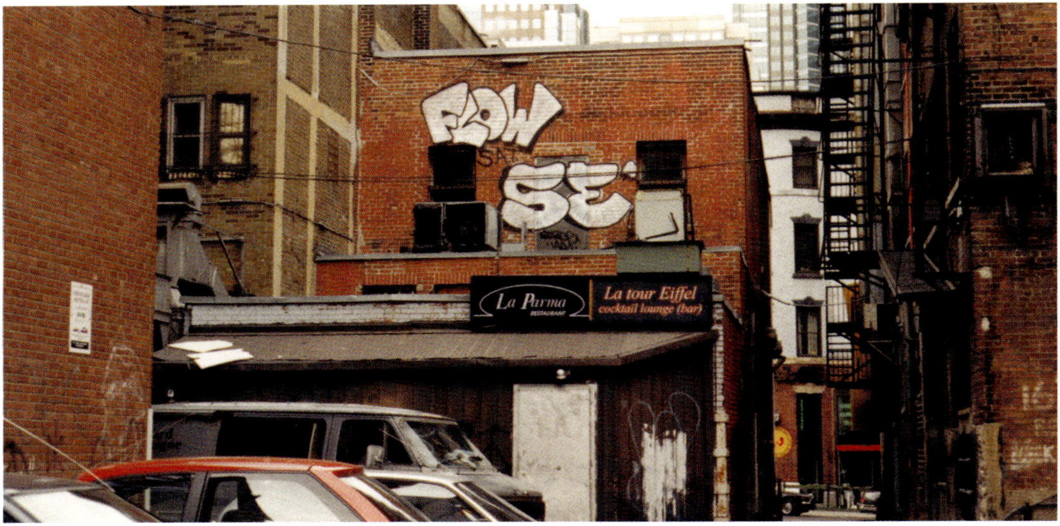

So there was no blueprint for what you were doing? You just rocked a few spots and the media picked up on it? You were more of a household name than most of the graffiti writers now, because even though there were other graffiti writers around, you were the one getting all the press at that time.

At the time, there wasn't too much stuff, piecing-wise. But I was doing pieces. Maybe I'm not remembering correctly, but there weren't very many pieces, and I was doing pieces that were legible. Some graffiti writers were writing for graffiti writers and the hip-hop community. I don't know if I was writing for the public, but it was very accessible to the public because it was legible and colorful, and I guess people like to see the colors, and they understood it. They knew what it said, so they understood what was going on.

It's funny, 'cause you went from wanting to get your name up for a reason, to slowly fading back when it got more popular in the city—when the city started to get saturated—but you still keep painting. Most of the press that you've done is from back then, too. At one point, you had to be hyped to be getting the attention, but later on, did that become a problem? Did it affect your writing in any way? A lot of people wouldn't have been driven to continue if they'd already got all the accolades, you know?

No. I just kept on doing whatever I was doing. Like I said, I started off on my own, and I didn't know anybody that did it, so I pretty much have done graffiti for myself.

Another thing that's funny is that about three or four years later, by '96, '97, you stopped concentrating on the city and you started painting trains—freights, right?

Freight trains, yeah.

How did that happen?

For a while there, I would go out a couple of times a week or whatever. But I never really bombed, like, throwups and tags. I basically just did simple pieces, just going out a couple times a week. I had access to an apartment downtown, so that's where I stayed. Once something gets popular, I shy away from it and move away from it. I got out of hip-hop in '84 because breakdancing was used in commercials and stuff. So by those years, there were a lot of writers—well, what I think was a lot of writers—there's probably more now, but they're all crappy. You know, all those white kids who think they're going to do whatever, and they're in it for a couple of months, and then they're gone. So I've basically been all over [the parts of] this city that mattered to me—you know, not St. Michel or whatever—but I did what I had to do in the city, and I just wanted to go on to something new. So, freight trains travel, and we'd see freight trains from San Diego, so I figured they could see our trains, you know, might as well.

That's another thing. Who did you paint with originally?

Originally? Nobody. When I first started painting, I didn't know anybody who painted . . . nothing like that. Then I met one writer, painted with him a couple of times, and then there was a place in Montreal called Redpath, which is basically a place where all the writers could meet other writers in a friendly environment. It was an abandoned warehouse; there was a courtyard in the middle of the building, and you could bring your lunch, you could bring a radio, you could bring a stool. You could spend all day there. Writers come in and go out, and you meet all the writers from Montreal there, basically. So I met a bunch of writers there, and then I met one guy called Seaz, and just hooked up with him and ended up painting with him for a whole bunch of years. Everywhere that I'd paint, he would be next to me, or everywhere that he'd paint, I would be next to him. Very rarely, for a couple of years, did I paint alone. And if I did, I'd feel guilty. Or he would make me feel guilty.

So that takes us to what year, approximately? 1996,1997?

Yeah.

When you started painting with Seaz, you started doing other kinds of spots. You started hitting buses, and you started hitting rooftops with more simple stuff.

He had a car, so that made me more mobile. Before that, I was on foot and public transportation. When I hooked up with him, I got a little bit more mobile, to get other spots [that were] farther out.

Tell me about SAT.

SAT started off with me only.

It was a crew of one?

Yeah. At the time, there were two crews in Montreal. There was DTC and THC, and I guess I liked having that little accessory for your piece, so I started a crew on my own called Smashing All Toys, SAT. Later on, I got Seaz into the crew, after I was painting with him for a while. It was definitely not one of those things where you let every Joe in the crew.

And after SAT, you had another crew.

I joined TA, Team Autobot; that was Seaz and a bunch of people I had met at Redpath. After that, after a couple of trips to Toronto and meeting people from Toronto and Ottawa, I got into another crew, called KWOTA.

Which is?

Which is a crew of higher-class painters.

The upper echelon? The crème de la crème?

Yeah, a couple of people from Victoria, Vancouver, Toronto, and Ottawa. At the time, I'd say that apart from Virus and them, even though I've never really cared for their work, there was AA Crew and KWOTA Crew for Canadian crews, basically, and TCM Crew from Toronto, which was like Ren, Kane, Recka, and Daser. Those were the three crews that were known across Canada. But I'd say KWOTA was the better crew, and I got asked in after our first Under Pressure jam.

Who was your biggest influence in graffiti?

I have people that I look up to, like their work or whatever, but it didn't influence me.

Example?

Shame 125, Skeme. That was a while ago, though. Now I don't really notice much.

Do you keep up to date with what's going on in Montreal now?

No.

Really? I mean, do you ever stop and look at a throwup, or—

Well, the walls speak to me. I notice stuff all the time. But I don't really keep track of who's up more than who . . .

Who are you checking for?

I've kind of disassociated myself from graffiti a little bit; I just do my own thing now.

Why did you dissociate yourself?

'Cause there was too much crap goin' on, and I just do my own thing.

At one point, you were doing three trains a week. You've obviously slowed down.

Yeah. Last week I did three, but that's out of the norm. I just went crazy. I racked a whole bunch of paint. No—I got a, a whole bunch of paint. So yeah, I've slowed down.

You've slowed down, but do you think you'll stop?

No. I hope not.

Do you think you were addicted? Or do you think you are addicted to graffiti?

Yeah. Yeah.

Have you been arrested?

Yes, I've been arrested.

For graffiti?

The first time, yes, for graffiti. The first time was when me and a guy from France tagged a little T-shirt booth at a street festival at night; we got busted, and went to jail.

What did he write?

Sigh. Another time, I got busted for doing freights, me and three other guys. We got charged with a quarter of a million dollars in damage.

Which is probably the biggest graffiti case in Canadian history.

Yeah, probably, because they charged us with doing everything that was there, like on the whole train line that was parked. They charged us with tags from Chicago and stuff. And [the train is] owned by Canada, so it's not city property. That's like different court system and everything. A different jail system, even. So then I broke my probation. I had a curfew, and I wasn't allowed to have spray paint, and I wasn't allowed to be on CN or CP property. Then I got busted on CP property—not doing anything, just taking pictures—and I told the cop, "Okay, I'm sorry, I took pictures," and then I went to prison for one night. Yeah, I went to jail for like three days, prison one night. That's it. So I got busted for graffiti twice, and breaking probation [one of those times].

Very few people have touched the subways here, but you have.

Yes.

You've painted different things. You've taken risks.

Like the tank?

Like the tank, yeah. Can you talk to me about painting the tank? 'Cause that's not something that very many people would think about painting.

Uh, I was looking for places to paint, walking along the train tracks, looking for trains, saw a couple of tanks or whatever in the army yard—

Like on an army base.

Yeah.

Aren't those guarded?

Usually, yeah.

Who were you with? How did it happen?

It was me and Cole and we just did it. Actually, there was a little hole in the fence. So I don't know why there was a hole in the fence, but we went through there, and it was a little scary, like risky—

Did you get photos?

Yeah. Went back in the daytime, and had to sneak in, and got a picture.

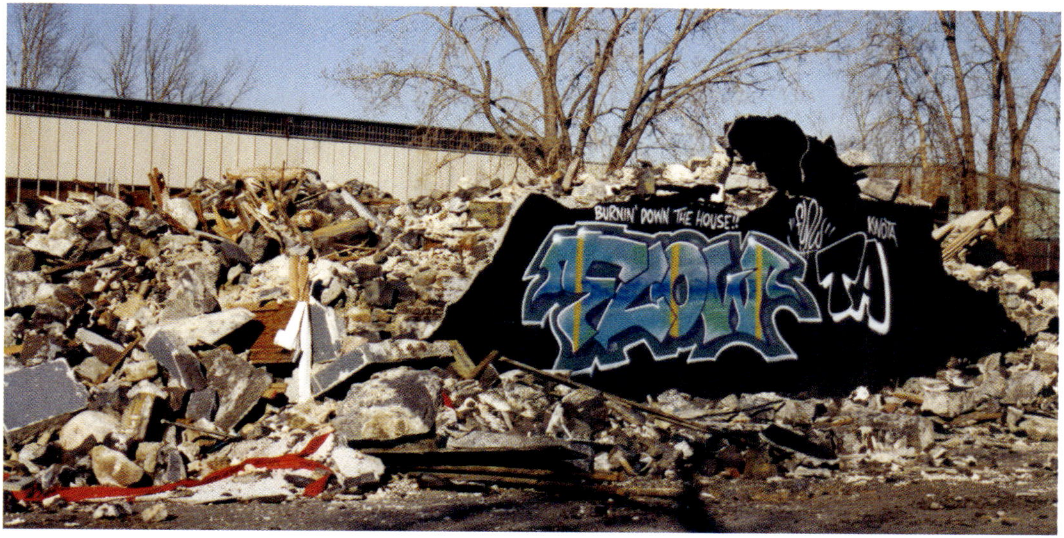

What's your favorite thing you've ever painted?

Well, the big piece I did at Redpath caught me a lot of wreck. That was good. And it was nice and clean and so forth. The tank was fun.

The tugboat?

The tugboat was alright.

The burned-down house?

The burned-down house was alright.

Where was that?

On the highway.

I think you're probably the only person in the history of the world to do a burner on a tugboat.

That's the only thing that was left. I've done a burnt-out car; I've done trucks; I've done the inside of a helicopter that was crashed in Ghana, West Africa . . .

You've painted a lot of weirdo things.

I've painted a lot of different things. Before, [the only thing left] was an airplane, but I did a helicopter. I did like an outline throwup in a marker. So that kind of covers the air. So I've done land, air, and sea. The tugboat, it was wintertime, and I just hopped across the ice and jumped up on the tugboat and did it.

This was in Montreal?

This was in the Old Port in Montreal. Once summer comes along, that's where everybody goes, so a bunch of people saw it until they buffed it.

You painted on Christmas Day?

That's how I celebrated Christmas: going out and painting. I told my family, "I'm not going with you this year," and I painted a train and a burnt-out car.

You just found the car?

Yeah, it wasn't far off the train tracks. I saw it and I was like hmmm . . . my mouth started to water. It still had the Ontario plates and everything on it, so I guess it must have been a stolen car. They did something, and then parked it and torched it.

Isn't that kind of incriminating?

I don't think they're stupid enough to think that I would have had something to do with whatever happened to the car previous to my painting it. I don't think the police would be that stupid. Why would you want to sign a crime like that?

One time, I was leaving jail after getting arrested for doing graffiti, and they were carrying my stuff down, you know, in jail you get your stuff back, shoelaces and whatnot. And I had a big, chunky white thing on a big brown wall next to the prison, and one of the guards said, "You wouldn't happen to be Flow, would you?" And I said, "No, but I wish I was, because he's got nice work." And the cop was like, "Okay, yeah."

Has graffiti been a positive force in your life?

Yeah.

Do you regret anything about it?

No. 'Cause like I said, before I got into graffiti, I had some problems, and then graffiti made me have to talk with people, and be more open with people, so I guess that's a positive thing.

What about cross outs? What's your stance on them? Would you cross somebody out?

If they deserved it.

Would they have to cross you out first?

Probably, yeah. That's probably the only thing that would drive me to crossing out more.

But I think that's funny, because you did get crossed out a lot in the mid-'90s.

By Bloo? That was the first person that used to cross me out. But that's all he did, so I couldn't really retaliate that much. All he did was cross out.

All he did was cross you out?

Pretty much. Well, at first, then yeah, pretty much.

Was he crossing Seaz out?

I don't know if he did. Maybe it was Seaz.

You started graffiti with a specific goal. Did you think you'd stop when you reached it? I mean, you left your mark, but the thing about graffiti is that your mark fades, and you have to keep putting it up. Do you feel satisfied with what you've done? Do you think you've accomplished anything?

I'm satisfied. I think I had an influence on graffiti in Montreal a little bit The young people now don't really know my name, but people who were never into graffiti back then, like older folks, they still remember my name from back then, so that's good.

What do you think about magazines?

At first I liked magazines because I didn't have any exposure to graffiti, so when I first got *IGT* and *Skills* mag, those were the best things I'd ever seen. Then got some other stuff, like *Tuff Stuff* from Switzerland, some more magazines, but then at one point, there were too many magazines and the *VideoGraf* was alright. When I first started, there was no Internet, but now you can pull styles off the Internet. You can bite from everywhere, so I'm not too crazy about all that graffiti-on-the-Web stuff. Now there's a few less magazines, but at one point there were too many magazines. But I guess then the Internet cut out a bunch of the magazines.

Do you think it's a false fame?

It could be. It's just like *Style Wars* only represents a couple of people; it doesn't tell the whole story. Same with magazines, you know? They don't tell the whole story. There could be people up in the city, but seeing as this guy doesn't like that guy, he's not going to put him in the magazine. So you never heard of the guy.

Is graffiti a part of your life now?

Yeah, I guess you could say. I'm a partner in a company that does a magazine and an event. After just dissing magazines . . . ironic.

How do you feel about legal walls?

No comment.

Why not?

Because I hear people shitting on legal walls, and I guess the negative outweighs the positive, so I hear a lot of people shitting on legal walls. Legal walls are good; I don't mind.

How do you feel about getting paid to do graffiti?

The first time I got paid to do graffiti, I was ecstatic: I got paid to do graffiti. I was gonna say it's like getting paid to have sex, but hookers do that. I was getting paid to do something that I loved, so it was good.

Do you think there has to be a balance between legal and illegal stuff?

Nowadays, I don't care. Just do what you're doing. There's all this "you gotta do this, you gotta do that," and I guess to a certain degree I subscribe to that. I don't care for people who've just come up doing legal pieces and never bombed anything. It kinda bothers me a little bit. Yeah, I think you gotta pay your dues. Like I said, I'm not too crazy about people just coming through on legal walls and trains out in the sticks.

That's another thing about the freight movement, like risk versus reward. It gives everybody a chance to do graffiti, seeing as how there's layups everywhere. But for you, being somebody who lives in the downtown core, and having to paint in more dangerous spots, how do you feel about those kids painting in buttfuck nowhere?

It should say on the train: "This was painted in buttfuck nowhere, so that's why we had all day to drink beer and smoke and do our piece," or whatever, you know?

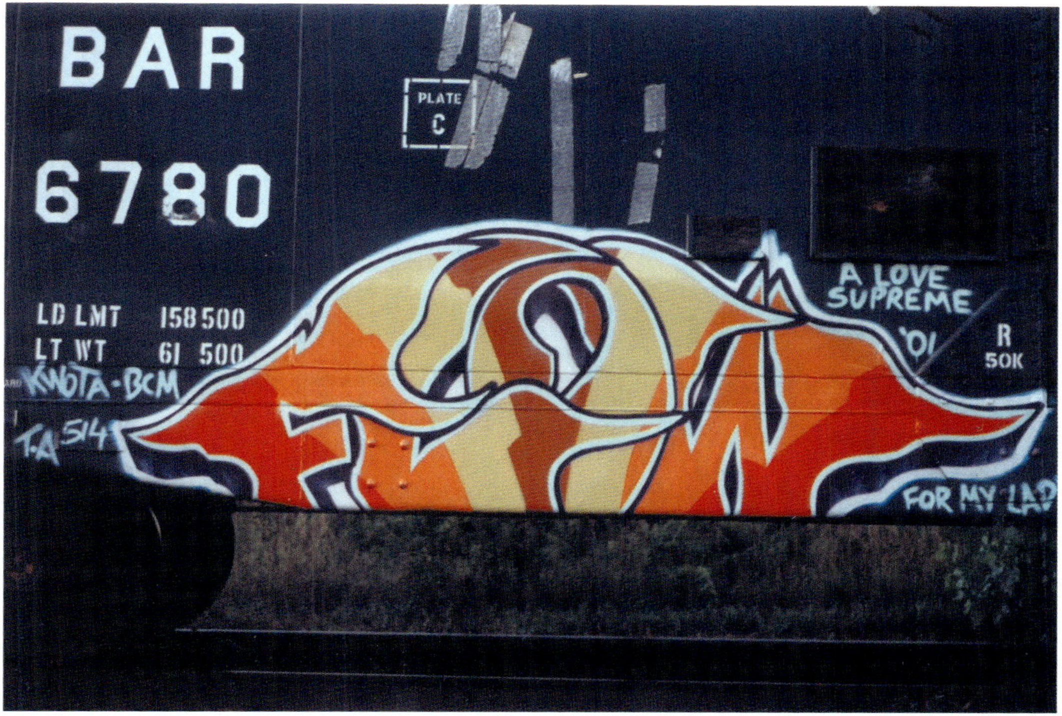

What makes somebody not a toy?

For me, it's just skills. What's a toy? To me, a toy is somebody that does ugly stuff and never progresses, never evolves. Just continuously does ugly stuff. Also, it's like somebody who goes over people when they don't have the right to. A piece goes over a throwup. A nicer piece goes over a crappier piece. There's a whole food chain, so if you're going to do something crappy over something that was better than what you did, that's pretty toy.

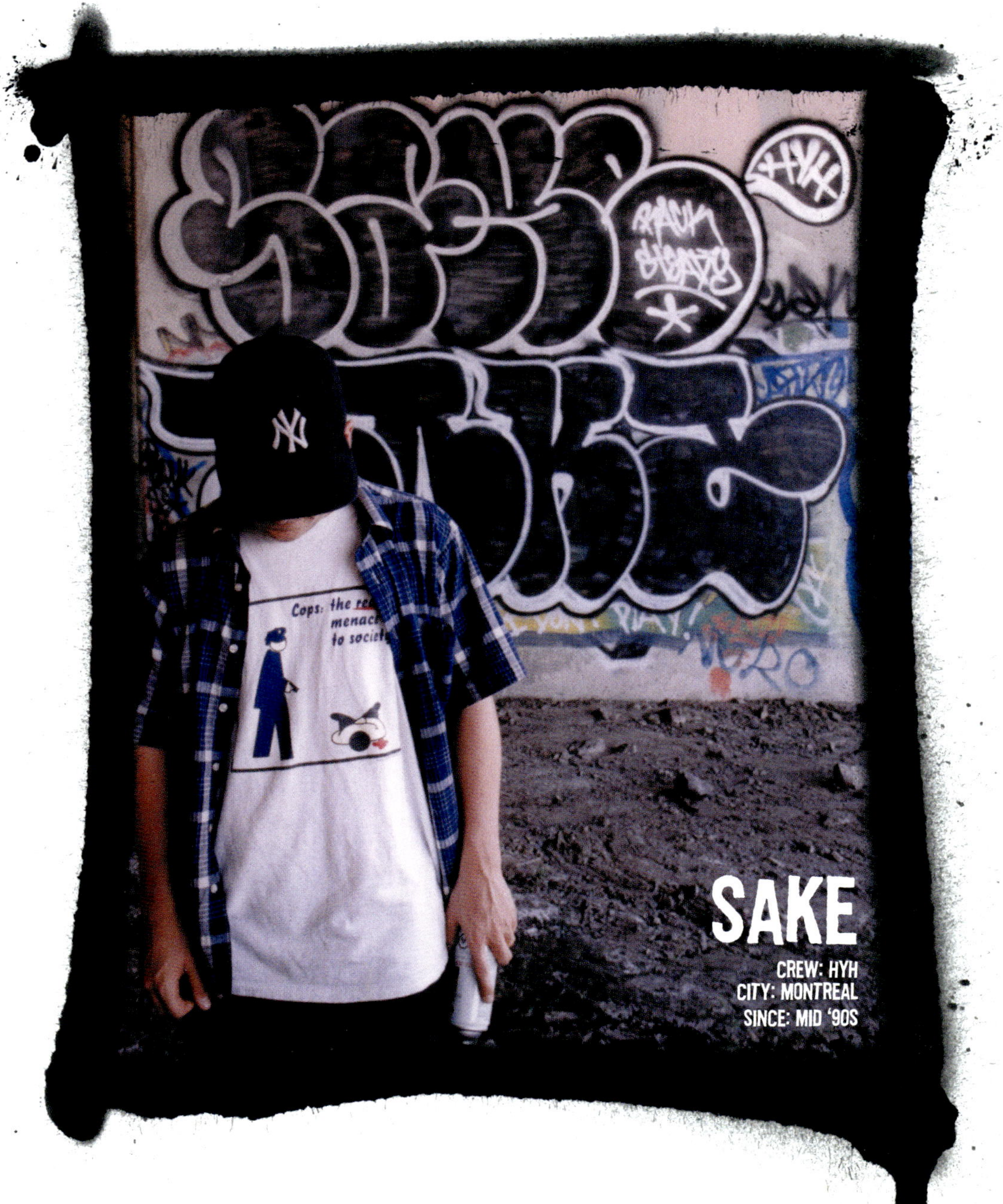

SAKE

CREW: HYH
CITY: MONTREAL
SINCE: MID '90S

Sake has been a black eye on Montreal for a while now. He's known for having locked down the Island of Montreal and its highways. From the downtown core to the suburbs, he has peppered the city with everything imaginable—fill-ins, tags, blockbusters, and lean-over rooftops—name it. Many consider him to be Canada's bombing King.

How many years have you been writing?

I've been writing for around eight years. I played around with a few names at first, for like a year and a half, and then I chose to stick with Sake.

How did you first get involved?

I got involved in graff because I had a big silver Pilot marker at home when a friend was over, and he got the bright idea that we go out tagging. From that day on, I was hooked like a junkie. I had no idea what I was doing, but I stuck with it, and now it's my way of life. I never leave the house without one of my various tools.

If you didn't know what you were doing at the beginning, what made you stick with it?

Boredom, I guess. I was at an age where I had nothing to do, and even though none of my friends tagged, it was good that they were around. We'd be out walking somewhere and I'd stop and tag and they didn't care. I tagged all around my neighborhood at first, but I didn't realize that anybody was going to notice it. I only realized that it mattered when a friend told me in a bar one night that there were some kids who wanted to meet me. I talked for like a week after that, about how there were some kids who were actually excited to talk to me. It was then that I realized that people really paid attention to graff.

Eight years in, what's your favorite marking device?

The can is king; there's nothing like the feeling of a can with a fat cap. Just run up to a spot and get loose. I love everything about it: the sound of the paint coming out full force; the fumy tags; color combos . . . that and any dark ink that's mad permanent and drips to the floor. The list could go on and on . . . .

What's your favorite type of spot to hit?

I've hit almost everything you can think of: rooftops, highways, street levels, riot gates, trains, subways, subway platforms, mini-ledges, building ledges, tunnels, trucks, and water towers. My favorite shit is stuff that is death-defying; shit where you have to worry about falling to your death, doing your shit nice, and the cops catching you, all at the same time. A spot being dangerous makes it more interesting to do than just walking up to a wall and painting it. It should get you more respect, too, than some legal guy who can have the cops drive past while he's doing his piece. I love hitting highway signs in Montreal, 'cause it isn't easy. There are only crisscrossed bars to climb, and no platforms to walk along. I love painting in the subway 'cause of the danger.

One time, a friend and I hid in the subway tunnel while the system was still running 'cause we wanted to hit a spot near a tunnel exit in a major station. There's no space to hide in Montreal subway tunnels; when the train is coming, you have to roll up into a ball, unscrew the lights in the tunnel around you so that you don't get spotted, and pray that the subway doesn't hit you. So anyway, we made it to our spot, and we did our shit. I did a three-color readable, and we took flicks the whole time. To be careful, we ran on the way out, which was smart, 'cause while we were running we heard an intercom announcement saying that there were people on the tracks. Had we not run, the cops would have seen us coming out of the tunnel, and we had the camera on us with the flicks of us doing it, as well as three cans of paint. We made it to the escalator, where subway cops looked at us, but they just kept on going. We walked past the ticket booth, past more cops, then got outside, where we had to walk past like six cop cars. Had we lost our cool, we would have been busted.

Have you been arrested?

I've done more graffiti than anybody in this city, and I've been busted once. Meanwhile, there's suckas who get busted five times in ten months and quit.

What do you wish you had known before you started?

I wish I had known how to deal with cops then. I wish I'd have known what a piece or a throwup was. I had no idea what was what for at least a year, because, like I said, I was the only one doing it out of my friends. The guy who got me started fell off in like a month, and I'm still here. I only saw a video about graff (*VideoGraf 8*) after being into it for around two years. I guess if I would have known what was up from the start, I would have started piecing right away and not gone through all the stages of development: tags, throwups, blockbusters, ground-ups, stickers . . . . I'm glad I didn't know what was what at the start though, 'cause I learned everything by myself—using caps, tagging, developing my throwup, and just going out and destroying shit. In the end, I guess I'm happy I came up that way, 'cause I'm happy where I am now: on top. Who knows, maybe if things had been different, I would have ended up a legal bitch . . . .

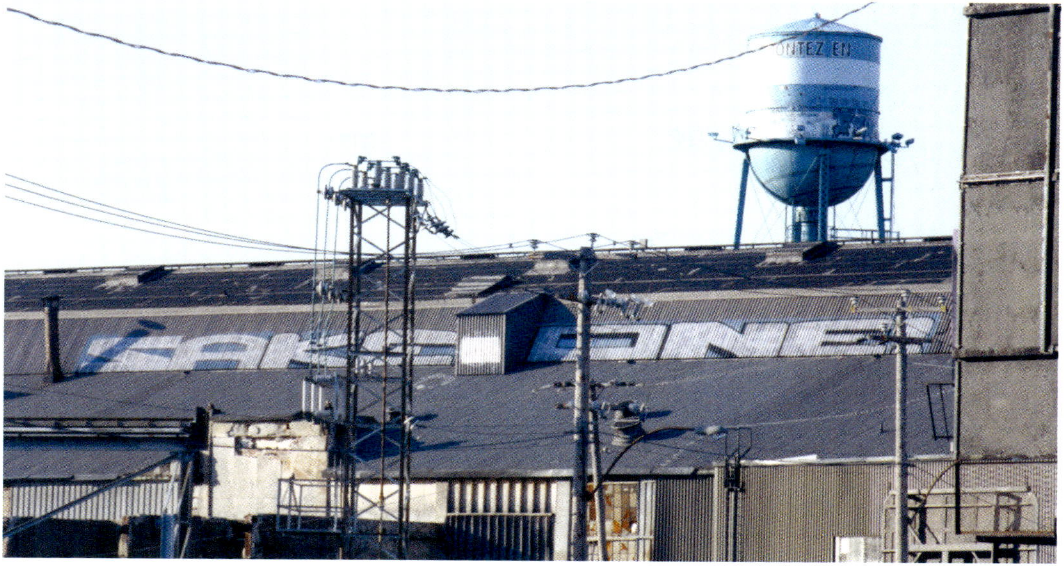

If biting is wack, where or how are you supposed to learn? Is anything really new at this point?

I guess biting is inevitable when you get started, especially with all the magazines and videos available now, but you gotta cool that shit down quick. Some people can't do anything but bite. If they try something else that's their own, it's just not happening. It's cool if you bite when you have no clue what you're doing, but after a few months, you've gotta dead that. What's the point of doing the same thing as someone else? Nobody can say that everything has been done; you can always come up with some next shit.

When is someone no longer a toy?

Just 'cause someone has style, it doesn't mean that they're not a toy. If you come out just doing legal walls and freights in nowhereland and you haven't put a dent in the city and you only exist in flicks, you ain't shit. Nowadays, you gotta rock the streets, the subways, the highways, trucks, trains, and walls. Keep graff in your heart. You gotta keep going, no matter what. No matter how many people diss you. Know your history; know where it all originated. Pay your dues. Maintain and go for yours, and that's when you're no longer a toy.

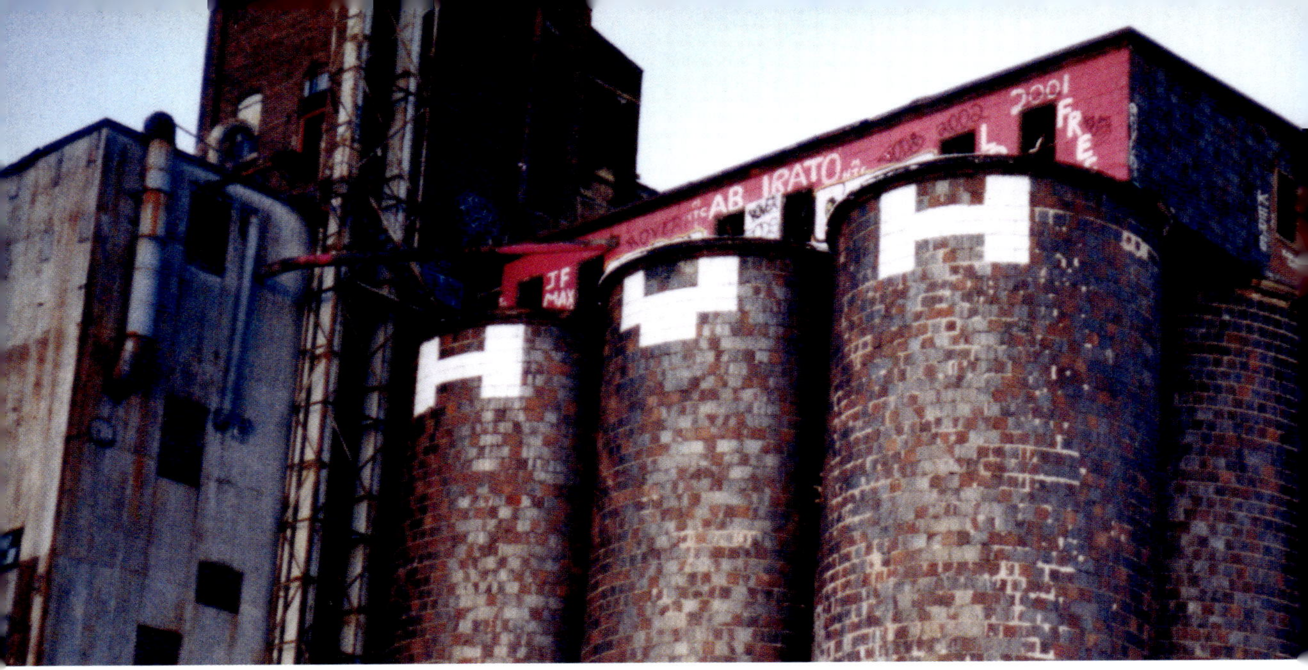

So is getting paid to do legal walls graffiti?

Legal walls are graffiti-influenced art. When I think graffiti, I think illegal shit, because graff is vandalism. What you do can't be considered graffiti when it's acceptable—it lacks the adventure and the rawness. It's fine to get paid for contracts, but when you start to pride yourself on legal walls and getting paid, then you're a joke. It's cool if you paid your dues for years, or you do your share of illegal stuff, but if you think you're this ill writer 'cause you have all these legal walls running, you're dead wrong. Is it hard to sit in your house, draw what you want to do, copy it on a wall and then show your mom and dad what you did? And how hard is it to do your stuff properly when it's legal? I challenge any piecer who has never bombed to do their shit on the corner of a busy street and make it come out as nicely as it does on their little legal walls. Just because you're using spray cans doesn't mean that you're doing graffiti.

How often do you go out strictly to paint?

Never. I don't work like that. For huge spots, yeah, I plan it out, but usually I just carry paint everywhere I go. So I could be coming home from a party or whatever, and just go off on the walk home. It's easier that way. Also, if you always have paint on you and you end up chillin' in another neighborhood, you don't have to go back for the spot—just take it there and then. I end up painting real often, 'cause if I don't paint for like two days, I feel like I haven't painted in months.

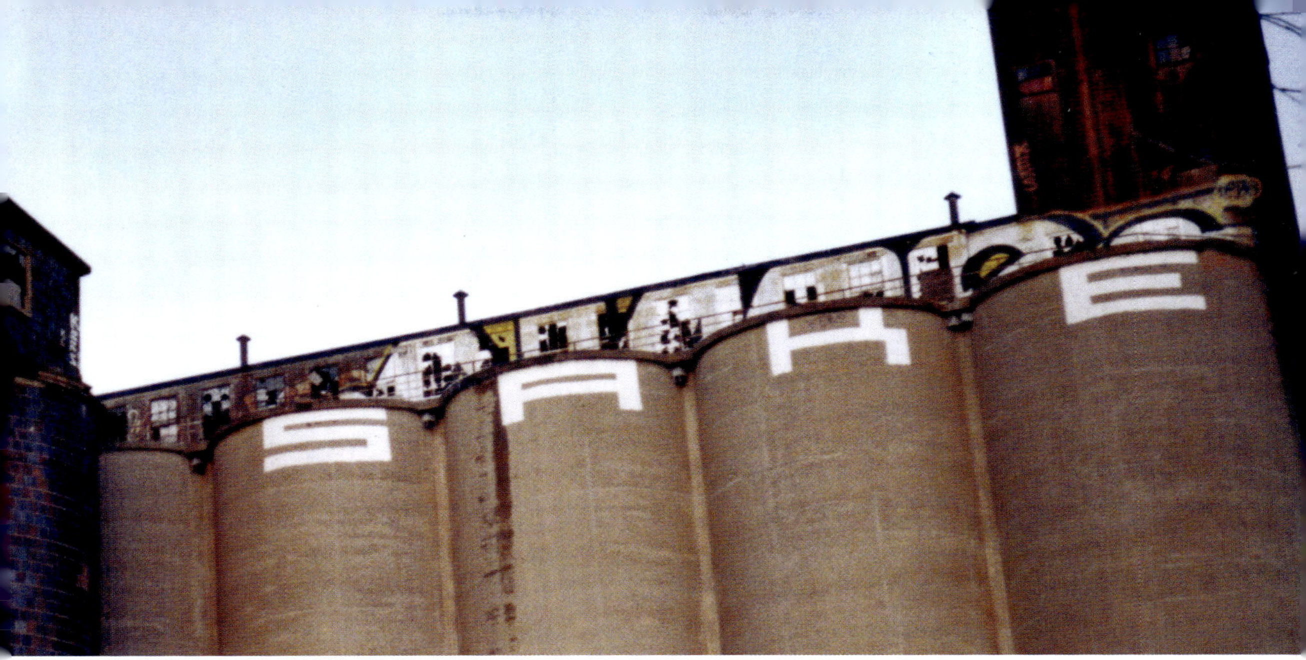

You're known for racking huge amounts of paint and markers, right?

First time I remember stealing something, I was in Kindergarten, and I've been stealing ever since. I rack everything that I use to get up. It's senseless to pay for graff supplies; it would be a never-ending expense for me. It's funny to see someone spend a hundred dollars on paint and then have the spot crossed out, gone over, or buffed. If I paid for all the supplies I use, I would be broke. I use racking to supplement my income. For example, I'll rack markers, keep some for myself, and sell the rest, then I'll buy stuff that I can't steal with the money I make. Graff has made me into a klepto, but I'll never steal from a friend. That shit is wack. Thanks to racking, I walk around town flossing in free clothes. I see racking as a skill. It's like painting; you have to be mad aware of what's going on around you so you don't get caught.

Do you have a policy on cross outs?

My policy is simple: go over me and I take the spot back. Go back over it again and it's over. I take everything you got. If somebody thinks they can take what I got, they better just give up their career, 'cause they won't be able to keep up with the pace that I'll be going over them at.

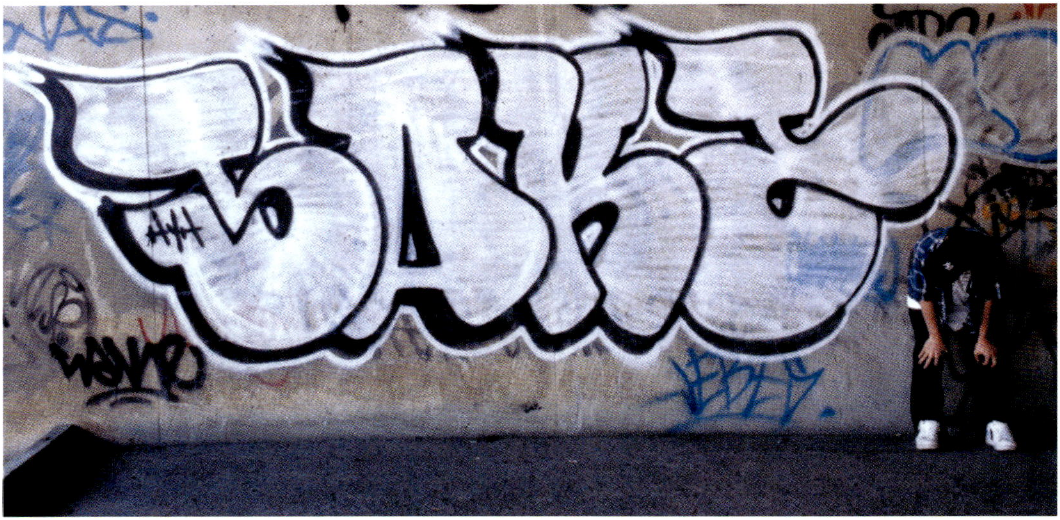

Who do you think is a well-rounded writer, and who do you look up to?

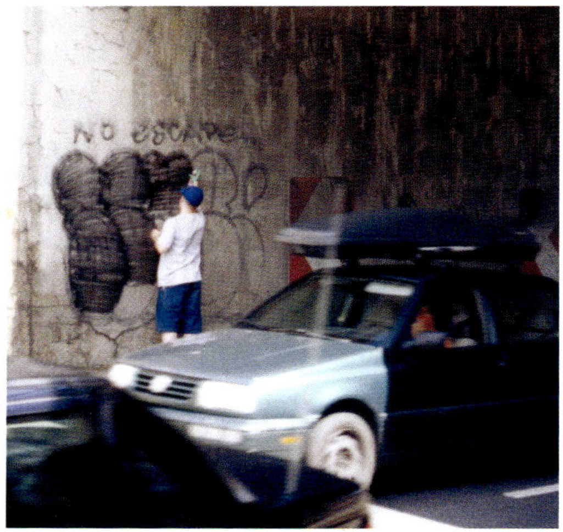

There are tons of guys representing to the fullest around the world, but I honestly don't look up to anyone. I'm anti-hero—no other writer is above me—I'm never gonna bow down to anybody. I'm never gonna praise anybody for doing something that I could have done myself, or have done myself in the past. I respect people who have love for graff and who've made it part of their everyday lifestyle. I like guys who aren't worried about seeing a dime out of writing, guys who are always willing to break their backs for graffiti, willing to risk life and death to get a spot.

Do you go bombing alone or with a crew? Is there a method to it?

It depends on how I feel. If no one's around, I'll go solo. I like bombing alone. I can hit what I want, there's no one around to get me busted, and there's no arguing over spots. You can never really trust someone one hundred percent. There are times when people say, "Yeah, I'm looking out," but then you turn around and they're watching you paint instead. Next thing you know, the heat's coming. When you're bombing, you need to remember to check parked cars' windows, 'cause somebody could be sitting there calling the cops. I always bomb now like there is someone watching, 'cause you never know. There's always someone around. The question is, do they care or not? Sometimes you can't avoid being seen, and that's when you pray that they don't care, because you could get vamped or arrested. I used to not care at all about who saw me when I was painting. I remember one time, downtown, I was painting a roll-down gate on a store and a woman and her family watched me the whole time. She's standing there with her kids, watching me paint, and they're all smiling! Now that I've made a name for myself, though, I have to worry more about who's watching. What I've really gotta watch out for now is undercovers rolling up—they'd love to bust me and stomp me down.

Is writing an addiction to you?

That describes it perfectly. An addiction; that's exactly what graffiti is. It's plagued my life and my mind every day since the day I started. As much as someone loves basketball, football, spinning records, breakdancing, emceeing, whatever . . . I love graffiti. I met a DJ who told me that he respects writers more than anybody else in hip-hop, 'cause graff is the element that he thinks is the most low-reward. Emceeing, DJing, and breaking can help guys get out of lives of crime or bad situations, but the more graff you do, the deeper into crime you get, and the more serious the consequences of getting caught become. A lot of people say they're down with hip-hop 'cause they dress out of rap magazines, but they don't even know that graff is a part of the culture. I've adjusted my whole life and where I live for graffiti. Some guys quit graff 'cause they say that they get nothing out of it. They quit 'cause they say it doesn't help them get girls, or that all it does is ruin their clothes. I can't understand that.

Any regrets at this point in your career?

I guess the one thing that bugs me is that people know what I look like. Too many people know who I am. If I could go back, only a handful of people would know who I really am. There's mad bitches out there who talk so much shit. I've seen them all come and go over the years. Who knows what those bitches say behind closed doors?

What's your ultimate goal in this?

I don't have one. I always plan to come up with new throwups and new tags, so that I keep my shit fresh. But overall, I just paint 'cause I love it and it's part of me.

Would you say graffiti has improved your life?

It really hasn't. Getting arrested or harassed is wack. I mean, I've been dropping a marker tag and have almost gotten beat down by vigilante storeowners. The only way graffiti has improved my life is that I've got hook-ups now and places to stay for free in countries all around the world. Also, there's stupid shit that's cool, like how I can meet somebody for the first time and they'll give me free stuff just 'cause I write Sake. I'm always happy in the moment that I'm doing graffiti, and it gives me gratification, but at the same time, it could bring me down.

One afternoon, I was painting with two friends on the outside of an abandoned building, where we could completely be seen from the street. A cop car rolled up on the other side of the fence. For a few seconds, they stared at us . . . until we ran. We hopped the fence on the other side of the yard, but they chased us in the car and cut us off. Thinking mad quickly, we jumped back over the fence and decided that we should try to hide out in the building. The only way inside was through a broken window, so we made our way in and tried not to get cut up. Nobody ever painted inside that building 'cause it was way too dark, night or day. Now we were inside this condemned building, there's dirt and bird shit everywhere, the floors are fucking broken, there's old wiring hanging down, and none of us had a flashlight. It was either maybe get hurt, or get busted. I said that we should make our way to the roof, so that we could look down to see if they'd left. We saw that they were still there, so we decided that we'd wait them out. Twenty minutes later, we think we hear another van pull up, and the next thing we know, we hear fucking dogs barking. The cops called for the fucking K-9s. So we went back into the building, my friends hid in a vent, and I climbed into the ceiling. I'm in this ceiling, there's so little room that I can't take full breaths, and I know that there's cops in the building. I thought that I was done. They walked around yelling for us to give ourselves up, but we got lucky and they never found us. I waited in the ceiling for like an hour and a half. When I finally climbed out, it was fucking dark outside, and I still had to make my way out of this building without falling through the floor.

We got lucky that day, but those are the times when you wonder what you're doing. There have been nights where I've been running for my life, tripped on something, wiped out, cut my arm, and I have to tell myself to get the fuck up and keep running. I end up in some ditch, seeing stars, gasping for air, and wondering to myself, "What the fuck am I doing this for?" But then I make it home, go to bed, and the next day I'm back out painting again like nothing ever happened.

How long will you keep painting?

I can't say. I don't know what will happen tomorrow, but for now graffiti is in me, and until it leaves me, I'm gonna be around. I can't ever imagine a time when I won't be up. People always say, "Oh, I'll never stop," but you can't say that. All I can say is that I don't ever want to stop painting.

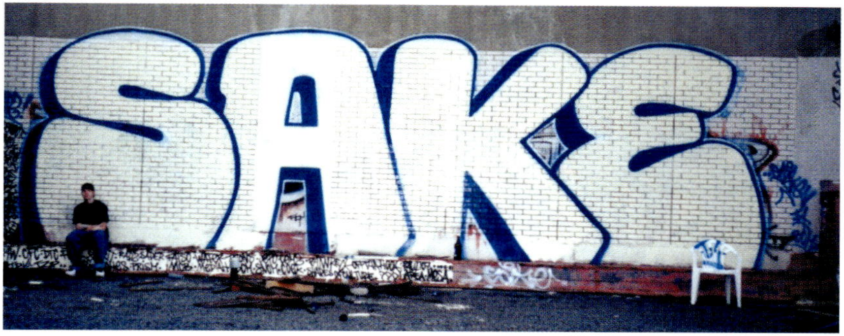
SAKE

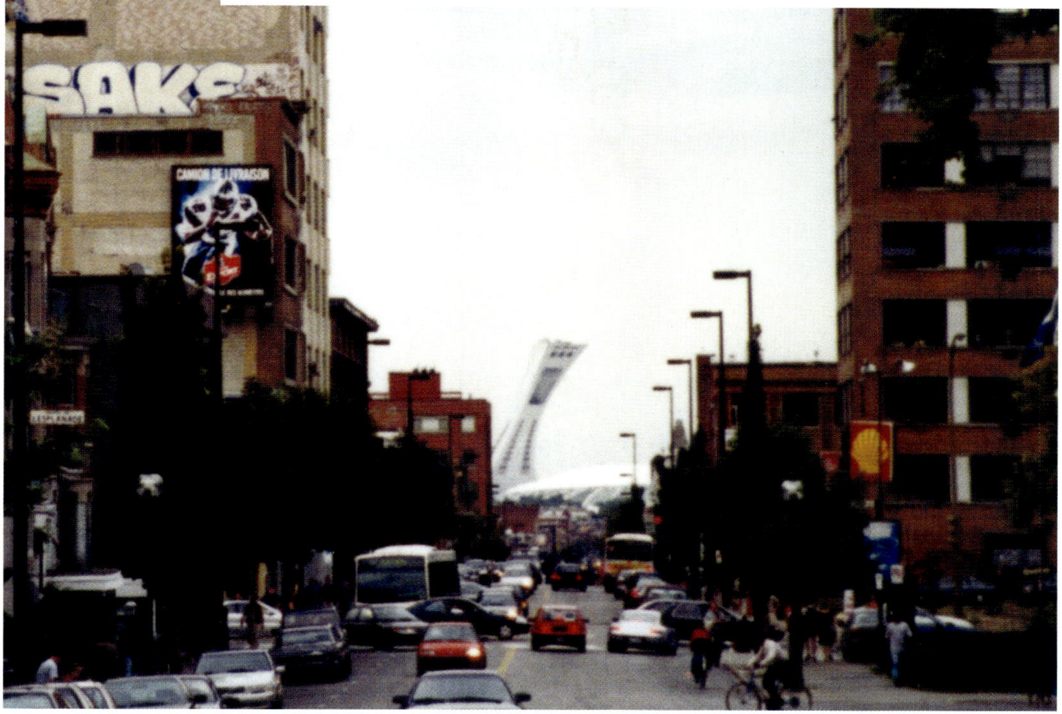
CAMION DE LIVRAISON

MIN

CREW: RTW
CITY: BROOKLYN
SINCE: LATE '70S

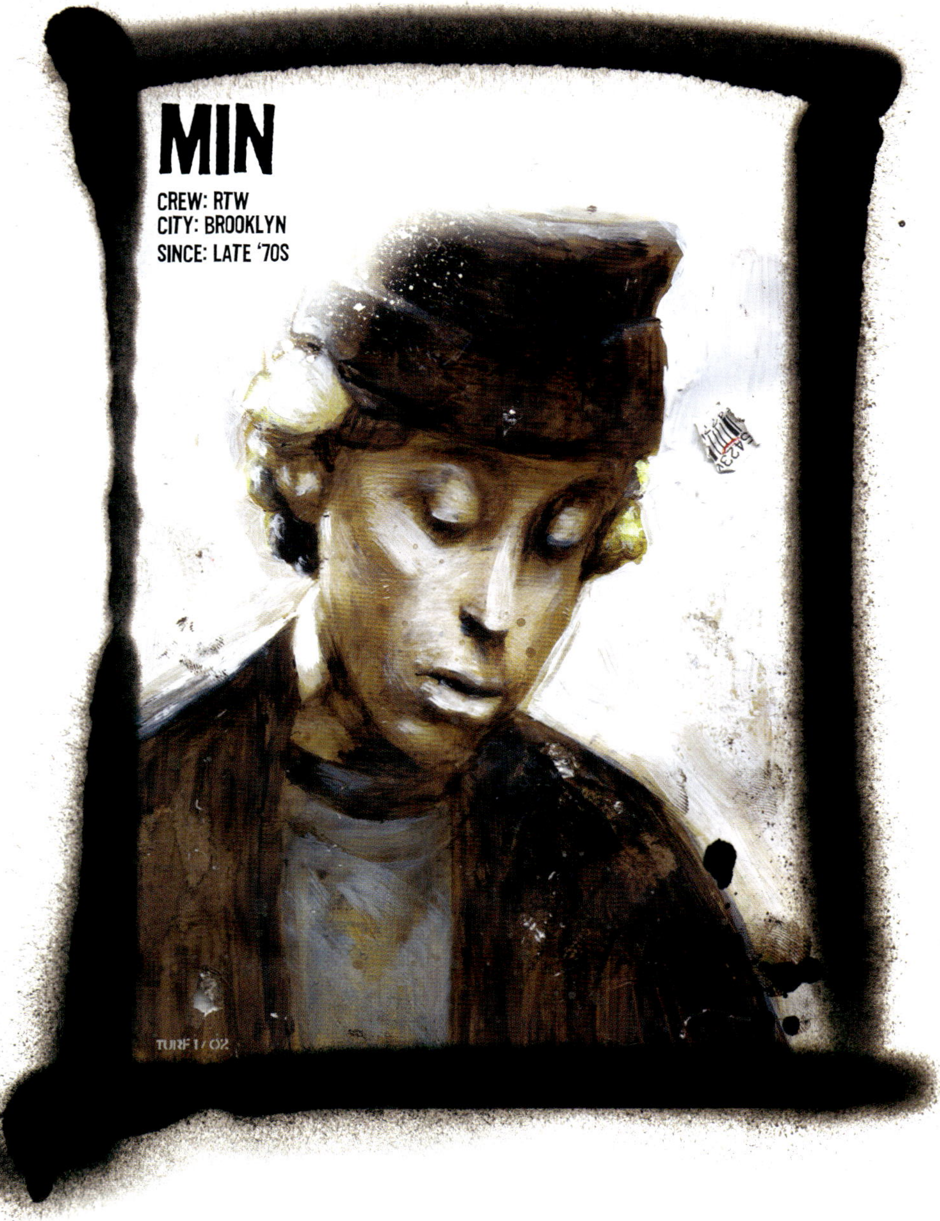

A lot of kids around the world quote you and know who you are because of *Style Wars*.

Yeah. It's weird, because when I did that movie, I wasn't even at my peak. I peaked after that. That's when I went, like, nuts, you know? So at that point I was bombing and I was good, but I wasn't like the all-time true legend I became after that movie. That's when I went bananas on transit. But yeah, I did have some pretty, like, original quotes in that movie that I definitely do hear people quote. Like when they do quote things out that movie, there are things that I said that they do quote. Yeah, there's Skeme with his mom . . . .

And then there's you with the "We gotta get together, bro" . . .

And Cap and his Lucille Ball hairdo, and the 2 Yard used to be an art museum and all that, and it was like that.

When did you start painting?

Well, I started writing in '77. I started writing on the 1 line, with like Zephyr and Revolt on the insides. I was about twelve. And we took King of the Ones and then from there, like I branched onto other writers and just got older and went to different lines, and we just kind of all expanded, you know? It was kind of a slow process for me at the beginning, and then towards the end I had written with so many like top famous writers that what I had learned and created with my own art became like my own original style and my own contribution to graffiti. It was like there really wasn't nothing for me to do anymore at the end. To me, you know, like I quoted in movies and stuff like that, to be King was to do everything. You have these dudes, they're talking about "Oh, I'm King." You bombed one line. I bombed like every line. I was King of every line except for the 6 and the 7. Literally King: insides, outs, top-to-bottoms, whole cars, window-downs, wildstyles, insides—all that. It was weird. There was a lot to graffiti besides just writing your name on a train, you know? There was the whole fighting element, taking people's paint . . . . It was weird; graffiti changed a lot, like from what you probably know about it and what it really was back when I used to write, you know?

I don't know about New York now, but in my experience with writers from other parts of the world, kids talk a lot of shit but it's rare that they're throwing down.

That was the difference. Like, me, when I used to bump into dudes I had beef with, I never talked. It was all about just like whatever. And it wasn't even if you went over me, [but] if you went over the dudes I wrote with, because that's what creates unity. That's what creates power. When you meet a dude and you didn't even go over him, you went over his boy, and he gives you two black eyes just for going over his boy, you know that their crew has unity and their crew has strength, and that individual has strength besides his graffiti. Because you could be the baddest graffiti writer in the world, but if you don't have respect as a man, it really doesn't matter all that much, because when people see your name, they'll be like, "Oh yeah, he bombs a lot, we see him on every train, but he's a sucker." Instead of, "Oh, I see that nigga's name on every train, yeah that's the man." You know what I'm saying?

When did you get down with RTW? Was that the first crew you were in?

Well, RTW is mine. Bill Rock made up RTW, Rolling Thunder Writers, and he gave it to me. And I made it rock the world. That was my crew. I don't know what you've heard . . .

And is that the only crew you were ever in? Were you in other crews?

I was in every crew. I was in every crew, just about. I mean, everybody put me down and asked me to write their crew; I just didn't do it. I wrote OTB a little because I was like really cool with Mad 2—he used to bomb and he was from my era, and he was definitely a King in his own way. What else did I used to write? TVS a lot, but that was basically family; TD, the Destroyers; WOW, Words of Wisdom, I used to write a lot—that was really about it. I was down with everything. I wrote CIA and TOP, stuff like that here and there, because they were old famous crews and I had respect for them. But all I really wrote was RTW, my crew, because that was really all that I was interested in—me.

What were your active years?

That I did the most damage? '82 to '85, I wrote graffiti like every day.

And that's insides and outs?

Yeah, everything. Window-downs, burners, top-to-bottoms, silvers with nice regular letters with coloured background characters, top-to-bottom wildstyle burners with styles on ridgies, window-down burner IRT styles on BMTs, you know, me and Kel were partners for awhile, we like took over the RRs with burners, you know, I had a few, like, big partners, like I was partners with like IZ The Wiz for a while; I was partners with Quik a while with throwups; I was partners with Duro; I didn't do all that much bombing, but I did some bombing with Dondi. Dondi was more, like, into a different type trip than me, you know what I'm sayin'? Dondi was more into like a mellower-type thing . . . we were more like from the wild type than Dondi. RTW, if you met us in the yard and you weren't down with us or down with people we knew . . . we robbed you or took your paint. That's really what graffiti came to. It's like everybody was going over everybody, so it was like whoever we caught, we caught. It wasn't just about like, "You went over us," because we weren't really catching everybody that went over us, so whoever we caught, we just did what we had to do. Then people who did [go] over us knew that when they [got] caught, they were gonna get it. If you were doing what you were doing to our names, just let it be known that what was gonna happen was gonna happen when we met you.

Did you find it hard to get out of? Like, did you get uninterested at any point? Because I'm sure that at one point, you thought, "This is me, this is the rest of my life."

Yeah, it wasn't that I got uninterested, it was like this: it was at the point where there were a few writers that were like constantly going over me on the BMTs, and I would catch them at discos, 'cause I used to club a lot, beat them down—I mean like serious beat-downs—and the next week they'd be going over me again. And then they'd be going over me with my own style, they'd be like bitin' my style and goin' over me, like as if they made up my style, but they goin' over me with my style. So I was like, "It's at the point where I'm gonna like have to kill these dudes," you know, and then I figured it was just like there weren't really many big writers writing anymore, and I was like the last of the big writers. I said, "Let me be the last of the Kings and just do my thing," and just quit. 'Cause like one of the last cars I ever did was that Shy 147 whole car on a ridgie, did you ever see it? Wow, I'd like you to see that. It was really . . . it was beautiful. 'Cause like he was one of my best friends and he died from cancer. He was twenty-three. You never heard of Shy 147? Yeah, he's a old IRT writer.

One of the reasons I'm putting the book together is because I was really curious to know, straight from the horse's mouth, about what was really going on. I'm not trying to read it in a magazine and wonder if it's true.

You wanna know the thing? The thing that's the worst thing about that is, those magazines are giving out totally false information. Totally false information. Ninety percent of the stuff that you read in magazines is like total trash. Didn't happen—guys that are sayin' they did this, they did that—they didn't do nothin', you know what I'm sayin'? They were running if they seen me in the yard. And they twist stories around. So that's kind of like why I'm . . . disinterested in the whole thing. And part of the reason that I did that thing for the *Style Wars Part Two* was because Henry's like a father to me. Number one, Henry Chalfant. And here and there, now that it's like a new millenium, I like to set things straight. Because dudes that really know about graffiti and know who I was, when I talk, they know it's fact. It's not me like blowin' my horn; it's not me like pretending to be something I'm not; everything I'm sayin' is like raw. That's what happened, whether you like what I'm sayin' or not, that's what happened; that's the truth.

Between '82 and '85, to king a line, what did that mean in terms of throwups, pieces, insides? Give me an example, like how many throwups is that per week? How many pieces is that?

Alright, if I'm going, like it would depend upon what line. The E's and F's were the ding-dongs. Those were INDs, alright. I would hit that with throwups; I would hit that with like NE throwups—I wrote NE. That was my throwup name. I would go to all the yards, all the layups, and another yard—the two biggest yards—one was in Queens, one was in Coney Island, Brooklyn. I would catch it from one side of one borough, one side from another, and then in between, in layups. I would hit every car, both sides, and then what I'd have left, I'd jump in on the insides, and sometimes I'd do like some nice top-to-bottom lettered pieces, you know? I never really got busy with, like—I did do some burners on them, you know, like really nice pieces—but nothing that was like a IRT-type style.

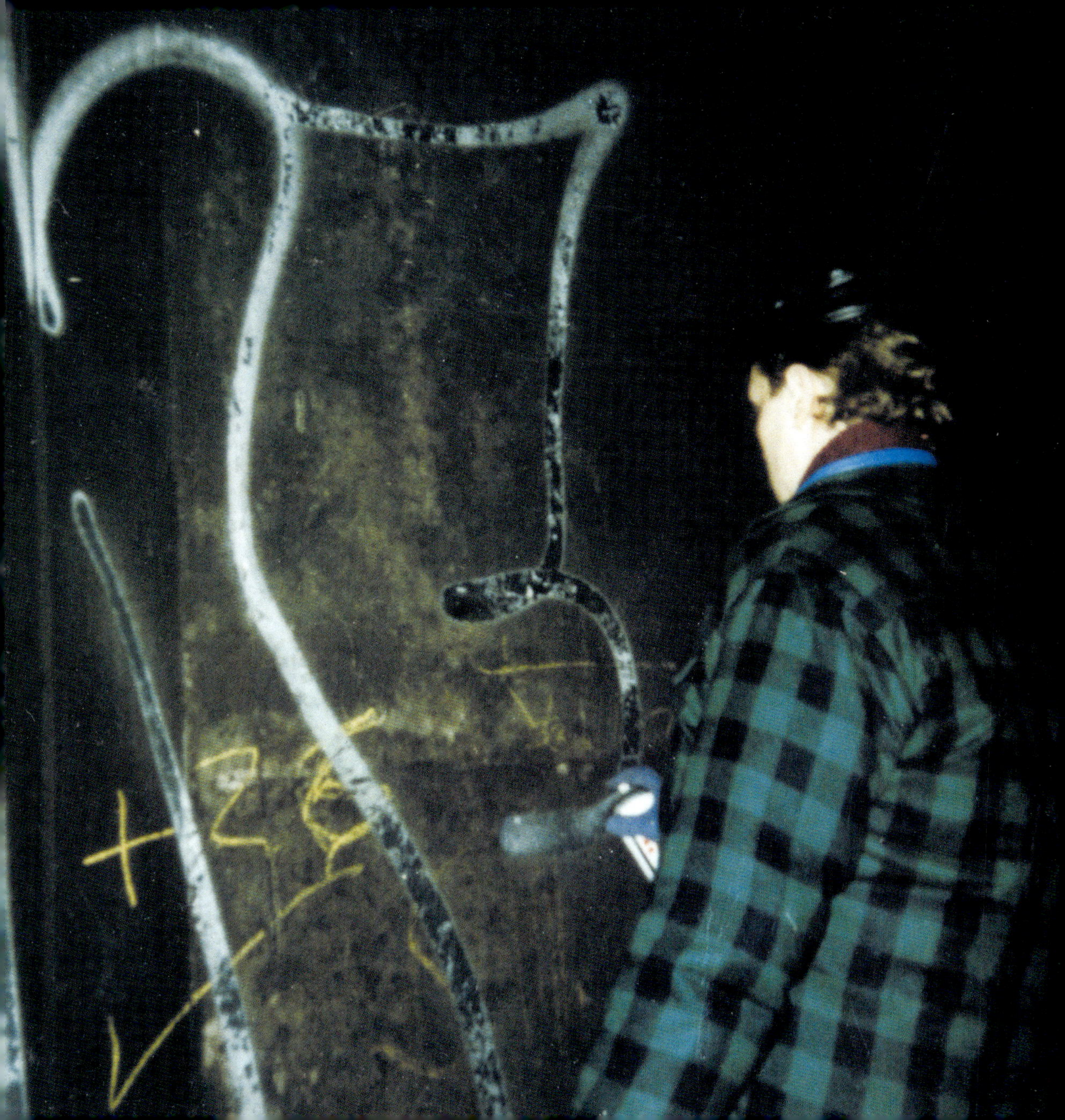

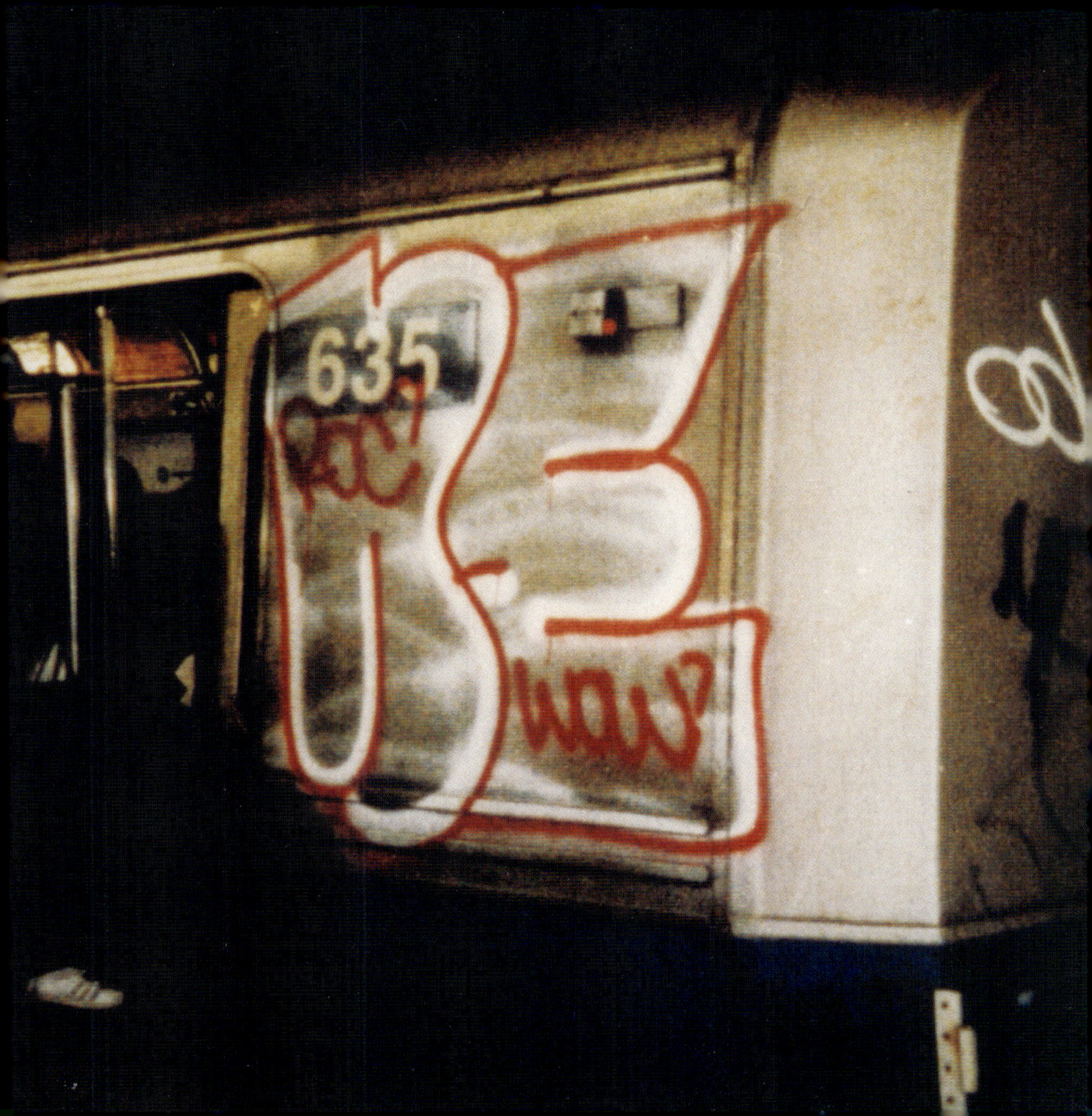
635

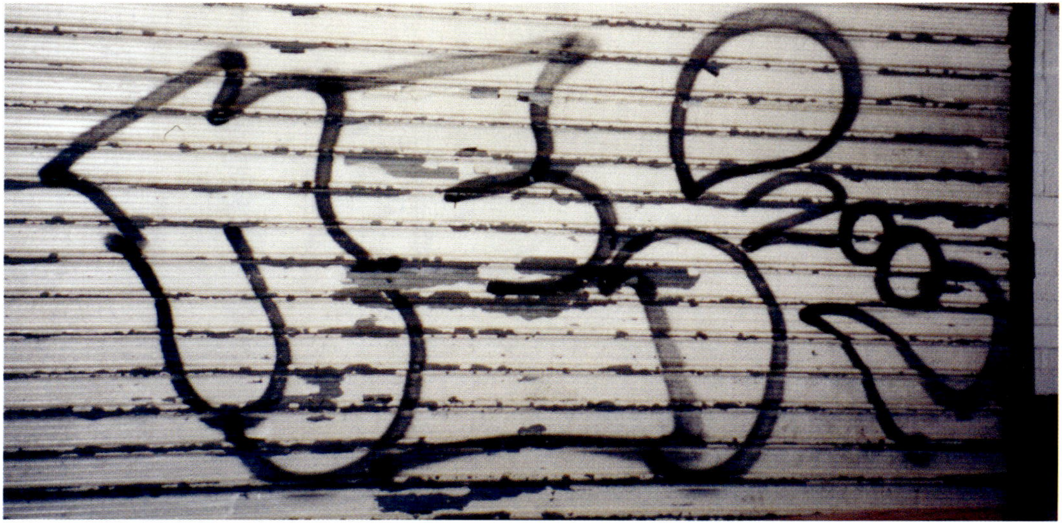

But at one point you were doing whole car wildstyles.

Oh yeah, totally. That's like what I ended my career with. On the BMTs, on the RRs. It wasn't even the R then.

To be a King in the '80s, that means you're fighting other writers, you're fighting the buff—you're fighting everything at once.

You're fighting everything. You're beating the buff, you're fighting writers, you're fighting hardware store owners for their paint. You know, it's like you're doing everything.

So does that mean you go out one night, you do forty fill-in throwups and like—

I used to do a lot more than that.

Give me an average night.

An average night . . . um, Head Lanes, every car both sides, so what's that, a hundred? Between eighty and a hundred throwups was an average bomb for me.

How many cans of paint is that?

Thirty, forty.

Did you make your own markers? Did you fuck with ink?

You know what I used to do with markers? I used to take like a Pilot, pull out the felt on the inside, cut it in half with a piece of glass, like on the inside of the yard, fold it in half, then there'd be nothing on the inside. Fill the inside up so it's nothing but ink, then plug up the end of it, and it's like a big, fat tip. And then like I'd slice it a bit with the glass to make it even bolder and fatter and drippier, and since there's no felt on the inside, when I'd hit the panel, it would be like an explosion of ink, just like ppptthththhhhh . . . you know what I'm saying, and it was just like, booom!

What kind of inks were you using?

Well in the beginning it was all Flo-Master. In the '70s it was Flo-Master, Flo-Master opaque—you know, opaque was like the stuff you couldn't see through. That's what opaque means: you couldn't see through it. Used to have like pink, baby blue; we used to mix colors. Then, like in the early '80s, we used to use store ink, and then Marsh. I used to like to take the supermarket ink, the purple ink, and mix it with like red Marsh ink, and it used to have a nice color to it. When they'd try to buff it, if you'd catch clean cars, the red Marsh would come out, but that store ink would seep into the metal, practically. It was almost impossible to get off.

Do you have any regrets about graffiti?

Yeah, I do have regrets. I wish that we could've been—I wish that more writers that were like real writers united more against that guy Cap, and put an end to, like, the destruction that he did to the IRTs with his stupid throwups.

Did you ever become friends with him after?

No. I would never become friends with that dude. I mean I've met him, afterwards, years after. The beef was so old, it was ridiculous to even think about fighting over it unless the guy started disrespecting me as a man—then that's something different. But I've met him, and he absolutely wanted—the first words out of his mouth was, "Graffiti's dead, man. You know I don't want no beef, graffiti's dead."

What year was that?

That was like '89. No, not even, excuse me—that was like '93.

Do you think graffiti is an addiction?

Definitely. That was like my drug.

How?

It was just like, that's like what I . . . I mean, I used to, like, leave girls in my house and go bombing. They'd be like, "Yo, you're going bombing and leaving me here?" And I'd be like, "Yup. What, you don't like it? Leave." Nothing came before graffiti when I used to bomb.

Do you think graffiti improved your life?

No.

In no way?

No, I don't think it did. Because honestly, I came from like a really good background. I came from like a family with money, you know, and I kinda like messed it up. I used to go to private school when I was young, when I was like really young. So, I come from a well-to-do family—my father owned a pharmacy on Madison Avenue for years—so I didn't come from like the same background as most graffiti writers, but I wound up falling into that category, the way I was living my life and the things I was doing in my life. I was basically living in train yards, and train yards are in the ghetto. You know what I'm sayin'?

How far into your writing career did your parents find out?

They knew I was always into it. My father remembers me . . . I mean, I've been looking at trains since I've been about like seven years old. I always looked at the trains, and it always fascinated me. And it was really weird 'cause I always remember seeing up like LFD 3, LFD Ohm—that's really the way that it was pronounced—and you know, FDT 56 . . . . Then, like toward the end of my career, I would meet these guys and they were like admiring me; they were like, "Yo man, you're, like, the King!" It was weird, because I remember being a little kid and looking at these guys and admiring them and being like, "Wow, I can't believe these guys do that." It took me a little while to figure it out, because I knew that they weren't doing it in the train station, but I didn't know about the whole yard thing and that it was like a totally organized type thing. You know, to be a King, you have to be very organized. Everything has to be very organized.

Did your parents forgive you at one point? Or at least accept that you wrote?

At one point, yeah. Well, my father is an art collector, and he actually loves my graffiti—he just didn't really dig it because it was illegal.

Name three dudes that you think reached King status in the '80s.

In the '80s? Fuzz One, myself, and . . . King, as far as like, overall everything?

Like all-city, everything, complete package—did it and didn't do it for a year; did it for like a while.

Me, Fuzz One, and hmmm . . . lemme see . . . that's a tough one, man . . . I really didn't think there was . . . I mean, I think maybe I gotta give that guy Quik a lotta credit . . .

Wasn't he in your crew?

Yeah. Well really, that was the only comp I had, was dudes in my crew. Dudes that roll with me were basically the ones that were giving me any kind of competition, and it was all my paint.

What do you mean?

'Cause I used to be like an incredible shoplifter.

You used to rack for everyone?

Yo, I used to go and rack—I used to have so much paint, it was like unbelievable. Quik used to rack up, but I had dudes like Beau, you ever heard of Beau? I racked up all his paint. Rich, I know you heard of him; racked up all his paint. That was all my paint. All of Kel's whole cars in the '80s. Like, in the early '80s, all those whole cars with me—all my paint. All that shit was my paint—all of it.

There were restrictions, though. Wasn't paint getting locked up?

Naw, I used to go to Long Island, man. I used to go with that guy Sach, who used to write with IZ, and he's like a big dude, man. I used to stand behind him and he'd, like, lean in front of me and I'd just walk out with like twenty-five cans a store; twenty, twenty-five cans. We used to come back with his mother's station wagon filled with paint.

Nowadays, obviously, you walk down the street, you notice tags, you notice throwups. Who's destroying now? Who are you checking for?

I don't. You know, like to tell you the truth man, I don't really, like, pay attention to graffiti anymore, unless it's like an old writer that I see up. The stuff that I see on the street now sickens me. I'd rather like look at like . . . I don't know, man, I think the stuff they're doing now on the streets make the streets look bad. Because to me, one thing that made graffiti so exciting was that it was a moving art form. That's why you never saw many tags of mine in the streets. I mean, I tagged up in streets; I have street tags 'cause I've been through a lot of neighborhoods and I take a tag, but I never concentrated on taking the streets. Because the thing that gave me excitement about graffiti was watching one of my whole cars like race through the station at like forty-five miles an hour, with streams of colors, and it would be like rolling thunder, you know—the noise, the color, the excitement of seeing it flash by, trying to focus in on it, and by the time you try to focus in, it's gone.

There's a lot of mysteries about you, dude. A lot of dudes want to know what's going on with you now. Like, what do you do?

I could get into that. . . . Yo check, I'ma call you back, man.

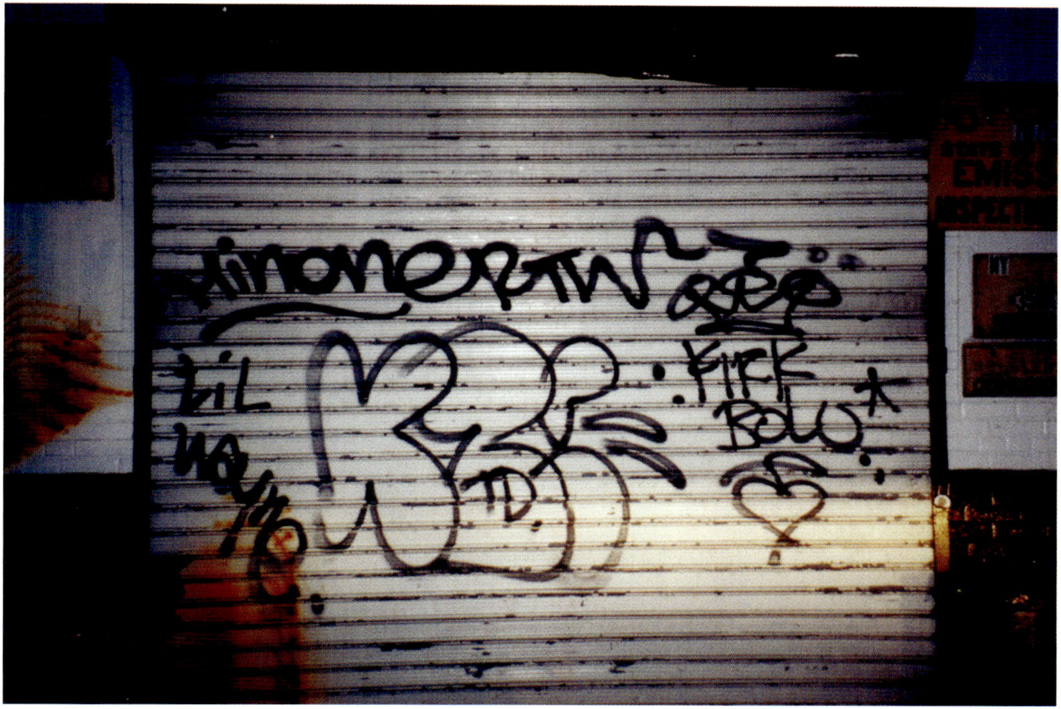

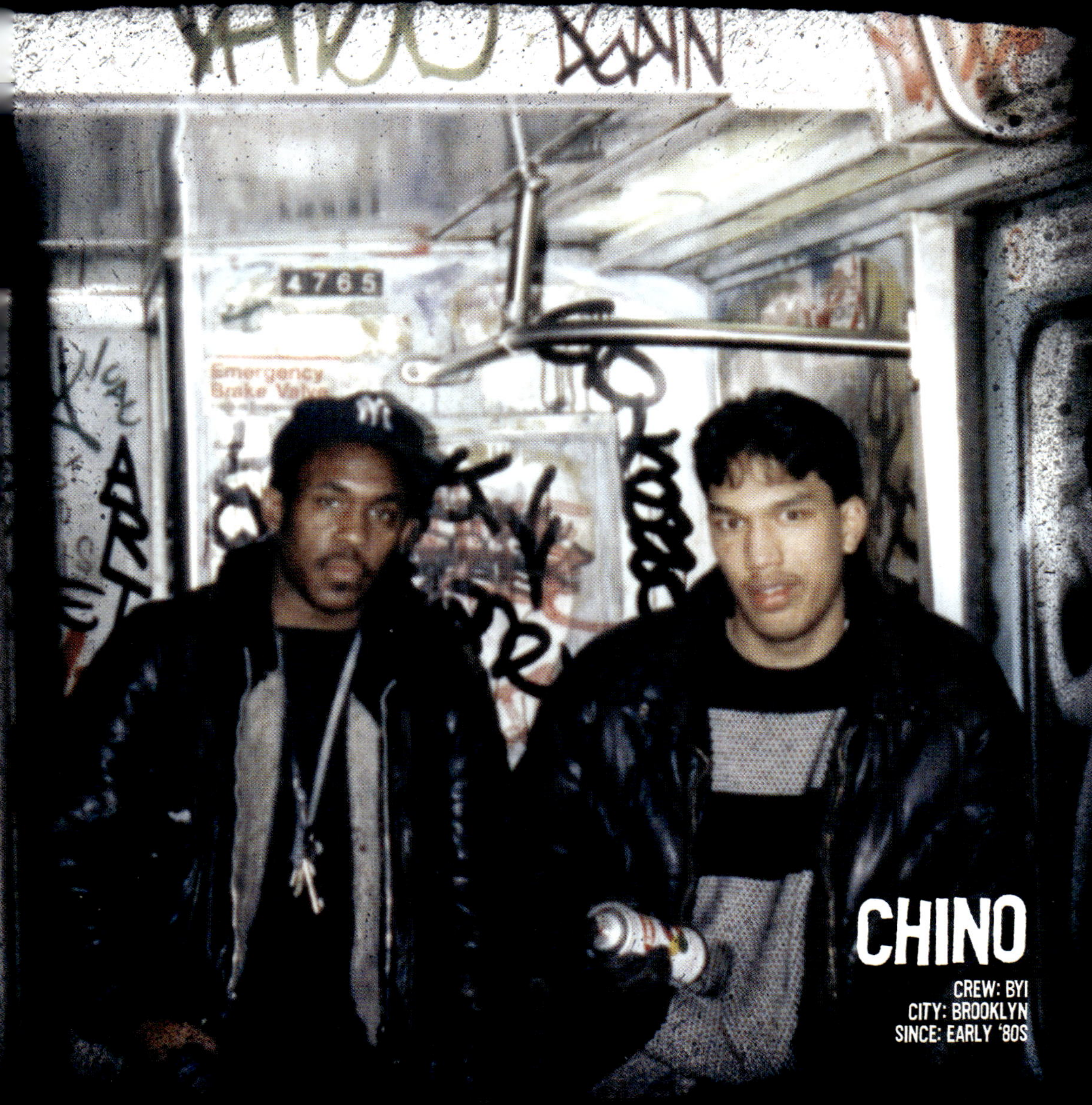

CHINO

CREW: BYI
CITY: BROOKLYN
SINCE: EARLY '80S

Do you remember making the transition from hitting subways to streets?

We moved straight from subways to streets. Once the trains went out, we just continued on the streets. Writers like OE, P13, AS 2, and a handful of others, like Blade and Comet, Ros on the highways, Lock and Lil Man uptown, Chissey and Johnny B in Astoria, and Pray—there weren't too many people systematically doing streets. So when the focus shifted from trains to avenues and streets, I was definitely a part of that first wave of strategic street bombers. Easy, Joz (RIP), Josh 5, Tekay (Track 2) , Magoo, Trim, Charm was doing streets with us between bids in prison . . . there was a handful of guys out there. I remember riding through streets in Manhattan after we smashed 8th Street . . . me and Look TPA were the only two names that were consistently up on that strip, with the exception of a Lust piece. Then, suddenly, 8th Street was just the spot where writers were climbing onto people's fire escapes and bombing the sides of people's homes, and the gates were destroyed.

With throwups or tags?

It started with a tag, and then eventually someone would do a fill-in somewhere, and the bar would continue to get raised. ZU, Voke, SZ (Sez), JA, and others continued to climb higher and higher to get the highest spots. Writers started targeting fire escape spots on abandoned buildings, and doing rooftop spots and things like that, so it was, like, people continuously trying to outdo each other until there was eventually this explosion of names on places were graffiti hadn't existed previously. It got to a point where even I would look at the streets and be, like, this shit is disgusting. I can't even find a single tag of mine these days because it's probably buried beneath three layers of throwups. When we first started, there weren't too many people doing streets strategically, I think. Joz was one of the first people I had talked to that really had all the major avenues: Canal St., 8th Street, 14th Street, 34th Street, 23rd Street, 42nd, 59th, all the major cross streets, and then the side streets, the FDR and West Side highways, off-ramps to the bridges.

So it was Manhattan first?

Brooklyn. For me at least, Brooklyn, definitely Brooklyn. I always had [good spots] in the downtown Brooklyn Fulton mall area; I grew up in Fort Green, which was really close to the (Albee Square Mall) Fulton Mall. For a long time, even before targeting streets, I always had tags in that area just because it was a really popular shopping area. I knew it was just a good location for high visibility; I was guaranteed to get some airplay. People would always see whatever you did down there, so I targeted that first. Atlantic Avenue was close by, so we would catch Atlantic, the off-ramps, the Brooklyn Bridge, Manhattan, BQE (Brooklyn Queens Expressway); anything I saw whenever I was in a car driving around. You know, like, shit, that's a dope spot—remember this location so I can come back and smash it the next night. Then I start branching out. Queens was easy because my girl lived in Astoria, so we (me and Look, then me and Tekay) smashed Astoria, hit Woodside, Corona, Flushing—all of these neighborhoods under the elevated 7 line. Usually always under the elevated subways. So we had a lot of stuff underneath the B line to a certain point in the line, at least until we reached Bensonhurst.

In a very strange way, I guess there's a great deal of racial tension that still exists, [but] it's not at the surface like it was when I was growing up. There were certain yards and certain areas that you needed to stay away from. You know, like me bombing in an Italian, Greek, or Russian neighborhood wasn't a good move; I stood out like a sore thumb. Someone would always say something, and then there would be problems. If you were in a Dominican area (like 175th & Broadway), the same shit would pop off. We were more comfortable in the hood; we had less headaches in the hood. I did a lot of Queens, a lot of Manhattan, not too much in the Bronx. I really didn't have any interest in the Bronx. Crack was really flourishing, and the Bronx was just dirtier than any neighborhoods in Brooklyn. One thing that was clear: it didn't seem like much was sacred in the BX. Dudes were writing on people's homes and churches. There would be a fill-in over the window to somebody's fuckin' house; you'd see some old woman staring out of it in the daytime, surrounded by a throwup. There was really no interest in the Bronx, for me. I had a lot of peoples in Queens, Manhattan, Brooklyn, so I just wanted to get up where I thought it would be best appreciated, best received, I guess. You know, anything you do in Manhattan, I think it is pretty prime real estate.

In all those years of doing streets, we were only pulled over by cops a handful of times (maybe four or five times), and there was no repercussions. The cops weren't interested in dealing with six, seven hours' worth of paperwork for street bombing. Besides, there were bigger crimes being committed on the streets, and street bombing wasn't the phenomenon, nor the problem, that it is now. If you get stopped now, you are going through the system. You are gonna get arrested. At very least, it's a twenty-four hour process. [Back then] cops were like, "What are you doing here?" I'd usually say "My girl lives right here," or "My boy died. His folks live across the street; I was just going to write Rest In Peace . . . I don't ever do this; that's probably why I got caught." Stroke their ego for like two seconds, calling them Officer, and after a couple of tense moments they'd usually say "Get the fuck out of here." They'd often ask, "How'd you like me to write on you or spray your face?" I'd always respond, "I wouldn't like that." Just play the game and say what they need to hear so you can get up outta there.

Back then you'd rarely ever really get in trouble for that shit, and quite often, they'd let us leave with our paint. They wouldn't search you, and we often had weed on us and shit like that. If they wanted to make an arrest, they had a legitimate one in front of them. But again, they didn't want to deal with the paperwork. It's a different city. Mayor Lindsay was the first one to coin, or at least classify, graffiti as a "quality of life offense." Rudy Giuliani was the first to pursue prosecutions under those quality of life offenses. The game's changed. We were getting away with murder with Mayor Koch and David Dinkins. David Dinkins was, straight up—fuck being the laziest mayor—maybe the laziest human being on the fucking planet during that window where I think the city needed him the most. Under the Reaganomics era, crack flourished. During the Reagan/Bush administration some real crazy shit was going down in this city. We went from having a mayor that just didn't give a fuck, to someone that really enforced Gestapo-like tactics. Civil rights and the Constitution went right out the window, and things began to change under Giuliani.

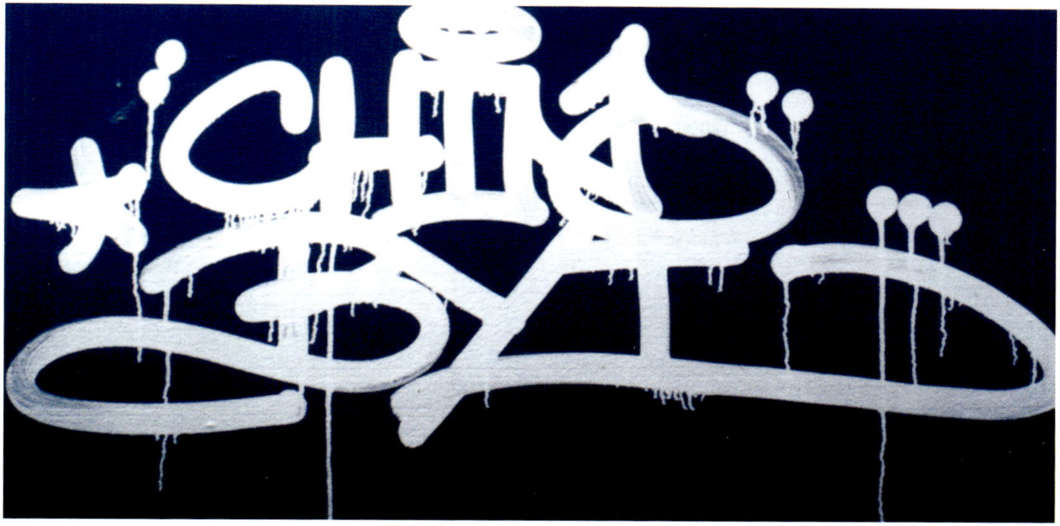

But again, for all those times we got stopped for doing streets, or even the subways, during those six years I bombed trains, I found myself in the custody of the law twice for bombing subways. One arrest resulted in one day of community service, which I think is a very fair exchange for the amount of subways we destroyed. If anyone reading this has ever cleaned subway trains as a result of community service, they'll tell you that they kept you there until lunchtime. You always worked a half-day. How much work you decided to get done that day was just on you. They (MTA supervisors) would be like, "Who wants to scrub the walls?" Some fools would actually raise their hands. Then it would be like, "Who wants to sweep? Who wants to mop?" Eventually, if you didn't raise your hand (like me), the supervisor would be like, "OK, well just help him." Helping him meant me sitting there, telling you "Yeah, you missed a spot over there." That's what community service was all about. It gave you an opportunity to meet other writers that had already been arrested. Jail, for some people who get arrested for very small infractions and go inside [get locked], [means they can] then learn more about crime than they ever knew prior to being locked. It was the same thing; we were connecting with kids from all over the city who were like, "Yo, D Yard is fresh right now. Do you wanna come through and blaze it?" It's strange how that system works. The guy that was actually running the MTA [Metropolitan Transit Authority] community service program would often brag about who he had there. I remember hearing him say, "I had Boe [WOW crew] here recently, and I had PJ once, and Seen . . . " This guy was always talking shit about who got caught and who had to clean trains.

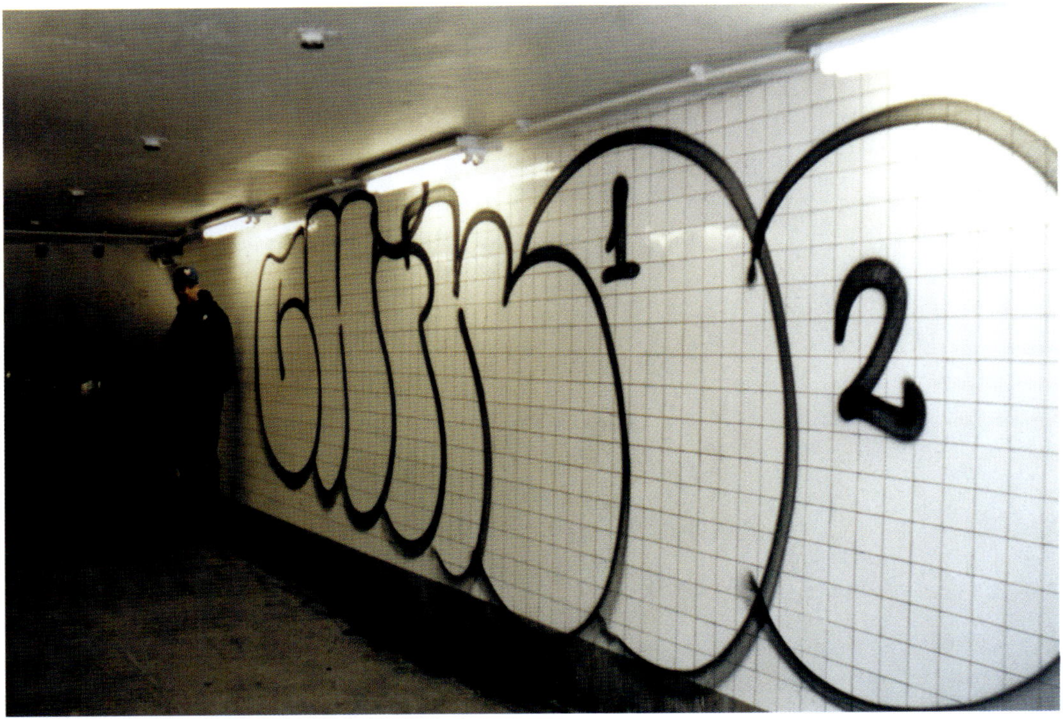

I can't imagine writing being hectic, like it was in that era, in other parts of the world. What do you think makes a kid somewhere else go all out like that? What's the motivation?

Maybe this a bad comparison, but it's like a suicide bomber or a kamikaze; that somebody that's willing to risk life and limb—some even dying—for something they believe in. Like Christ on the cross. There aren't that many people that are willing to die for shit they believe in, or are this committed . . . . A lot of people send me stuff, and lots of people ask, "How come you don't run current graffiti?" Honestly, my take on the whole situation is that I wrote for fucking more than twelve years. Consistently, from 1982-1994, without one inch of desire [to eventually appear] in a magazine, video, or in a book. That shit came MUCH later in the game. Once there were venues, rather than have somebody on the outside looking in handle our culture, why not? I was an active participant; it wasn't a spectator sport. I got my hands dirty for a lot of years; I got stitches, and cut, and a very minor criminal record behind this shit. Why not? If anyone can talk about it, why not me?

In all those years, I've watched a lot of kids come and go, and there were kids that were real hot for like six months that ended up in a little bit of hot water and came to pieces and disappeared. It's like Cost and Revs. Cost got bagged, and kinda disappeared. And understandably so, man—they hit him in the head with a lot of fucking years of community service. But Revs kinda continued in his own direction, and continued to do his thing, and it was just over the years, longevity. Cope 2, he's committed to what he does. I've said this before: he survived at least three administrations here, like Koch, Dinkins, Giuliani, and now Bloomberg. He is like that fucking Energizer Bunny, man. He's still ticking. He writes on all sorts of shit.

Cope's survived all sorts of wars—all those Vandal Squad rumors about him being, like, a snitch and blah blah blah. I know a DJ in Perth, Australia, he called me and asked, "Is it true that your man Cope is a snitch?" A rumor the Vandal Squad started. The Internet has definitely changed the game. You know, something happens in Brooklyn, and they know about it in Bangkok the next fucking day. As far as recognition goes, whatever shine Cope gets, I think he deserves. To date, I don't think any writers have painted, bombed, or collaborated with as many different writers as Cope has. Graffiti, that's his shit. If James Brown is the hardest-working man in showbiz, then that's what Cope is to graffiti. That's my opinion. He's just on some longevity shit, like some KRS shit.

When you were writing, did you think you'd ever stop?

No, but as I've matured, most of my focuses have changed. I've worked hard over the last ten years, doing lots of still graffiti-related shit. Not to sound arrogant, but there's just not much to compete with right now (I'm talking about bombing, not collaboration murals or clean trains). During the subway era there was just so much good graffiti on the trains, it made you want to be with those people with an interesting tag name and a dope signature or hot throwups. In the beginning I think most writers, including myself, all eventually aspired to earn the respect of those writers and have them become your peers. It was one of my earliest motivations to write. I just don't see much of that in the current state of recent local graffiti. I see guys copying guys that have copied off guys, and now they're not sure who they are biting off of.

I'm generally very respectful, but I'm also a grown fucking man, so in spite of the props you might be entitled to for doing what you did on the subways, I've learned to respect a person on a more human level. [I've] got a lot more love for my real friends than I do for some cat that was all-city and blah blah blah, who I don't know from a hole in the wall. I could go on for days about all the writers I grew up looking up to that I've met that try to hit me up for like ten, fifteen dollars every time I see them. It's all good between friends, but don't ask me for shit with a dollar sign attached to it right after introducing yourself. There's no reason why, at forty-five, fifty years old, you're still living at your mom's house (unless one of the two has a medical condition that may require some routine assistance). Otherwise, there's really no good reason for any of that shit, you know what I mean?

I've seen firsthand what happened to some of the guys I used to look up to (so many pitfalls). I've worked hard to try to get some shit done. I've got some projects in progress that I'm working on currently. So me writing graffiti, or a comeback anytime soon, is [not] in my best interest. There aren't as many incentives to drag me back into the game. No one wants to be the recurring news blurb on NY News 1.

Do you think you'll get sucked back in?

Wherever I've traveled, regardless of [whether] it's for business or pleasure, I usually end up writing on something. It could be South Beach, Buffalo, NY, or LA . . . we smashed shit in London; we did tons of streets out there. We did subways in London—my man Oker kills trains out there. Oker keeps London subways on smash. Dels and Oker, just killing shit out there. Keo recently forwarded me a page [from the *12oz. Prophet* site] regarding Oker's shit, and there's photos of probably about twenty-some odd whole cars he has running there now. He was in New York for maybe two months, and he probably did trains about seven, eight times: whole cars, window-downs, all sorts of shit. He's always doing something somewhere . . . France, Holland, Amsterdam, etc. . . .

I never thought I'd stop. A big reason why I think I've slowed down is a lot has changed. I don't need someone knocking down my door, looking for me, right now. The people I may have wanted to maybe impress while I was interested in impressing them have probably been left with some sort of impression at this point. I wouldn't say there isn't enough good competition, but the game has changed completely. None of these gates around us have graffiti on them. None of these walls around us have good pieces on them. Fifteen, twenty years ago, there was a Web piece on this wall right here, and all these gates were smashed. In hindsight, when you think of some of the names of the people that were up, it was mostly all good graffiti by quality writers; it was established, reputable shit. Some of these newer kids might last six months, a year, tops. Six months later, it's some next kid. I don't necessarily feel the need to compete at this point. A majority of the people I've met in my lifetime are familiar with me in some capacity; it's all good. I enjoy it when people phone me from overseas and are like, "Yo I'm staring at this Chino tag I saw outside a restaurant in fucking Belgium," or outside their hotel in Germany. Fly me overseas and I'll lose my mind. I'll do streets and hit trains like I'm seventeen again. While outside of New York, I'm more inclined to bomb, and I'll carry a can with me twenty-four hours a day, no matter where we go while I'm on vacation, just hoping to catch a good spot.

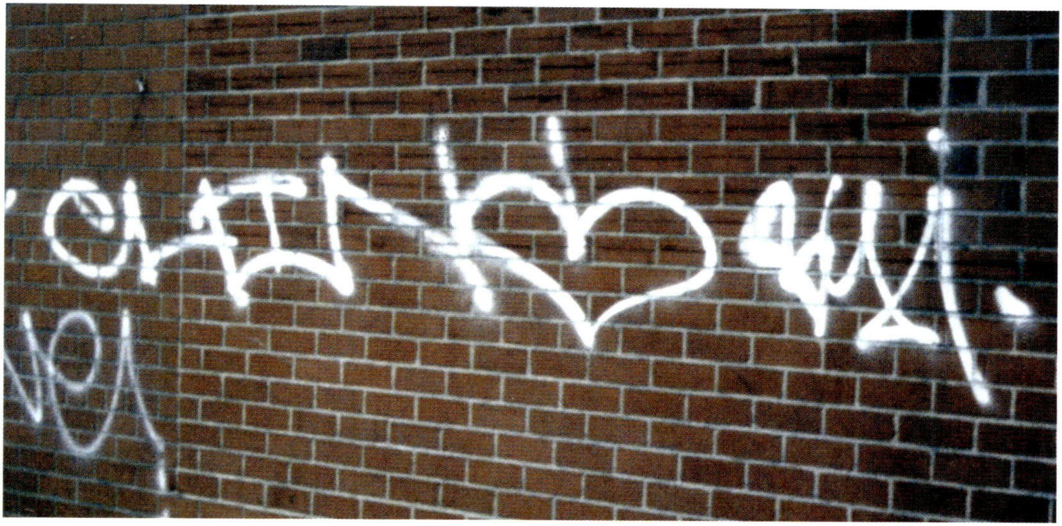

How did you come up with your name?

Everyone in my family had a nickname. I experimented with a bunch of different names before I actually wrote Chino, a name that my Uncle Vidal (RIP) had been calling me since I was a baby. All my brothers and my cousins have interesting Latino nicknames, so in comparison to some of the family nicknames, it was one of the kinder names. Everyone had really fucked-up nicknames in my family. Mine wasn't so bad, and it just made sense when it came time to find a tag.

Do you think you were addicted? Or do you think it is an addiction?

No doubt. I dropped out of school in the seventh grade—I stopped going to school when I was maybe eleven years old. I was actually left back due to a medical reason; I had an infection in a bone in my foot and they thought they might have to amputate some of my left foot. I was in the hospital for like forty days. I was used to being ahead of my class and I rarely had to study, but I missed far too many days of school without an assigned tutor. The shit I learned in school stuck to me, and I was a good student. But unfortunately, my two-month hospital stay exceeded the amount of allowed absent days you can have during the course of a semester. The year I was left back was the same year that I was really getting into graffiti (getting my feet wet in the game), doodling on everything in my mom's house, had probably stolen my first Magnum and Pilot and shit like that . . . .

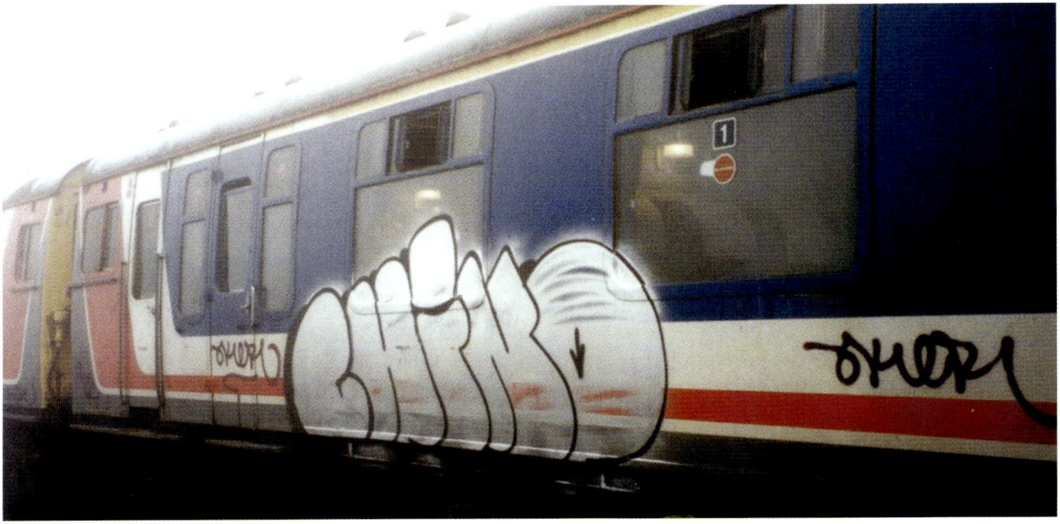

Did you kill your room?

Mostly the inside of my bedroom closet, [and] areas in the building I grew up in, like the staircases. One of the images in Espo's book, *The Art of Getting Over*, has my boys Disk CWK (Craft Work Kings), my boy Rae, and (Joe) Craz from Park Slope, chilling in my old staircase. Peep the flick—there are just layers and layers of tags. That's my old staircase; it's where I went to practice handstyles [or to] test markers, mops, paint, and caps. That same stairwell led you straight out the building to the street, [without] having to walk out the lobby, so me and my boys always bombed it en route out of my building. My hallway and the outside of my old building eventually got destroyed.

Being held back completely contributed to me losing interest in school. I got shuffled from school to school and became more and more bitter. My mom eventually placed me in a junior high school in Brooklyn Heights. It was very strange because we grew up in the hood, and Brooklyn Heights is a pretty affluent area. My mom thought if I was away from my friends, away from the hood . . . in a nicer neighborhood, in a more diverse atmosphere, surrounded by students from good homes, maybe it would rub off and I'd be reinspired to pick up a book besides my black book. In some of the other schools it was so easy to get lost in a crowd and slip through the cracks.

The new school had much smaller classrooms, [so] my mom felt like if I were missing, it would be a concern for my teachers, and it was. There were only three classes in the whole school, so if you were missing, it was on some everyone knew type shit. But it didn't stop me from cutting class anyway; the majority of my time was spent benching subways and riding the train. I remember cutting school when I was twelve to attend the show at The Graffiti Aboveground Gallery (the graffiti gallery show in *Style Wars*). Prior to the show, most of the good graffiti I saw was on sides of fast-moving subway trains—so fast that my inexperienced eye often couldn't always process what I was looking at. That gallery show was probably my first opportunity to see good graffiti by established artists, and really sit there and just study shit.

As for school, I was a constant truant. My education took a back seat to graffiti, and although I remained enrolled in school until the ninth grade, I only made it because my old principal told me if she held me back she would have to spend another year having to deal with my shit, and besides, she felt sorry for my poor mother. The bathrooms in my junior high school were bombed; I was writing on everything. Essentially, [the] principal told me she promoted me and pushed me through junior high school in order to avoid not to have to spend an extra year [with me] . . . like that was such a bad thing? Big ups to Miss Kasindorf, anyway.

During my freshman year of high school, my mom came in to a parent-teacher meeting, and the teacher said to her, "I only wish that your son would show up once so I could see what his face looks like." I felt bad that she came all the way to Williamsburg only to find out that I hadn't been going to school at all. My guidance counselor suggested taking my GED . . . so that's what I did. I dropped out in seventh grade. The majority of what I learned growing up was on the streets, hanging out with cats from around the way that were a lot older than me. I was looking at a lot of graffiti. So while most of my friends and two brothers were in school, I was getting my feet wet and learning the whole who's who in graffiti. I traveled places all over NYC, just to look at graffiti in different areas. A majority of the city's swimming pools would just get destroyed. Come summertime, there would be all these pieces in Marcy Pool, Red Hook Pool, or McCarran Park.

I made some sacrifices. In hindsight, maybe made some wrong decisions. The lack of a proper education hasn't hurt me a bit. Eventually, I went back to school. I attended college at SUNY Buffalo for two years. Without studying or anything to bridge my new full-time college schedule with my sixth-grade education, I managed to maintain a 4.0—which was an accomplishment for me—for the four semesters I was in school.

So I don't regret anything. Some of the important things in life—family, relationships, and education—definitely took a back seat to graffiti. For a lot of years, it was my primary focus. Everything took a back seat to graffiti. We would go to my grandmother's (RIP) house for Thanksgiving dinner, and I'd need to break out early because we were going bombing. Christmas Eve, the whole family is dressed up, and I'm the only one with a marker, ink, a pair of sweats, and a change of clothes in my bag, and I'm breaking out right after midnight so we can go do trains. Everything took a back seat to graffiti.

By 1982, paint is caged up, right? Like you can't get paint in the city?

No, I think there were a lot of places that had paint unlocked, up until the later mid-'80s. There were still tons of stores you could go to and rack paint, like in the early to mid-'80s. And then towards the later '80s, the mid-'80s, you know, we started traveling further outside the city, going to Connecticut or Westchester. One of my favorite routes, and I'm probably never going to go back there again, was along Montauk Highway, en route to the Hamptons. I had a girlfriend that had a summerhouse out there, and after I met JA, his dad had a house out there. Pooling our resources, man, we were able to live out there. None of those places we were stealing from outside of NYC had cages on any of the paint. There were tons of places in the city that didn't have any of their paint locked up; it was still accessible. I know in high school, probably 1984, I was doing a lot of racking locally. . . .

When did you start painting with JA?

That was towards the later end of my graffiti. Subways were on their way out, you know, and he was, like, a younger cat that was very active. As per usual, Ven introduced him on some real hater shit. Don't get me wrong—Ven's my man—but Ven called me one day and was like, "JA did a fill-in and went over you, and if you want you can find him here." We had smashed the D Yard a couple of times years earlier, and we caught a handful of IRTs [number trains], some that ran for a minute, until JA did some fill-ins on the trains' insides and went over me.

After calling JA and threatening him, about six months later, Ven brings him around, and is telling me, "Listen, I know you don't like him, but he's a really good kid." The same guy that painted a fucked-up picture of JA was suddenly trying to draw a new picture for me. Anyway, we met, he was cool, he was very motivated. He was still young and still learning the ropes. He started getting up at the tail-end of subway graffiti. I think the only spots to catch trains at that time was at 111th in Jamaica, Queens, the Uptown IRT layups at 140-something, and Tishman, the 57th St. layups.

So you would go in the yard without anything? Knowing that you were gonna be able to vic somebody for their shit?

Hell yeah. Astoria and Kingston, man. Especially Kingston—it was a gold mine. I remember Vandal Squad caught Wolf AOK there. It's fucked up—they raided the layup, and while he was running they screamed "Freeze, or we'll shoot!" And he just stopped. After they had him cuffed and he was in the station, they let him know, "By the way, if a cop ever yells 'Freeze or I'll shoot!' and you're in the tunnel, keep running." Because if they miss you (the intended target), the bullet will ricochet, and they could end up shooting themselves. They won't shoot in the tunnel unless they absolutely have to. The cops enjoyed taunting him with the whole "you stopped for nothing." They told Wolf, "The only reason why we come to Kingston Avenue layup is because on any given day, we know we can catch a bunch of toys here." And that's why we went.

A couple of people (writers) have approached me on some, "Yo, what's the deal, Chino?" Trying to give me five and there's all this love and I'm like, "Where do I know you from, yo?" They're telling me shit, like, "You once shook me down over here and you took this from me." I'm still trying to figure out where his head is when the same kid starts almost boasting about "Yo, but I tell niggas about that shit all the time," and I'm sitting there like whoa! This is fucking crazy. It could be another horrible analogy, but it's like survivors of the Holocaust. Guys that bombed and wrote subway graffiti, they all seem to have something in common that really does brings them together, you know? It's a common experience that we've all survived, [so] to some degree, we can usually, at very least, identify on that level.

All the beef shit is really behind me. Back in the day, there was so much ego involved; it's an extremely egocentric sport. Most writers you met that were already established always fronted like they never heard of you. Now, I could talk graffiti with just about anybody. Finally, some of the older guys [were] able to admit, "Yo kid, you had the streets smashed." I remember meeting this old school writer who told me when we met that I had the double Rs locked down. I'm sitting there like, "Wow, this is crazy." He's someone I grew up seeing up. During that era, when I was actually seeking that praise, I would have never gotten it.

We have reached a point where we are so far-removed from the situation, everyone's matured a great deal. Egos aren't quite what they used to be; people are a lot friendlier now. I said it before and I'll say it again: The game has changed, the rules have changed. When I started writing, if we saw you in the schoolyard, we'd run up and it'd be like, "Yo, you guys write?" And you'd probably be like, "Yeah, what do you write?" You tell me your tag and ask, "What do you write?" So that you wouldn't start crossing my shit out after we robbed you, we wouldn't say anything as we'd proceed to dig in your pockets. Now I got your money, and I know what you write. Ten out of ten times, when graffiti writers met it was real hostile. It was always hostile, you know what I mean? We could walk up, see you guys just sitting here like now, and it wouldn't have been anything more than [Chino stands, walks past me, picks up my bag] just keep walking.

When some of the newer kids first came out, we'd cross them out just because. It's like they said in *Style Wars*, traditions are passed down from one youthful generation to another. That's all we were doing. When we started getting up, lots of the older guys hated on us, and I'm sure it happens wherever there is graffiti. So in the spirit of just trying to pass the baton on to the next generation, everyone that started getting up when we were established, we just started nipping them, dripping over them, or just straight going right over their shit. As I look back, [I] think that when more established writers started going over me, I was just like, consider it a privilege. Like, you've reached a status where we can go over your shit now too; you're no longer beneath our radar. There are lots of guys I'm now cool with that I was introduced to downwind of some real tense shit.

Was the fighting graffiti-based, or do you think it was just about being a kid in New York?

I think it was the era. You didn't get in too much trouble for fighting.

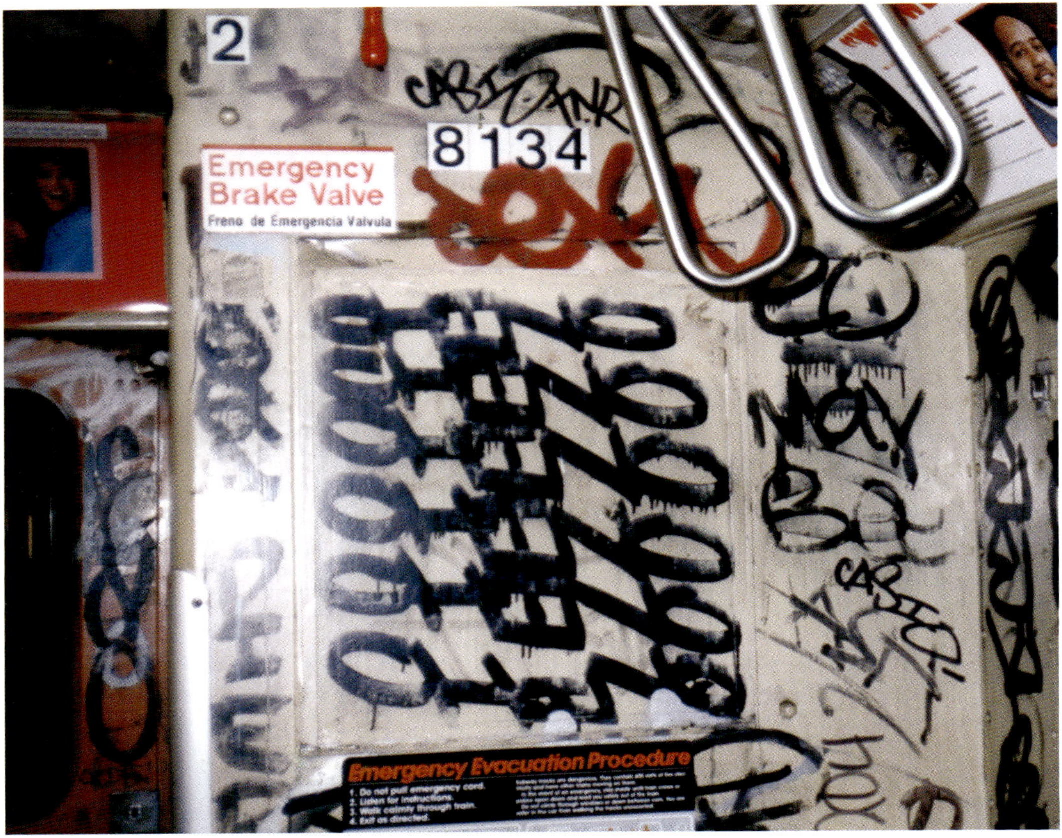
2
8134
Emergency
Brake Valve
Freno de Emergencia Valvula
Emergency Evacuation Procedure
1. Do not pull emergency cord.
2. Listen for instructions.
3. Walk calmly through train.
4. Exit as directed.

But do you think it was a graffiti thing, or do you think it was a New York thing?

Throwing joints was far more common during that era. People were catching ass whoopings over nothing on the daily. There was an absence of a police presence in my neighborhood (like most in the early '80s), there were little if any legal repercussions, and if you fought on the street, big fuckin' deal. Parents were beating their children in the streets; cops were beating crooks up in the streets. Today's New York, as I see it, it's a lot of Wall Street yuppie types; lots of folks that have moved here from Colorado or came here from San Francisco; an NYU student from Berkley who decided to stay. I'm not hating on anyone . . . everyone in New York got here from somewhere. The majority of people I grew up with were second-generation New Yorkers. Their grandparents moved here from either down south or Puerto Rico, our parents grew up here, and so did we. We didn't just move here from some other city. The lines that separated most communities were clearly drawn right in front of you; you knew not to go into Bed-Stuy, Bensonhurst, Brownsville, or East New York and walk around like shit was sweet, because someone that knew the block and knew you didn't live there was liable to put a rusty piece of metal in you and take your shit. No matter what neighborhood you were in, if you got out of pocket, there was someone there to put you in your place. If you didn't play your position and you got out of pocket with some older cat, you were gonna get it. I wouldn't dare hit a kid half my age, but when I was a kid it was the norm for a thirty-year-old nigga to whoop on a fifteen-year-old—it was another one of those traditions.

New York was just a different city on the whole; the flavor was different. There was a lot of lawlessness going on. This was an era where if you got caught with a gun it wasn't such a big deal. [This is] before guns were felonies or there was a year-in-jail penalty. There was just a different mindstate. People were just on a different vibe in New York. People don't get mugged the same way they used to in New York. I've seen guys get their shit took on crowded streets, in clubs, and on subways. In those old '70s and '80s movies that take place in NYC, you'd often see someone get their shit snatched on the street in front of everybody. It could have been happening in New York—it was common—don't sleep!

There used to be ads in the subway that said, "Springtime is chain-snatching season" (for real).

There's still posters that tell you to tuck in your jewelry and turn the stones [on your] rings to face your palms, [and] beware of pickpockets. Although it was more prevalent growing up, crime ain't going anywhere. It happened all the time. Some big nigga (like Deebo in *Friday*) would walk into your subway car and start shaking someone down—lifting your shirt up to see what's in your pockets, patting your pockets down, digging through them—that shit happened every day.

I grew up in an all-Black neighborhood; I was one of the few kids in my neighborhood with straight hair. This was the early '70s. This was the tail-end of the Civil Rights movement, and there was still racial tension in the hood, straight up. In elementary school, there was one Irish kid, named Michael, and there was an Italian kid named Frank. Between them, Dennis, and about five other guys, we were the only non-African American students. Like Common said, I stuck out like a nigga on a hockey team. People saw me. I was the first one that stuck out in a crowd. I grew up fighting because it was routine that I got my pockets dug—usually by some older cats, gang members, or a group of kids your age—it didn't make me a sucka. Everyone I know was getting their shit dug back in the day at some point or another. You didn't tell the teacher, you didn't call the cops, and you handled your lumps. I don't regret a second of it. I'm cool with it all.

Times have changed. Crime isn't as rampant as it was when I was growing up. Stripped cars on busy avenues up on cinder blocks, missing all their wheels, people getting mugged on the subway right next to you while everyone turns their heads. I've bombed streets in some busy areas like the Village, midtown, or even in quiet residential areas at like 8:00 p.m., walking around with my cans, coppin' tags, and no one's said shit. Now there are hotlines; you can call up when you see shit happening, and someone will dispatch a police car to that location. Everyone's got a cell phone right now, and people are less accepting of crime these days. In 1982, if someone was getting beat down, you just kept walking by, and you were happy that wasn't you.

When you look back, what do you think you'll remember the most about writing?

I guess some of those near bullets that you almost caught, like getting raided, and having to jump off a subway platform onto a roof in order to escape. Those moments where you're curled up in a bush and the cop kicks the branches as he runs past the bush looking for you, [and you're] sitting there trying to control the heavy breathing, convinced that he was going to hear your heart pounding through your chest. Those moments where you're sitting there, telling yourself, "Fuck, if I get out of this, I'll never do it again" . . . only to turn around and do it the next day.

Surviving those moments probably stands out the most. There's so many good things that I remember from graffiti, too many to narrow down any one moment. The first time I saw myself up on a train was big. I'll always remember the summer of 1985 and the amount of subway insides we were killing. On the weekends, I'd hit the RRs at the elevated Astoria layup in Queens Friday night, hit 45th & 53rd layups in Sunset Park, Brooklyn, Saturday morning, bounce over to Sheeps Head Bay layup and kill the trains parked at Cherry Hill. Bay Parkway was sweet. We were also hitting B's and D's at the Coney Island Yard (the Dewey). At that time, they buffed those trains every so many days. So we were smashing them every day, just to stay on track. Me, Blas, and Rae had this idea that if we killed subways the whole summer, by the time September wrapped around and kids went back to school, we would have the insides smashed. So whoever was down to go bombing that I was cool with rocked: it could have been me and Rae, or me and Trim . . . Dape, Trech, Blas, Hero, Mesk, Suey. Tekay (Track 2 TNR) right before his comeback . . . me, Tekay, and Hash, Paulistic did some bombing . . . it was me and whoever was down to go do some insides. You don't wanna go? I'ma holla' at him. He doesn't wanna go? I'ma holla at him, but shit's going to happen.

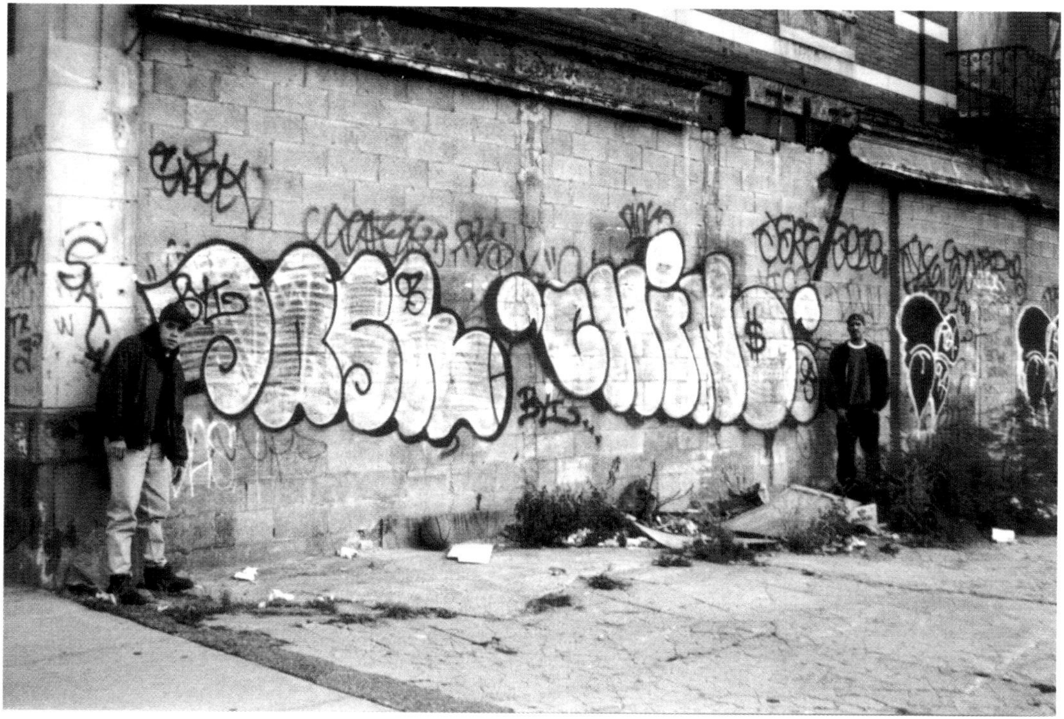

Life was simpler. I didn't need to work as hard; everything I needed was in front of me. Meals were prepared at a certain time, so I knew there was food at home and I didn't have to buy my own shit—just steal shit, sleep late, write on subways. To quote IZ The Wiz, "When you're a King, people either wanna write with you or fight with you."

I remember a time when lots of writers wanted beef with us. I knew we were doing something right, to get under so many people's skin. We were definitely making a mark. Most of the people who we were trying to get the attention of somehow gave it to us, either by way of respect or disrespect. Either way, our stuff was getting recognized. So maybe it's that era of graffiti for me. We really did just live and sleep graffiti for most of that summer . . . .

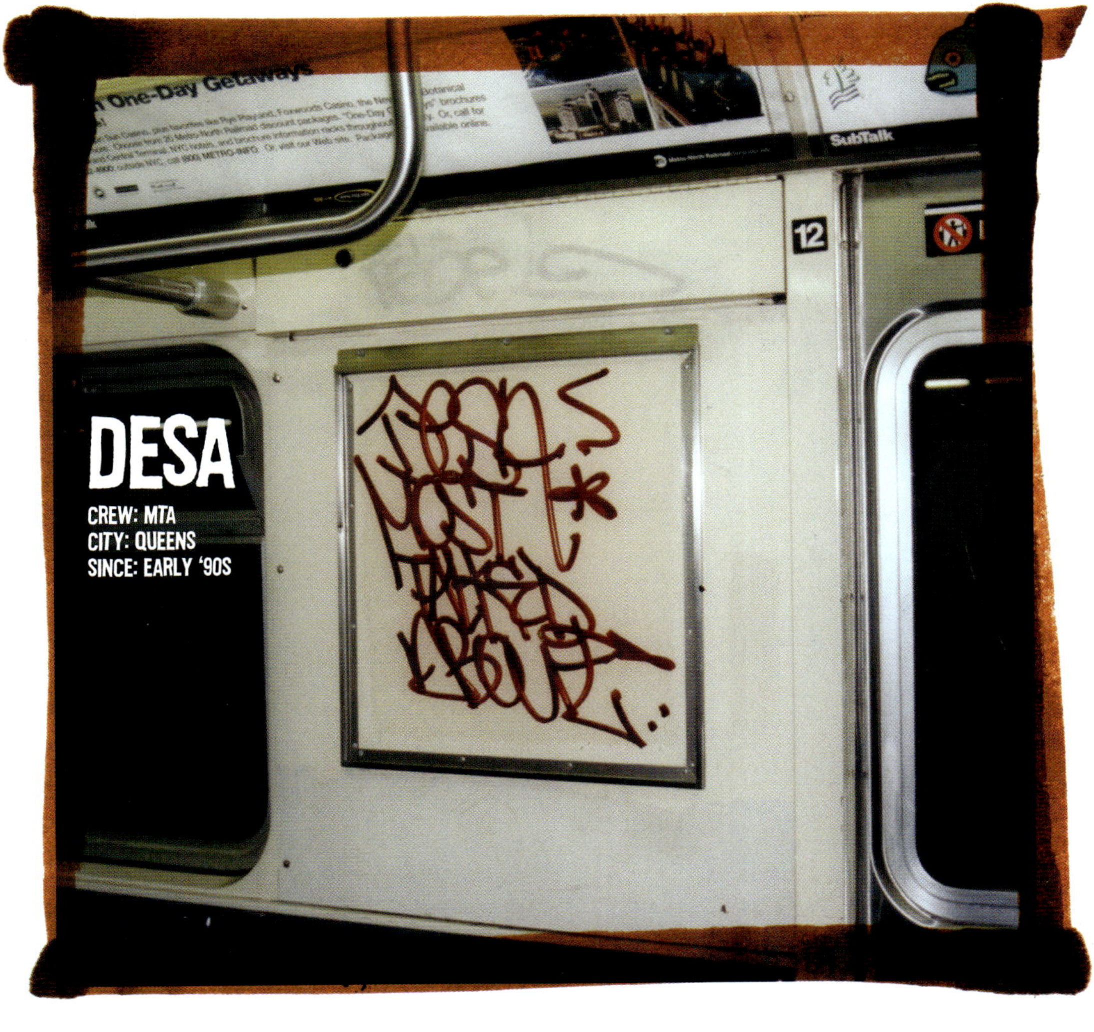

DESA

CREW: MTA
CITY: QUEENS
SINCE: EARLY '90S

The Wannabe Has-Been that Never Was

Where did you start painting?

I basically would do Queens, and like, Brooklyn. And then, like 'cause where I lived at the time, the neighborhood was kinda like well known because of the train yard, and they had a sanitation truck lot around there. A lot of big writers, subway writers and street writers, did those trucks in the '80s, so when I was younger, I lived near the lot, so I was able to see a lot of older writers doing the trucks.

Who was bombing garbage trucks at that time?

This guy Visa, he was from Green Point, Brooklyn, I think. He and Saint TMR hit a bunch of trucks; those are two of the bigger names. And plus I knew them from seeing them up in the streets and on the subways, so that gives you more of a reason to do it, because you see 'em up on the subways, then you see 'em up on the trucks in your own neighborhood, so you kinda get excited.

And that's pretty much how you got into it?

I've always been interested because I rode the trains since I was so little with my brother and my mother, and then, you know, when I was ten, eleven, by myself. I moved to Brooklyn in like 1987, so I had to travel back and forth to Queens to hang out with my friends and stuff. At that time the trains were really getting cleaned, but the neighborhood I was from was basically the last lines to get cleaned, so I got to see whatever was left because they didn't clean those trains until the last minute. I'd take the C, and transfer to the L, then transfer to the M, so I would wait for a train that was full of graffiti instead of getting on a clean one. They had the ones that were still bombed, then they had the ones they painted burgundy, and then they had other ones that were stainless steel that they finally cleaned up. There were still quite a few that were painted in '88, so basically I would ride the trains just to see that.

What were your active years?

I was off and on because of the trouble I got into, so it was like '91 'til '94. I had already gotten in trouble before that, but I just didn't care; I just kept doing it, you know? So '93 is when I got arrested for some trains, for doing insides on trains . . . that's when a lot of my trouble started. I got charged with a felony, and I had already been in trouble before that for the graffiti, and threatening to like burn down like people's houses and shit, the anti-graffiti programs. They were trying to put me in jail for that, but since it was my real first offense (I had been arrested before that, but I was under sixteen), in New York, it's like if it's something minor and if you're fifteen and younger, your parents can come and pick you up. All those other times were like minor things, up until I got arrested for the threatening and other graffiti charges in '92. So when I went to court, they wanted to put me in jail, because, like I said, in the area I was from I did do a large amount of stuff. So they basically were excited that they got me because at that time, the neighborhoods were starting to clean up. A few of the neighborhoods that surround where I hung out basically were bombed just because of the train yards. People from other neighborhoods would come to the train yard as they would come through, and put their names up as they're walking through the neighborhood or whatnot, you know?

Once the city declared graffiti was dead, they started to notice that all the gates and buildings were starting to get writ on now since the trains weren't painted. Before that, they really didn't notice it as much. The '80s and the '70s were just something New York City basically had to deal with when it came to graffiti. Once that ended and 1990 came around, they started noticing that the buildings were getting written on more and more, that it wasn't stopping. They cried and complained about the subways being so filthy, but then when they noticed it was on their houses, they were like, "Wait a minute—it isn't stopping, what's going on here?" In Queens, it's always been like that, from what I've heard, even in the '70s or the '80s, 'cause it was mostly all white, and some of the neighborhoods are more like suburban kind of lifestyle because of all the people that live there; it was mostly white, and some of the neighborhoods are very wealthy.

So they weren't happy about having the writing.

In Queens, the area I was from was, you figure like each borough, each neighborhood has a different police precinct, so the one where I was from, they covered four different neighborhoods in that part of Queens. So when I say like where I was from, I mean the four neighborhoods that that police precinct covers. In that area, one place did it more than the other, but it was like a domino effect; they all started to get involved. So when they got me, like I said, I did do a good amount in those areas, so . . . .

This is like tags, throwups . . .

Yeah, fill-ins, whatever. They kinda targeted me before that, because my name was around so much. So instead of just me and my friends getting gone after, they were cleaning some of my stuff, and only half of it, so maybe they figured I'd come back to fix it, and maybe they would be able to catch me. Once, my friend had seen them cleaning some stuff and was speaking to them about it, and they basically told him what they were doing and why they were doing it. So my friend told me, and he had gotten a card from them, so that's why I got their number. I kinda called them up, you know, sayin' stuff, but at the time, you know . . . .

You called the police?

Not the police. The anti-graffiti program. At the time I said a bunch of stuff, but it wasn't like—it was all child shit, because I wasn't going to actually do anything I said. It was basically a kid making idle threats, and they took it so serious because of who I was at the time. They wanted me because I was a big name, and they'd seen that they had a chance, and I basically made a very big enemy over that whole shit. I'm very not liked by them, by the Vandal Squad unit . . . .

So the Vandal Squad really exists.

Oh, yeah, they exist. They're going to people's houses like every day, either with a warrant or without, and basically getting everyone to admit to all these things, and arresting them. It goes on on a daily basis now, more than it used to. Years ago, they used to sit in front of your house, and torment you and follow you, but now what they're doing is what they've been doing in Europe: they're just coming to your house with warrants and taking everything. So people that are doing stuff today, it's not that easy, you know? And especially if they're not well educated on the situation that's going to be dealt to them when they approach 'em, you know? The cops are always gonna be around. And they need somebody to follow because now, especially because of the etching stuff, the windows on the subways are getting destroyed so bad that they gotta replace windows like every day because they're so fucked up that they can't see out of them. They're getting a little irritated over that.

When you were at your height, did you think you'd ever stop?

Well, I kinda never got to the height that I really wanted, or should have, because of all the trouble I got in. Because of all that trouble, it was more like I never had a fair shot, and I never, you know, I kinda like got my childhood taken away, in a sense. Like, all my friends were able to do anything they wanted in that category, you know, graffiti—

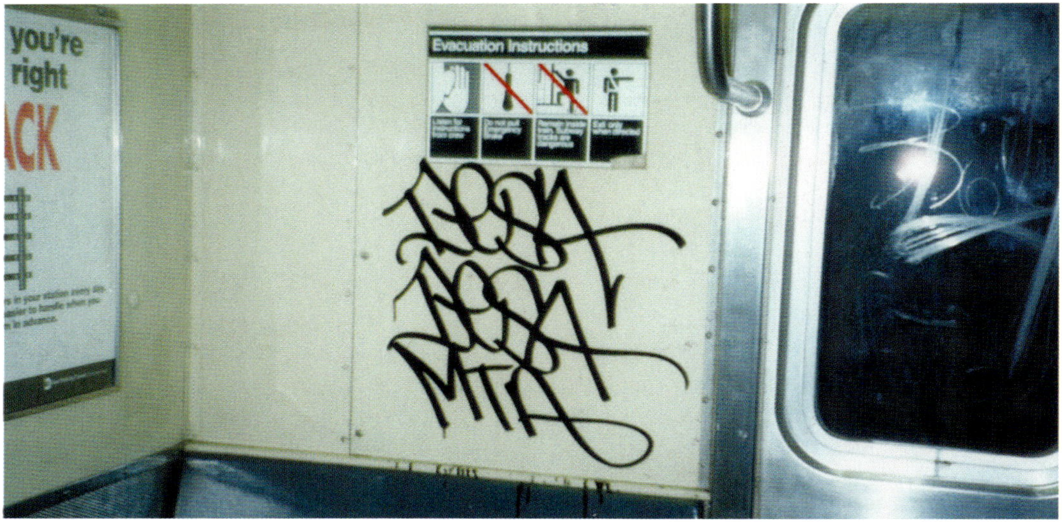

Who were you painting with?

When I first started, it was just basically me. The only one I really started to go and do things with was this kid TKA. JRC was the first person that I started to do more with, as in leaving the neighborhood, because he was two, three years older than me. At the time, he was the only one that was down to do anything. One of the reasons he wanted to hook up with me was because at that time, I was basically the one that had [the garbage trucks] locked. In the '80s, certain people would have it every two years, and then they would just fade out. I started doing it, like '88, '89, around that time—the end of that is when I had them—and I was the one that was on top up until, like, '92, maybe '93. After that, I kinda just left it, and they started cleaning them all over the city, so you really couldn't even do it anymore . . .

So when you were talking about writers that got to get to the point where you wanted to get to that you were writing with, who were you talking about?

My friends, basically. Like Giz, and VE, and I guess like SN, and even JRC got more than I did. The problems I had, it was either keep doing it like I was anyways, or . . . and I kept getting myself into more trouble. I had to just stop, you know. I couldn't keep doing it, because it got a little annoying getting arrested and put away. Basically, I got out, and I did it again, and then they put me away again.

How long did they put you away for?

One time was for insides, and they gave me a felony charge, so that's basically one to three years in New York State prison. You can't escape that; you gotta go up into the state prison system. So when I get out, that means I'm on parole, like a rapist, or a guy robbing a store or whatnot. They got work release programs here in the New York State system, but at that time, there was no more violent criminals being allowed, so there was a lot more opportunities for people to get sent home on work release, so that's what happened. I did half of the one to three in jail, and the rest I did on a program—you stay in jail two days a week, and you stay home the rest. It depends on your schedule; you can go to work and come back to the jail for the rest of your time if you don't have a permanent residence, or if you're a flight risk . . . certain reasons. But I had a place to live, and I never had a drug history like most other people, so I started out with two nights, and then after that, once you get close to your release date, they give you, it's called seven-and-0, meaning you only gotta report twice a week, so I did that for the six months until they let me off on parole.

As far as graffiti writers go, though, and sentencing goes, that's probably the longest sentence that's ever been given out for a graffiti writer, right?

In New York, yeah, as far as I know, but I know in California, there's been like Chaka, that was in, like, I think '89, 1990 or something, that he got put away, so, and then GK had a lot of trouble, you know, that was a more recent one. But for me, honestly, that's the longest that I've ever heard of, but I know some people got time, especially now, after the whole thing with me. I mean, there's this kid Korn that's been writing for a few years, and he's from Queens, and he did a lot, especially in Queens—

He went all-city?

Basically. What you can consider all-city nowadays. Like Manhattan and Brooklyn and Queens, and I guess maybe the Bronx. He did a lot, and he got arrested once, and then a television channel, Fox TV here in New York, wanted to do an interview with him because it was like high-profile a little bit with him—it wasn't as big as mine—but they basically tricked him, so he said, "Yeah, I'll do the interview." He had his face covered or whatnot, but he gave them a tape to air with the story, and I don't think he covered his face on the tape, so when they put the tape on the news, they informed the cops, so the cops went and arrested him for that. I don't know if he had probation with that, or fines, but he only did two weeks in jail, so for him I guess it's worth it, because he didn't have to go through what I did, you know? Two weeks in jail for what he did is, I guess, kinda good. But other than that, I mean, they don't care if there's anyone else doing it, you know? I'm the one that's gonna get them, like, good publicity, you know? Because a lot of them sit around, and they amp each other up, like, "I'm gonna get this guy, and I'm gonna get this guy." I'm the only one that's really been put away, when I really didn't do as much as I really should have to be put away for that long, you know?

They made an example of you.

Yeah, and they broadcasted it, you know, on the news, on MTV, *New York Times*—everyone knew about it, so it's kinda like, "This is what we're going to do to you." A lot of people get arrested; Espo had got arrested for a bunch of stuff, and he was goin' to court, and I don't know the outcome because it's been a while now, but he didn't go to jail, and that's what was done a lot, you know? Not like I wanna see him go to jail, or anyone else, but it's like every time I hear, "Oh, this guy's goin' away for graff," I just laugh, because he's not, you know?

So after you got out the first time, you went back to work and started painting again?

Yeah, [I was on] the work release program for six months. I had one to three years, so my earliest release date would be one, and then my second one would be two years. They always do it two months before time, so with me they did it after ten months, and I was approved for parole, so I had two months left, and I didn't really do much before that time was up. I kinda just was like, "I'm gonna stop doing this," you know?

At the time that I got arrested, it was like a really big blizzard, a snowstorm, so I took that opportunity to go out and do some shit, but unfortunately I got caught. Basically, before I got parole I wasn't doing that much, 'cause I didn't wanna push my luck with the program, but after parole—

You were like, "I'm gonna take my streets back."

Yeah, I figured I was gonna do a little something that I didn't get a chance to do—like I said, everybody else did what they were supposed to do, but I couldn't 'cause I was in jail. And that's when a lot of my friends actually did the shit. Coming home from prison upstate, being transferred to the work release facility in the Bronx, and I'm on the bus, shackled, with all these other inmates, and I'm looking, and once you get in the Bronx you start to see graff, and I see Giz and VE, Deck on the rooftops along the highway, so it was like, "Oh, shit, look!" And then, like I look around, I'll be like, wait a minute. They put me away 'cause they said I was they worst person in the city doing graffiti. I'm the one that basically gets everyone hyped to do it, and then all of a sudden, I get outta jail, and this shit's worse than it was before I left, you know? So it's kinda, like, it makes me laugh.

I kinda like started after the parole. That was what, three, four weeks, and then I got arrested again. I got paroled in the middle of December '95, and then I got arrested in the middle of January. And since I had parole, and I'm a high political case when it comes to that type of stuff, I got arrested by the Vandal Squad.

Where I did the location, I climbed up a fence that was basically like a two-story height right outside the train yard. I've seen that spot for years, and I wanted to do it, and Med from the Bronx, he had a big outline there from the '80s, so it was like, "Yo, I always wanted to do that spot," and I said, "To hell with it. Let me do it." And I just climbed up. Like I said, it had been a blizzard, so it was only a few days after, and there was still a lotta snow, and a lotta ice. I climbed up on this thing, and I did my spot, and then I climbed down. I went to the corner, and in the corner of my eye, I saw an undercover police car, a burgundy Caprice, and I said, "Oh God," you know? But I was already down and at the corner, so I saw them turn. I watched them in the corner of my eye, saw the brake lights, and I said, "Alright, they're gonna fuck with me."

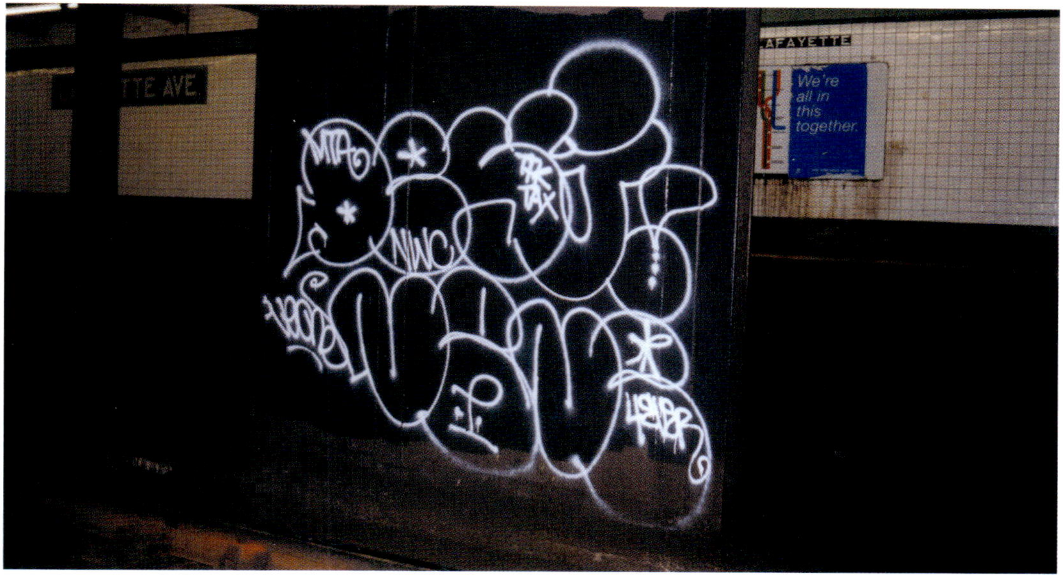

I had a pair of gloves that were full of paint, and I threw them under a mailbox as I walked. They were coming down the block behind me, but another blue and white regular patrol car was coming toward me from the other direction. So I said, "They've seen me, that's it," and I thought it was the regular police. So when the patrol car pulled up, it passed me only by two car-lengths, and stopped. The passenger cop got out, ran up on the sidewalk, and the cop backed the car up and stopped right in front of me and like ran out, and they put their guns on me and all that bull-shit, so I stopped, I went against the wall, and I figured why they were stopping me is because of what I just did. It turned out that they weren't; they were just regular patrol cops. They said that somebody just got robbed on the train station. He was wearing the same coat as I was, like a pullover fatigue army coat, and they basically stopped me for that reason, searched me, and then let me go because I wasn't the person. And [they] said, "Alright, we're sorry, go home."

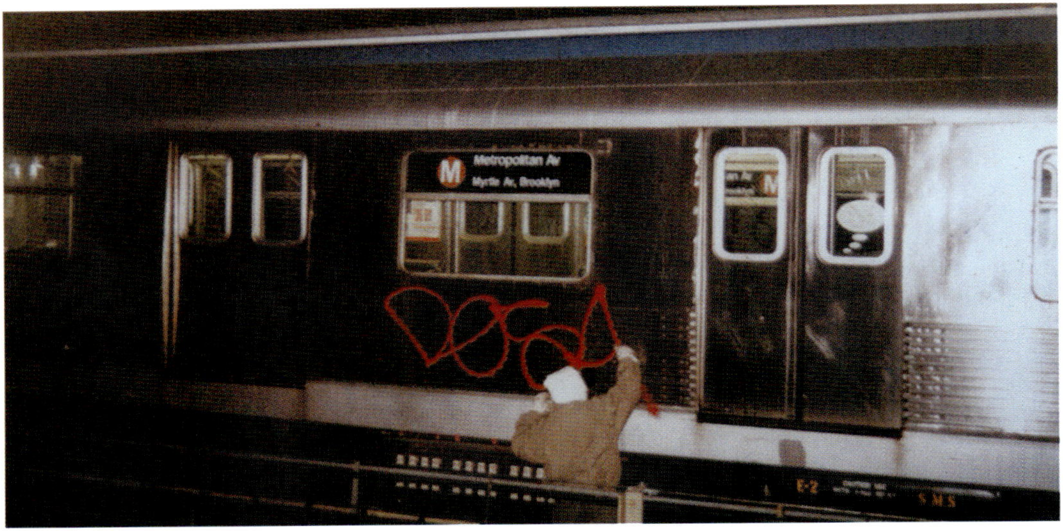

The other cops in the burgundy car pulled up, and I figured, you know, that's just regular cops. They were like, "We heard the call over the radio, so we thought, you know, we came to assist you or whatnot." I was like, "Okay, I'm going home now." This is around the corner from my house, basically. So I'm walking, and then the patrol car drives away, and the Caprice drives away, but then it stops and starts backing up, and I said, "Oh my God." So as they stop, they say, "Hey, is your name ______?" And I'm like, uh . . . and before I could answer, they say, "Your name's ______, right? Don't you do graffiti, ______, huh?" And I was like, "No, man. You crazy?" And they got out, and that basically was my answer to who they were. Once they said my name, I was like, "Oh, okay."

It was the Vandal Squad?

Yeah, basically. Same dudes that arrested half the people in the city, and start rumors about everybody—yeah, it was them. They got out, and I had a can of paint on me, so they searched me, then they put me in the car, drove around to where I did the thing. What happened was they thought I was in the train yard, because the spot that I did was originally an entrance to the train yard. So they thought I was coming out of there 'cause I was on the spot. We went in the yard, they drove around looking to see if I did anything, and I didn't, so they let me go in front of my house, and then they went around the block.

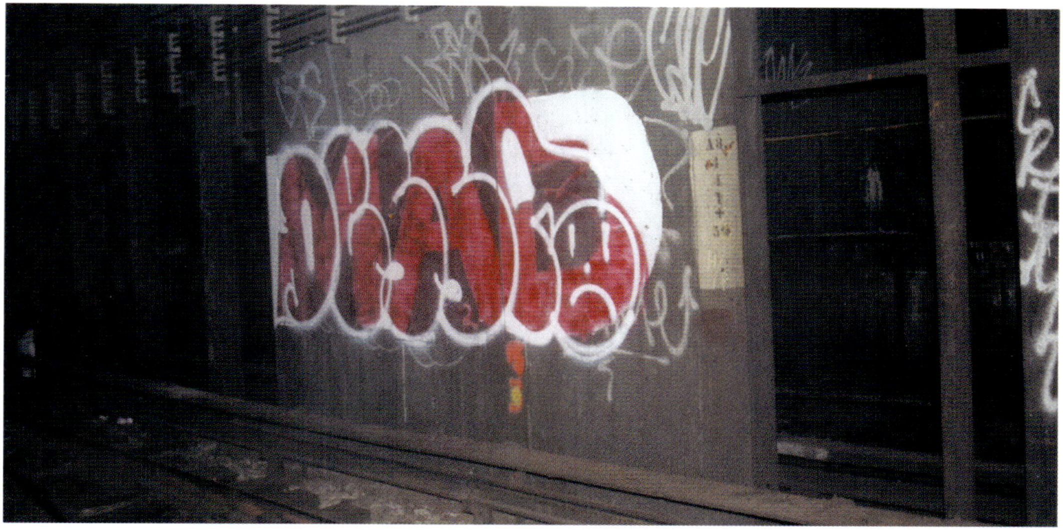

They made it back so damn fast. They were yelling and banging, and my mother was sleeping, so like an idiot, I opened the door. I tried to slam it on them, but they had kicked it in with their foot. So then my mother got up and was hysterical. I kinda just was like, "Fuck it. I'm making my mother crazy." But I didn't really think that I was gonna get fucked over again, you know what I mean? At that time, I really wasn't thinkin'. So they arrested me and took me in. They were giving me a desk appearance ticket, which is basically like a ticket, but it's an arrest. You get fingerprinted and everything else. They call the courts, they call the DA, and they get you a date when you gotta be in. So that's what they were giving me, but their lieutenant or whatnot came down, and was like, "No, this piece of shit is going through the system. So I was like, "Alright, here we go. I'm not going home. I'm stayin' in jail; I'm in trouble again."

Tom and Jerry, they was the two guys from the '80s that used to fucking arrest everybody. Yo, them two clowns came to the precinct to do their usual bullshit and talk to me, and try to be my friend, and so Jerry's there, and then I hear him on the phone talking to somebody about me, then I realize it's a reporter. And I'm like, "This fat bastard's callin' the papers. I cannot believe it." Tellin' 'em all this bullshit that I had just got out of prison, and what happened was I went out and I had a few drinks, and you know, I went on a binge. I couldn't control myself. A whole bunch of bullshit.

So they made up a story?

Basically, to make me look like a psychopath, like they did in the past. That was another point in my life where I lost my youth. That time, actually they could have probably given me a felony, but they didn't. They gave me a misdemeanor, so the most time you do is a year in city jail. The judge was an asshole, like most judges are, and what happened was that a police officer had just been killed, like that day, I think, or the day before—he got shot. So the guy that did it, he was in the court, and he was in Central Booking with us, so my luck as it is, he has to be sent out with me and the other person, 'cause three people go out at a time for court. So the judge was in a bad mood, so then the judge flipped on me and was screaming that . . . I don't know, probably I guess I was a loser. So they gave me fifty thousand dollars bail, which is ridiculous. And then my legal aid was like, "No, this is too much," and he said, "Alright. Twenty-five thousand." And that's it, you know. Like, it didn't make a difference because I had no money like that. So basically, it started another term of my being incarcerated.

So you did a total of about two and a half years.

Altogether, yeah, probably off and on. Plus I was on probation twice. I just finished being on probation, like seven, eight months ago, because one of my friends, Aks, and the other guy wrote on a pole. There's a new Graffiti Task Force unit—it's a few years old, five, six years—that's based out in the borough of Queens, but basically they got the power to go anywhere they want in New York City—any borough. They drive around, and just basically look for people writing, and arrest them. So that night, they were in Manhattan, and I was with my friends. I wasn't even standing with them—I was standing like three car-lengths away, sitting on a train station railing. So they caught tags on the front of a store with a marker, and on a pole. My friend Aks wrote on the pole, but my other friend was blocking him, so they didn't see Aks write.

When they pulled up, I knew immediately it was cops, 'cause I seen them get out of a car, and it's like, dead ringer. Cops, undercover cops, don't dress good. They're very horrible at trying to be undercover. These assholes don't realize it. It's like they're coming up on them, and I don't think they know until they pull their badges out. So I'm on the railing, like, "Oh, this is all I need," So I just stayed there, and when the guy came over, he was like, "Yo, come here. Are you with them?" And he started searching me. I was like, "What are you doing?" He's like, "I wanna know if you're with them." Then he stopped searching me, came back over five minutes later. I didn't leave because I said I was waiting for my friends, who like took off.

So basically, they took me in just to be safe, but then they found out who I was, so they charged me with writing. They basically charged me with actually writing on the fucking pole. The only reason they did that is 'cause they found out who I was. If you have a record from being arrested and put in prison, and you get arrested with one or two people that doesn't have a record, they want to put the felony charge or whatnot on the person with the record, because it's a guarantee that he's gonna be convicted of that charge, and it looks good for the cop. Ten, twenty years, it's like he arrested 500 people, and 400 of 'em got convicted. And it looks really good, you know, so that's basically what happened to me.

But wasn't your name in the paper recently, as well?

Yeah, the one in the paper was a few months back, maybe like six already. That was just because they're saying that I've been out doing all this stuff, and really the whole thing is, it's the anti-graffiti people from the community in Queens. Those people have a lot of power with like politicians, DAs, all type of shit like that. So it's like they can get favors done, you know what I mean? 'Cause they do other people favors. So they called a reporter from the *New York Daily News*, and talked to him about the situation. That person called the transit Vandal Squad and talked to the top lieutenant in charge. Because I wasn't arrested, they really couldn't talk to a regular officer and say, "Is he doing this? Is he doing that?" Because they don't have that authority—what if another unit was trying to build a case on me? So they talked to him, and this guy hates me, you know what I mean, with a passion, so—

But you haven't been painting.

Yeah, that's the thing. I haven't. So it's like they said all this stuff, and the *Daily News* reporter had to make sure that the anti-graffiti groups in Queens weren't just doing it because they wanted to get some more press on the situation. So he called the lieutenant of the transit Vandal Squad, he told them, "He's doing this, he's doing that," and like talked about like how much time I did in jail and whatever else. That's basically what the article was about.

There was another time before that, after I got arrested in Manhattan, that they were trying to give me a year. I didn't take it, so I was in jail for a few days, then I got bailed out, so I had to get a lawyer. The DA gave me a deal, and then he found out my situation, because he had no idea why I did all that time in jail, so he called up the DAs in Queens and in Brooklyn, and spoke to them and asked them why, so they told him. The deal had already been verbally talked about, so he didn't go back on it; he gave me three years probation. I was willing to do time in jail, but not a year for something I did not even do.

But you didn't do anything.

I know, but I have a criminal record, and I got arrested again for graffiti, and the cop was willing to come in. I was gonna go to trial because it's a misdemeanor, and no matter what, if you lose, you're still gonna get a year, and they were offering that anyways, so the DA basically told my lawyer, "I understand the situation, but if you go to trial, the cop is willing to come in and testify." Of course he is, because, that's his job. He's anti-graffiti. He arrested me. I'm like the star of the media. I'm the poster child of like anti-society, quality of life destroyer, you know? He figured he'd get his name in the paper, and he'd get like all these props 'cause he caught me. Meanwhile, he didn't even catch me doing anything.

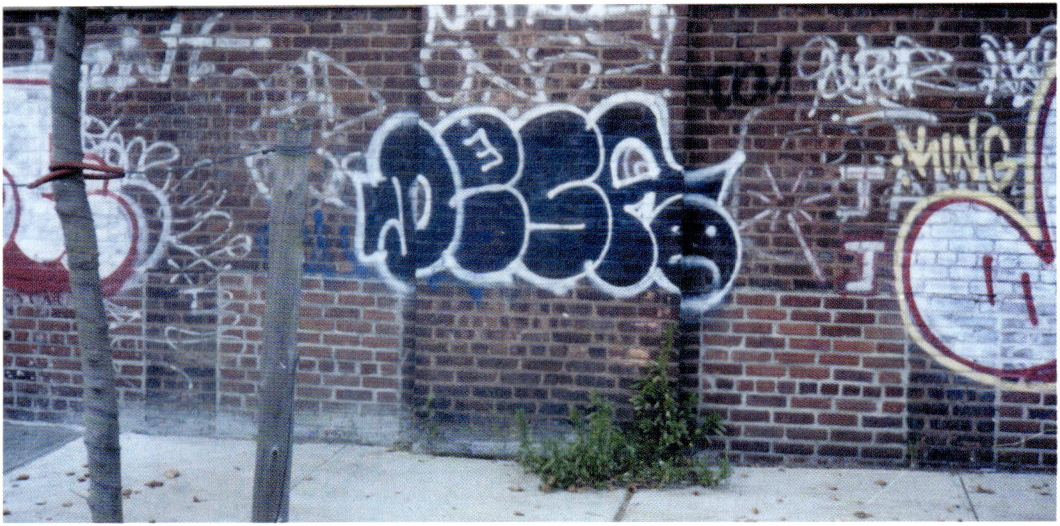

In the '70s and '80s, there was a lot of fighting, and there was a lot of beef between writers. Do you think it was the same in the '90s, with streets?

Not really. I mean, there was some. Me and my friends would have problems with other people. It would start over a little bit of graff nonsense, and then one of the people who had problems with us would catch one of our friends, or one of my friends would catch one of their friends and beat them up, and that would trigger a whole all-out war. But personally, like I don't consider having beef with people; I look at it as they have beef with me, because I want nothing to do with anybody that I don't know.

It still happens . . . dudes are just bombing the street and like, you know, some guy and his friends are in a car, and they see them bombing and they stop, jump out and be like, "Oh, what do you write?" take all their paint 'cause they've got the upper hand, you know that stuff still went on, and they took their hats, or their clothes. It wasn't like that in the train yards, it definitely wasn't like that—it wasn't that intense.

Crazy like that.

Yeah. It was like a lot of shit with me was that I was well known in my area, and then especially because of the articles in the paper, and TV, and all this other shit, what happened was I had a lot of people not liking me. Literally, that's all it came down to. Like me, I'd be the last person to try to think I'm conceited about anything, you know, but when it comes down to it, the only reason they wanted to, like, you know, stomp me, and go over me, and try to embarrass me and whatever was because they had like a—I look it as like they had a mental problem. They had like a handicap—they basically can't write, so they figure that they can fight better than they can write, and they figure that, "I'm gonna beat him up, and tell everybody that I beat him up." I feel bad in a sense too, because they don't know how to go out and paint, so that's how I looked at it, and I've always had problems like that.

But even now, do people still say, like—

I still have the problems, but I'm much older now, and if someone comes over and steps to me, I basically try to just like be like, "Yeah, yeah, yeah," and ignore it and walk away, because I'm not going to get into a fight over absolutely nothing. I'm not going to give him the satisfaction of fighting with me and then telling everybody what happened. Usually I walk away, and they get so fucking mad that I'm basically ignoring them and don't want to deal with them, they don't know what to do.

One of the last times someone came up to me on the train station, I was with my girl. We're walking to get on, and someone just got off. He was a kid, probably like twenty-one or twenty-two, like a Puerto Rican. I didn't know who he was. So we're walking, and all I hear is, "Yo son, Desa, yo," and I'm looking, like, "Who the fuck is this?" You know, he started with his mouth, starting all this bullshit, like I had beef with one of his boys, and I'm like, "Yo man, I don't know you, so I gotta go." And I'm trying to get on the train, and my girlfriend's holding door, and she's like, "Come on, come on!" And then I'm like, "Listen, man. I gotta go." He's like, "Yo, son, don't walk away from me, son, yo, son," Like he's this big-time killer. So I was like, "Yo, man. I don't know you, and I don't know what you're talking about, so I gotta go." He's like, "Oh, shit, you don't know me, son? Oh . . ." And I kept walking. And he's like, "Oh. You know what? Now you're not gonna know who I am," so I said, "Oh, okay, that's what this is about, then. Okay, I understand. Bye." So I just got on the train, so it was like all that because he was gonna step to me and say, "I'm such-and-such. What are you gonna do," you know? That's the type of shit I get into nowadays.

Basically, like, "I'm a new writer. Feel me."

Yeah, or an old one that couldn't get up, so they had to like fight for the right, you know? Sometimes I'll be on the train, or walking, and I don't notice the person coming or standing there, and a lot of times, I just got swung on, you know what I mean? It's like either you see the person comin' at you, or you feel gettin' snuffed in the back of your head. When you get into a lot of fights and shit like that, once you feel that first hit, it's like, you're like a fuckin', a cat, like the dog or someone tryin' to get the cat, and you've got that cat in a corner, and that cat's still gonna be able to get away from you because it's got so many skills at moving and practice. It's like if I get hit once, that second hit ain't gonna hit me because I'm dropping to the floor, rolling over, and like running down the block, you know? Because I'm not gonna get beat down over graff when it's not even like a real reason. I try to ignore a lot of it, because I basically look at it like they got beef with me, really, but what it means is they got beef with themselves, because I'm not even interested in what they got to say.

Do you regret graffiti?

Not really. I just regret—what I regret is doing what I did with the phone calls, the threatening phone calls, because when I did that, that's what really got me in trouble. That's what caused my lifetime of fucking hell. The transit Vandal Squad wanted me way even before that, and they'd never caught me.

There were a few times that they tried to get me. I was with my friend Giz and this other guy at this particular park in Queens, where the train pulls in to the last stop, and right alongside the train line is the freight tracks. While the trains were parked, I would go from one end to the other, hitting every car, then go out the hole in the fence and wait for the next train to pull in, and I would do something over 'n over until I got tired of it. What pissed them off was that I was doing it at seven or eight in the morning. There were so many people on the trains at that time going to work, they were forced to let the trains run; if I hit seven sets of trains, that's half of the morning rush hour service. Then all I would do was just sit back and wait for my throwups to roll on back from Bay Parkway or Coney Island in Brooklyn. I'd be sitting all the way out in Queens waiting to get flix . . . and they still came back in service.

So we were on the tracks, plus looking at freights and taking pictures. It was like in '92 or '91. What happened was I noticed three men coming, and at first I thought it was track workers or whatever, but then I hopped over to the other side of the freights, and all of a sudden I noticed one of them was on that side. I was like, "Yo, that's not workers. They're coming down after us." So we walked a little faster.

As we go through the hole in the fence and walk up onto the sidewalk, all I hear is footsteps and heavy breathing, and as I turn around, all I see is a gun in my face. I hear the words, "Don't fucking move." Now all I'm thinking is run, run, run, and run a whole lot more. I don't know how anyone else would handle this type of situation, but when a gun is stuck in my face, I'm going to do anything but stand in place so I can be shot. So I ran to my friend's house that was close by. Later, when I met up with my boy Giz, who was with me when that shit happened, he was like, "Yo, those guys were Vandal cops and as soon as you took off running, the guy with the gun was like, 'That was Desa, wasn't it? Tell him to stop writing on the trains, because this is not a game. We are not playing games with you kids. Just tell him we will be seeing him soon.'"

But that's how it was; it was really extreme. Like he stuck the gun in my face. And it's like they were there for me. Literally, not being bigheaded, it's like certain things that I did, like, they didn't get me, and I guess they got annoyed because they couldn't get me.

Another time, in 1992, while I was out to paint some trains, I ran into a little trouble while I was in the process of fillin' in my throwup. I noticed that there was someone inside the train car next to me, so I started to finish up what I was doing at that moment. Before I even got to finish my outline, I saw all this light coming through the train door, then I saw a shadow standing in the doorway, and I was a hundred and fifty percent sure that it was a cop and not a worker—a worker wouldn't be working in the dark. I had to make a move immediately so that I could be out the hole in the fence, and to get to the hole in the fence, I had to run past the open door where the Vandal Squad cop was standing. As I run past him, all I feel is a foot kicking me in my head, then I bounce into the fence and fall onto the third rail running board . . . instead of trying to grab me, this guy starts to stomp on my back as I'm crawling my way to the hole in the fence. I started to run as fast as I can, because this guy tried to stomp me out once, and I didn't want to find out what his next wave of rage was going to be.

Then there was the time me and Giz were bombing the upper level roadway of the Manhattan Bridge and we got chased by the cops. The only way off the bridge was to climb down this big round drainpipe that was connected to one of the beams that holds up the bridge. We had to slide down this damn beam all the way to the street level below.

When they had the chance, they got me. But that's the only thing I regret, like the phone calls, because all the other stuff was basically just graffiti and honestly, if they would have arrested me [for just the graffiti], I wouldn't have got prosecuted like I did. I was just another kid writing on trains, trying to make it look like the '80s or something, but when I did the shit with the Queens community people, they had a lot of political cause, so that was it. They were fuming. So that's the only thing I regret; making an enemy with them. And like I said, I probably wouldn't have been doing half as much if my childhood wasn't interrupted, and I was [able to go] through my phase, you know? Like my friends did.

But a guy like Veefer is still going, too.

Yeah, that's because he, in a sense, is like the average writer. But you know, he's up all over. He's like all-city, all like whatever, all like it never, so whatever, but . . . he's not gonna be prosecuted like me because—

He doesn't have the priors.

Yeah, and he didn't really personally, like, get them annoyed. It's just crazy—take what they did with John Gotti, and like Sammy "The Bull" Gravano. Sammy "The Bull" Gravano killed what, like probably more than twenty people. Or fifteen or something that he admitted to. And they let him get off with like five years, just because they wanted John Gotti and thirty other people. But probably altogether, like Sammy "The Bull" did more than any of those guys. Usually it's an assistant District Attorney handling any type of case, no matter what it is, from murder to rape and whatever, so when the head DA of the borough personally takes that case, takes interest in the case—

You know it's big things.

Yeah, and he's getting interviewed from the news reporters about me in his office. It's like this dude goes after, you know, mobsters that kill people, everything, you know, big time drug kingpins, like drug gangs all through Queens, and it's like I'm this little kid graffiti writer, and this guy is coming after me. And it's insane, they're like, "Oh well, we're going for him, putting him away, but you know, Sammy "The Bull" is gonna get off in five years and kill some more people, but as long as we got John Gotti, it's okay," you know? And that's basically how it is with me and the whole situation. They said it's gonna set an example, and they wanna teach me a lesson. But obviously, they're just doing it to make me suffer. To teach someone a lesson, you'd send them to school, you know? You don't put them in prison.

I'd go to court, to Supreme Court, and there'd be like thirty people representing the borough of Queens, like victims of my "graffiti assault," they'd say, and the Congressman was there, putting on a show because he was running for re-election or whatnot. When he was running, he put out flyers, stickers, and posters saying what they're gonna do, and what they'd achieved. He sent the flyers out to everybody in certain parts of Queens where he was running. The flyers stated that he was running for re-election, and on the things that he sent to the area where I was from, where I was most hated, he had put certain things he did, plus he put,"I had helped to convict the city's biggest graffiti vandal." He had that shit on his card as one of the things he did good. On top of that, the police chief and the Queensborough president signed a letter stating that they supported the District Attorney's office on the case.

That's crazy.

That's when you know they don't like you. A lot of people that I know, that I grew up with, still don't understand what happened to me, even though they know I was put away. I look at them when they ask me, "How you doing?" and I'm like, man, where the fuck have you been, man? You think this is like a joke, or a made-up story? I didn't go to a graffiti jail, you know? I didn't go to a jail with fuckin' little kids that wrote on their mother's wall with crayons so they had to be punished. I didn't go to some special little jail. I went to, like, real prisons, you know, with people that are in there for murder, you know?

How was prison life? Did people understand what you had done?

A lot of them knew me because I was in the paper; they knew who I was because of the article. Down the line, like when I moved to other dorms where I had to do time, everyone would get to know each other and talk about whatever, and it's like, I'd talk about me, and they didn't believe me 'cause it's insane. I had articles that I saved while I was in jail, like out of the paper, and you know, I got court papers, and I'd show 'em, I'd be like, "Yo, they're not playin', man." And then here in New York, the radio station Hot 97 had done a show on graffiti, like in '94, before I had got put away, and they wanted me to come on the show, but I refused because I didn't need any more publicity. It was annoying. Down the line, they had another show on graffiti. They had like another two. So it was one of the shows that was on in '96, when I was in jail.

I worked in the mess hall overnight, from like eleven to like six in the morning, seven in the morning. Because you're in jail, you need to do shit to pass the time. I had been sleeping, because coming back from the mess hall job, you're so used to being up, and you'd get back to the cell and you don't go to sleep right away. You sit in the cell, and wait to be locked out like at nine o'clock or whatever so you can watch TV in the dayroom, or you can just stay in your cell, reading a book, listening to a walkman, so I didn't get to go to bed usually until like two o'clock, three o'clock. By the time ten o'clock comes along, you've got to get ready to be picked up and escorted down to the mess hall with the correction officer. So I'm dead asleep, you know, and Hot 97 was on, and they were talking about me on the show, but it was probably the end of the show, someone in my house came in the cell and was like, "Yo, get up!" I was like, "Why? What's going on?" They're like, "They're talking about you on the radio." And I was like, "What? Really?" "Hot 97. Put it on! Put it on!" By that time they weren't talking about me anymore, though.

When they came to pick us up for the mess hall, I was looking for a guy that I worked with at night. He came right out, right away, and was like, "Yo, they were talking about you on the radio!" And then they were like, "Now I understand what you mean by, like, what they did to you," you know?

A lot of people liked me because I was still young, and I wasn't a knucklehead. I wasn't the average junkie with the bullshit stories about like he didn't do what he got arrested for, and yeah, he had a million dollars before he got locked up, and the cops took it, and the Feds took his house, and you know? I was just basically a real person. I never tried to put on a front. Even when they didn't believe me, I'd be like, "I don't care. I'm in jail, just like you. What the fuck's the difference," you know? So I never really had it bad, like in a sense of getting extorted, or beat up, or whatever else, you know? I was thinking the worst part of being in jail is the mental stress, you know what I mean? Because you think about it, [the people] you're in jail with like, eighty percent of them are drug addicts. I mean, come on, you're worried about a drug addict that can't even lift a can of fucking soda 'cause it's too heavy? That wasn't ever a problem. Yeah, I had some problems, but if you know what you're doing, you just avoid the fuckin' things in the beginning. I mean, just the mental stress destroys you.

Tell me about VE.

I met him in '91, and he was two years younger than me, so he had just started, basically, when I met him, and we started hanging out before he even got up, you know? So throughout the years, we were just friends with like our group and shit. Like Giz, and him, and a few other people.

Was it a crew?

Yeah, it was basically a crew. Like FTR, we were all from the same area, so one crew, FTR, Fuck The Rest, and like he did the same thing that he would have done before I met him, so like then I was there with them anyways, so it's like from then on, you know, we hung out, and it's like at a certain point, we were older. But there still was like Giz and everything, and I guess, you know, SN off and on, you know, people hang out off and on, and like a few other people—that was us. I guess like Giz or Double D came up with MTA and was like, it was just a thing they started, so it basically was me and Giz, and VE, maybe a handful more of people just that we knew from the neighborhood, but no one but like VE, Giz, SN, Ketch, this other guy, A1, it's like, you know, we were the ones that were actually getting up, I guess. And Slash, you know?

One night in the winter of 1992, me, Giz, VE, and Cend were painting this building along the subway tracks, in between two subway stations in Brooklyn. When we finished our throwups, me and VE climbed to the upper-level set of tracks to paint another spot where you can hang over the lower level of tracks. So now Giz and Cend are walking back to the station to wait for us. As we're painting, we hear sirens down below in the street. . . . From where we were standing, you can see the steps of the train station. By this time, the cop cars were already on their way up to the platform. We run to the other platform to catch up with Cend 'n Giz, and when we get to the platform I see two guys with work vests and flashlights trying to lie down on the steps at the other end of the station. I start to tell everyone that those guys are cops, but they're like "Nah, that's just workers." I said, "Okay, but I'm getting the fuck out of here."

As soon as I hit the tracks, the cops start running towards us, and now everyone is panicking, so I said, "Yo, let's go down those poles to the street." As I start to go down the pole, I see this van going real slow in the street, so I start yelling to go back up the pole. As I'm going back up, Cend has already landed on the ground. So the van spots Cend hitting the ground and makes a U-turn, almost hitting him. He gets up, runs around a corner, and crawls under a car to hide. Since the van went after him, I slide down to the street, run across, and start to climb a fence, but the fence isn't too strong, so it starts to bend, and I'm getting stuck on the razor wire. Now VE is running towards me, so I say, "Yo, VE, this way, come over the fence." So he looks at me stuck in the razor wire and starts to laugh and say, "I'm not getting cut up," then he just starts to run down the street.

So now I'm bleeding and still trying to get over the fence, so I just let my body drop to the ground and landed in an empty lot and just laid there bleeding. Then I hear over the police loudspeaker: "We got one." Now I'm saying to myself, maybe they are just saying that to fuck with us so we would think they left. But I know they're still driving around in circles, going around the block where I was hidden for like two hours. As the van is circling the blocks, I see Giz walk right past me on the other side of the fence with his hood on, and he just walks right past the cops. He sees VE in the cop car, so he just keeps on walking. I stay in the bushes for a few hours.

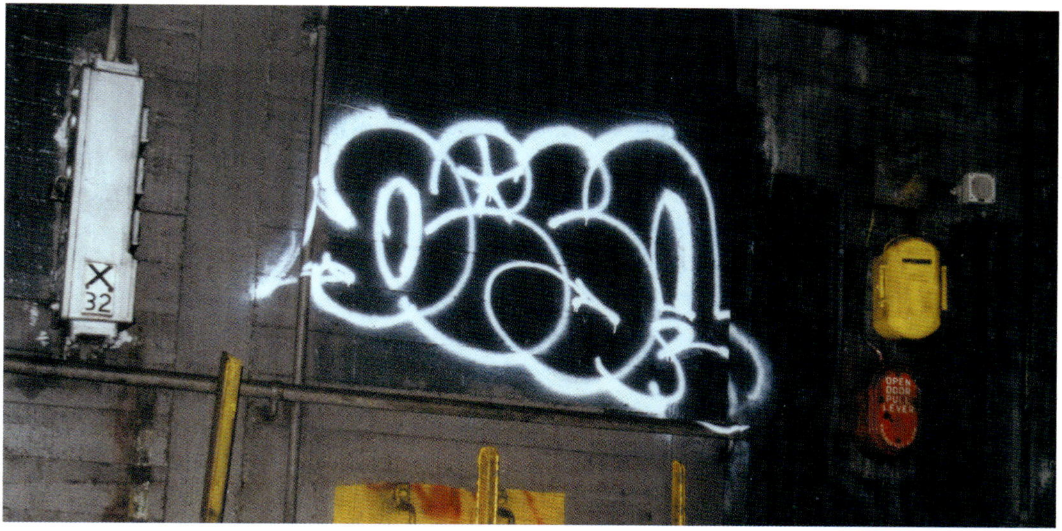

After I went to jail, I basically had to do certain things. When I got out, I had to be on parole and deal with all that, so I couldn't be going out and drinking with everybody, going to clubs like we used to do, and getting into these problems. I wasn't hanging out with VE that much at that time, because of that. Then I went back to jail right away, like within four weeks, so that's like another year that I wasn't hanging out with him. Then he died in '97, so I didn't get many chances to hang out with him before he died.

It's kinda like fucked up that I didn't get to do much with him. But you know, up until then, before that, he would paint, and he was getting up here and there, you know? And he's the type of kid that, no matter what you did, you'd have fun. He was like a wild but harmless person. The things he would do, he'd crack you up laughin'. Being on the train, and this Chinese guy was like reading the paper, and like the train is pretty empty, and he's like copping on the floor, like underneath the paper where the guy can't see him, and writing on his newspaper. Memories like that are just like bugged out to remember. It's basically just like having childhood friends, I guess, but doing graffiti, like anything, other categories, you know? But that's when he really started getting up, when there were times I was in jail, like Giz and SN and VE. Before that, '93, you know, we went on missions, and he was known, but it wasn't up until then that they really got well known because of the spots they were doing. They were doing a lot of fire escapes, so they knew what to do, and then they got a lot of recognition. I don't know what else, like, you wanna know—

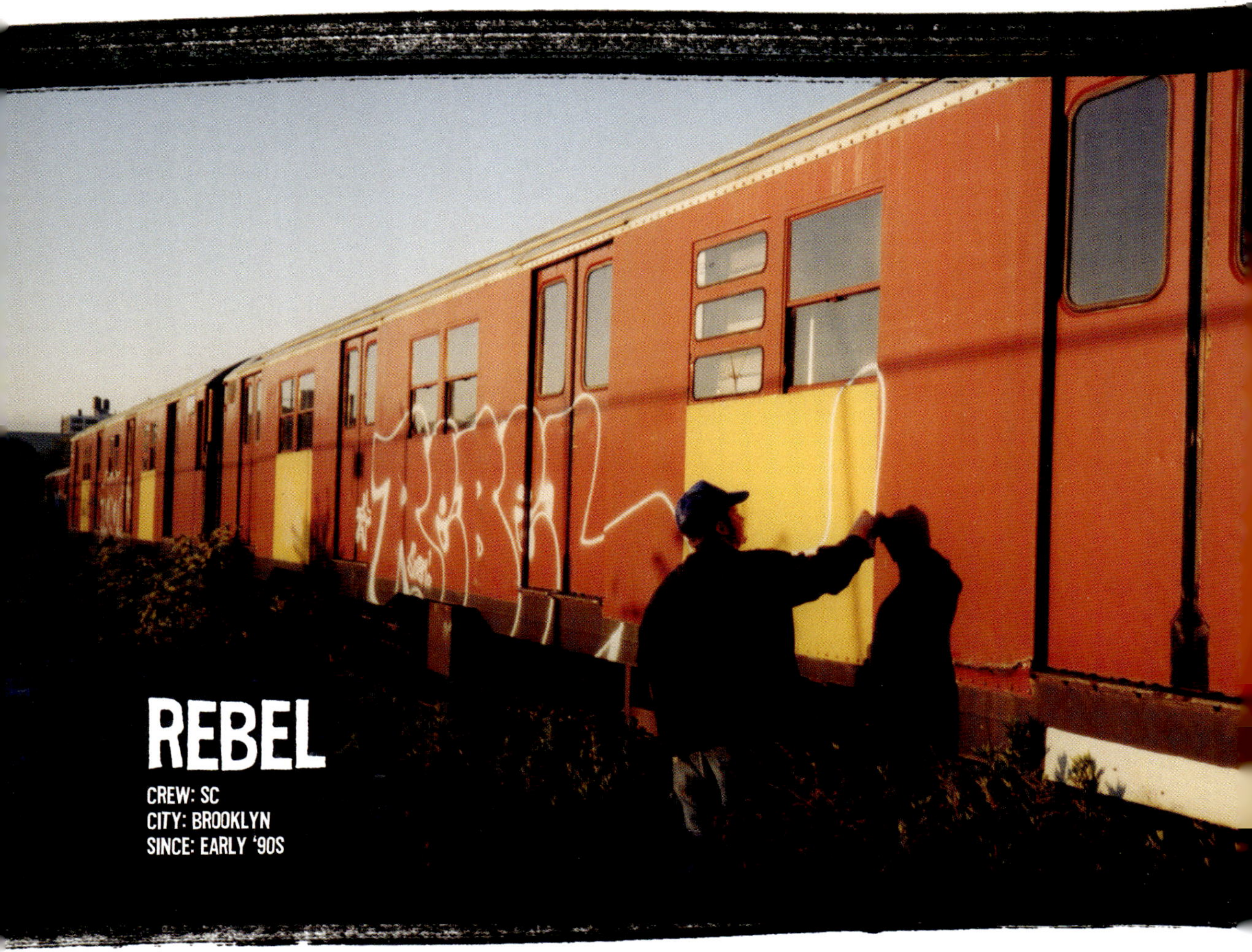

REBEL

CREW: SC
CITY: BROOKLYN
SINCE: EARLY '90S

What do you write?

The only name I write is Rebel. Although I like to piece lots of different names from time to time, the name that I am known by is Rebel, and I'll have that name until I die. It's not only a name; it's who I am.

As far as crews go, I'm down with lots of people and lots of crews. I'm not going to sit here and list them all. Basically, if you've seen any of my pieces, you know the crew that I always put up is SC, which stands for Style Crew. SC is more than a graffiti crew; it's a close-knit family that goes way beyond the realm of graffiti. The initial reason it was created back in 1991 was to organize my friends, because we all had the similar interests of having a good time and writing our names on stuff.

When did you start writing?

I started marker-tagging around my neighborhood in the summer of 1987. Upon my return from a trip out to California, I was hanging out on my block with my friend Pete, who was showing me a marker he had just made. It was a white Pentel he got from our local art store, and he added red Pilot ink to it. We had stolen from Chins, a neighborhood hangout where we'd go to play video games and practice the art of stealing instead of being in school. Pete was like, "Let's go take tags around the neighborhood." So I was like, "Sure." After all the crazy stuff we got into in Bay Ridge as kids, tagging sure sounded like fun! But I didn't have a tag to put up. So as we were kicking it on our corner, tossing out cool-sounding tag names like old mother jokes, Pete glanced down at the jacket I was wearing from my uncle's boat, called "Sloop Rebel." He was like, "Rebel." It sounded good, and it stuck. And that's where it all started.

There were a few writers on our block at that time, like Kaves, and ADM, TK, and the Verrazano Boys. They pretty much had tags all over the neighborhood. Also, there was Hi 5, TYVB, RS3, Ser, Bir, RR/Sase, Revlon, all the TBR guys, Reckless Eric, Gasp 69, Dek 5, Ant, Bete, Krook TBK—there were a bunch of guys around my neighborhood tagging.

We used to all pack in and take the bus ride up to the main avenues, but during our ride, we would absolutely destroy the insides of the buses! The whole bus was filled with high school kids, and nobody would care. We'd ink the whole place down with Unis filled with all sorts of ink! We would be tagging everything. If we weren't tagging, we were doing big scratch block letters on the windows. Before train windows were the way they are now, we used to destroy the buses. Some of the kids who wrecked the buses with me were Menz, Cort, Beware, Stun, Dren, and Ogre. We were killing the windows! We used to have so much fun! If it wasn't the PX-30s, we were making homemade markers out of roll-on deodorants and chalkboard erasers. The king of the homemade bombers was this guy Hi 5 from around the block. He always had the dopest drippy marker tags, with the freshest inks.

I remember taking the train with my father to work in the '80s, with my legs dangling off the seats of the R train, the lights flickering on and off, and just seeing a purple and black Haze on the train with all sorts of marker tags. The name that stood out among all the rest was Ant—that tag was everywhere!

After we kind of perfected the art of making markers in a few sessions with the older guys from the neighborhood, we would go on missions on the trains. Riding them every day after school, religiously, we would travel all over the subway lines, tagging. We'd get on the R at 95th, transfer to the N at 59th, take it to Coney Island, sometimes switching to the B, then back on the F, changing over to the D, doing insides and hitting stations all the way.

Around '95, I started hitting the scrap yard on a regular basis. We would go in and wreck the insides 'til the markers ran out and we got dizzy with the fumes. We used to bring all sorts of markers into the trains. We had unis, Minis, Bombers, paint markers, Pilots, Pentels, Magnums . . . you name it, we had it. I remember one time, shoving the eraser into the container of ink and using that as a marker. It was kind of messy, but it worked. We were going through ink like it was going out of style! One time, before a mission, I remember duct-taping a bottle of shampoo, filling it with ink, and doing insides, squeezing the bottle and watching the panel tags drip down to the seats!

Do you plan missions, or do you always have paint on you?

Usually I like to plan out missions, but I like to carry around a marker just in case there's a chance to catch a tag or whatever.

Do you rack paint?

I was never a huge racker, unlike some of the kids I know. I used to steal a lot in my younger days, but not so much now, as an adult. When you get older, you realize the consequences more than when you are young and carefree. I know kids that could steal the watch off your wrist while you're talking to them. For some, it's a way of life.

What's your favorite brand of paint?

I would honestly say Rust-Oleum, although I'd paint with any kind of paint. Belton and Montana make some really good paint, as well as a few other overseas companies. I grew up on Krylon and Rust-Oleum. After 1991, when Krylon switched from Borden to Sherman Williams, the quality of the paint took a turn for the worst. They discontinued a lot of the classic colors, and the thickness wasn't the same anymore. I don't give a fuck if it drips; that's graffiti. Graffiti's not supposed to look all fucking shnazzle-dazzle pretty, you know? But Krylon started sucking after '91. It started to become all watery. I mean, I paint with a lot of Krylon still, but it's a lot of old shit, like paper labels and shit like that. Nothing was as good as the smell of black licorice when you used a can of Borden Ultra Flat Black.

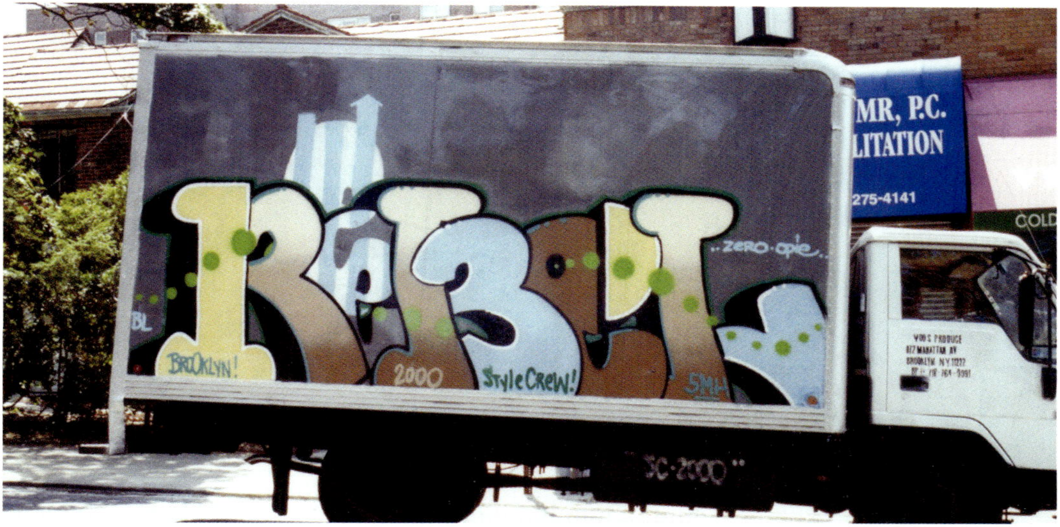

What was your favorite marking device over the years?

The marking device I think I had the most fun with was a 32oz. of Suave shampoo with an eraser tip in it that I could squeeze and fucking write all over the scrap trains with. That was my favorite marking device.

So that was like making a marker, sort of.

Yeah. Actually I'm looking at one that was a 6.5oz. of Suave shampoo. And we used to fill that with Flo-Master, Marsh, and Garvey mixed together. And just wipe all over the trains. The first couple times I went there, we made bombers out of Pilot markers and shit, and then ran out too quick, 'cause we were just excessively tagging, so I was said fuck it, I'm gonna make something, and the only thing that I could think of that I could actually hold in my hand without feeling awkward would be a shampoo bottle. So I just duct-taped the shampoo bottle so that the ink wouldn't eat through it if it ever did. I put massive amounts of duct tape all over the bottle, and then we just filled up the bottle with ink, put a cap on it, went to the train yard, took the cap off, slid the eraser in, and just went to work.

Do you make a lot of markers?

Yeah, that shit you've seen in *12oz. Prophet*, with those drippy tags? That's that Suave shit.

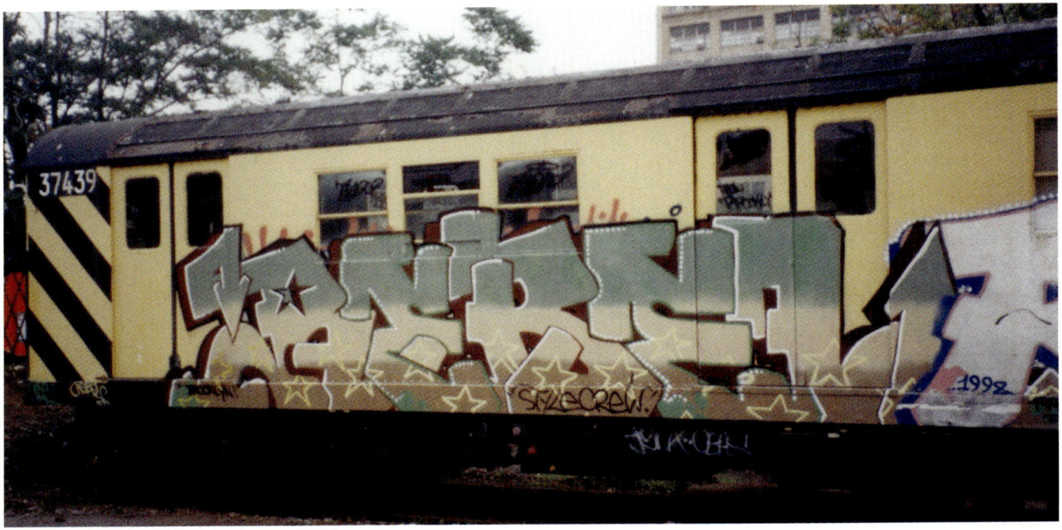

That's what that was?

That's the shampoo bottle.

And what about inks?

Well I remember when I was fuckin' young, I used to go to my mother's job and get . . . what are those papers called? Carbon papers, I used to just steal, like, all sorts of receipts with carbon papers, and we used to pile carbon papers in jars, and pour rubbing alcohol in it. And then after like a year or whatever, six months or however long we could wait without doing—we used to just let it sit for as long as we could think about it, and every now and then we'd shake it—that was like the first purple ink I ever used, 'cause it was like purple-blue from that carbon paper.

And that was permanent?

I don't know how permanent—I don't even remember how permanent it was, but it was cool because it had that purple tint to it, and back then I didn't really know where to get the fuckin' supermarket shit 'cause I was young and toy.

How old were you in this era?

Eleven, twelve maybe.

Whose work are you checking for now?

I see graffiti every day, whether I look for it or not. Most people don't even stop to notice something that is right in their face. Some are just too absorbed in their everyday lives. I grew up looking at it, and I'll continue to look at it. As a photographer as well as a writer, I tend to see things in a different light. There are tons of names in New York. I won't sit here and list them—anyone who follows New York graffiti should know. There are lots of Kings in this sport, as well as a lot of new jacks. Just learn your history and do your thing.

What's your policy on cross outs?

Don't cross me out, and I won't cross you out. 'Nuff said. I'm not really a fan of it, but if you cross me out, I'm going over you. I never really had any major cross out wars with anyone except the occasional jealous toy.

The whole purpose of painting is that you want your shit to run, not to get crossed out. Some dudes love it—I mean, it does amp you up to go do more shit, but to each his own, you know? If I was more of a bomber, and if all I did was fill-ins and throwups, then somebody lined my fill-in and my throwup, it's not a big loss, you know? But if I'm going out and I'm doing a fucking piece on a truck and some kid comes and does a throwup over it, I mean who ultimately loses that game, the guy who does the fuckin' piece, or the guy who does the throwup over it? You be the judge. I guess if all I did was bomb . . . I mean, it's kinda fun goin' out and raggin' people. But I'm sayin' when you're losing pieces with tags, fill-ins, and other bullshit, you're ultimately not gonna win unless you really don't give a fuck and all you're gonna start doin' is throwups from now on.

How do you feel about biting?

Everyone starts out copying something from somebody else. It's evolution. Whether it's copying out of *Subway Art*, someone's piece, or anything else, take what you see, get creative, flip it—change it and make it yours. Don't just carbon copy. There's no originality in doing that. Inspiration comes from everywhere—just open your eyes and realize it. Learn how to adapt it to your work.

Is there anything you wish you knew before you started writing?

When I started writing, in the summer of '87, the trains were still bombed a little bit out here. I wish I was more experienced with graffiti. I never got a chance to really hit them, with the exception of a few marker tags. Basically, I wish I knew people who were hitting them because my friends and I were mainly bombing the streets with tags and throwups. We didn't really start tagging the trains until a few years later, but by then, no one bombed them anymore.

How has writing improved your life?

I wouldn't really say writing has improved my life, nor would I say it has had a negative effect on my life. But I will say it has made me who I am today. I've had the best of times, as well as the worst of times, because of graffiti. If it wasn't for graffiti, I wouldn't know half of the people that I know today. I've met friends through this who I consider to be some of the closest people in my life. Who knows what my life would have been if it weren't for all of this? It's gotten me into a hell of a lot of trouble, and it's been a hell of a lot of fun. It's given me something to do besides fuckin' drugs and shit . . . if I had the chance to do it all over again, I wouldn't change a thing.

Any advice for younger writers?

Basically, learn your history, pay your dues, and respect those who came before you. Try not to go over old graffiti. If there's something you like, whether it's graffiti or anything else, put your heart into it—you get out what you put in.

Do you have any regrets?

Yeah, not being older when I started. Not knowing the right people, back when I was scribbling, to take me to the fucking trains. I wish I'd have bombed the trains when they were bombed.

What is your ultimate goal?

As far as graffiti, I have no ultimate goal, 'cause once you have an ultimate goal, it becomes more of a job than just a hobby and having fun. As long as I'm having fun, I don't give a fuck. I don't want to be the biggest graffiti writer ever. I could care less. I just got into it 'cause when we were young, it was riding skateboards, causing trouble, lighting off fireworks, and writing graffiti. That's what we did when we were young.

How long will you do this for?

Only time will tell. I'm not currently active like I was in the past. Everyone has their moments of productive work. Sometimes life and certain circumstances get in the way, but I'll always have a love for graffiti. I'll always try to be doing something.

Do you think graffiti is an addiction?

It's worse than crack.

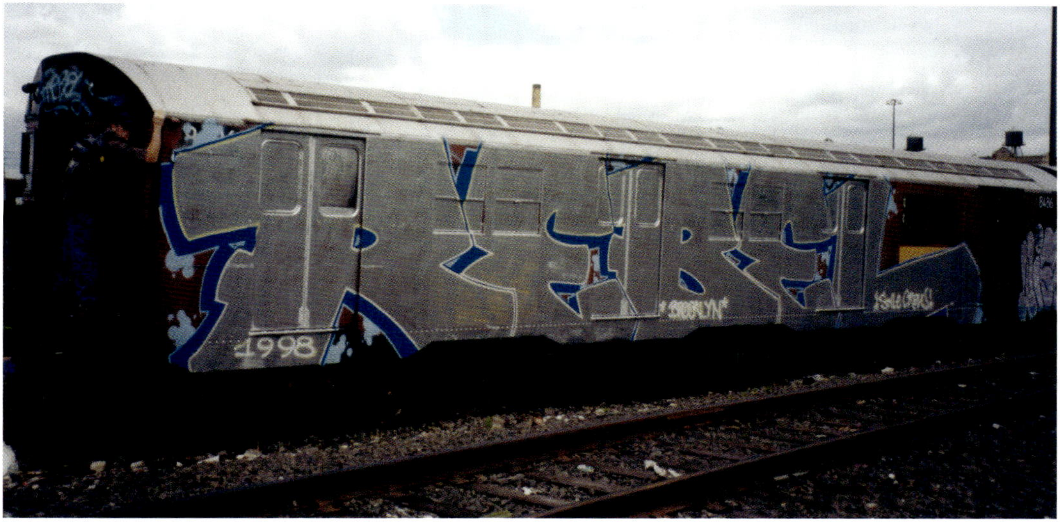

Why?

Just 'cause I'd have to write my name everywhere. I have to scribble on everything that doesn't move. And anything that moves.

Even now? Do you even feel that compulsion when there's, like, a piece of paper around?

I write on everything in my fucking house. Everything. Nothing is safe.

Where have you painted?

Most of my career has been based in Brooklyn, New York, but I've painted pretty much all of the East Coast, [as well as] St. Louis, Ohio, and California.

What's your favorite place to paint, and why?

I would have to say, hands down, it would be the Brooklyn scrap yard and the SC truck yard. The first time I painted the scrap yard was 1989. I was cutting out of school with a few friends, and we went to the scrap yard. We saw workers in there on an engine. But we went in through the front gate anyway. We walked in with a notebook and a camera, and told them we were doing a report for school. They let us right in. It was great.

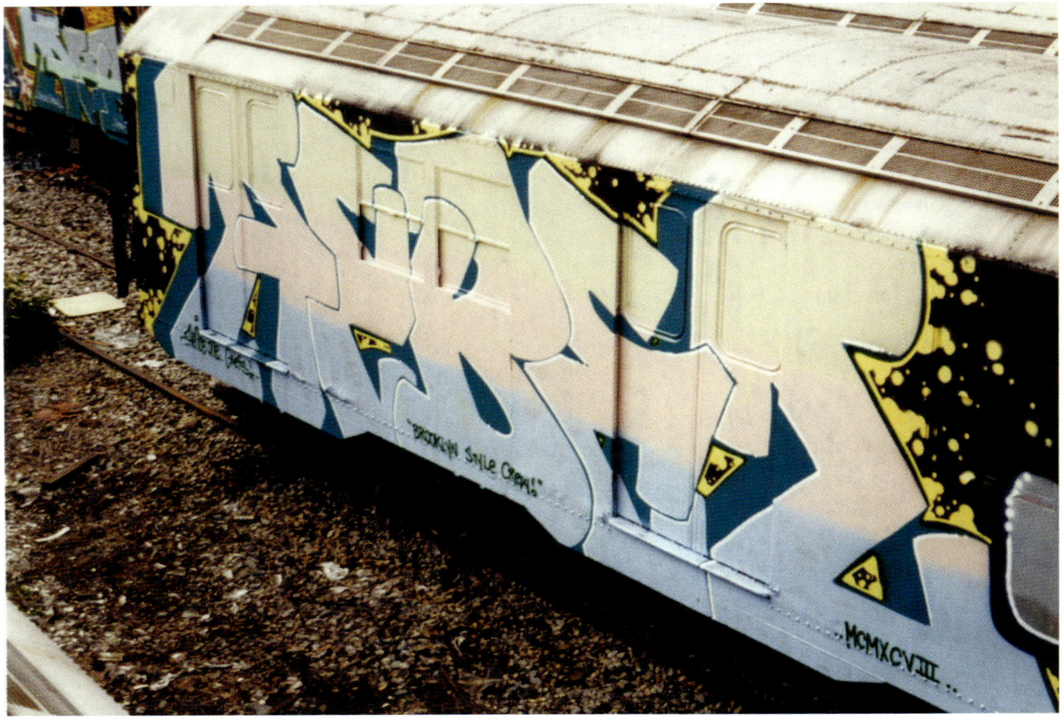
MCMXCVIII

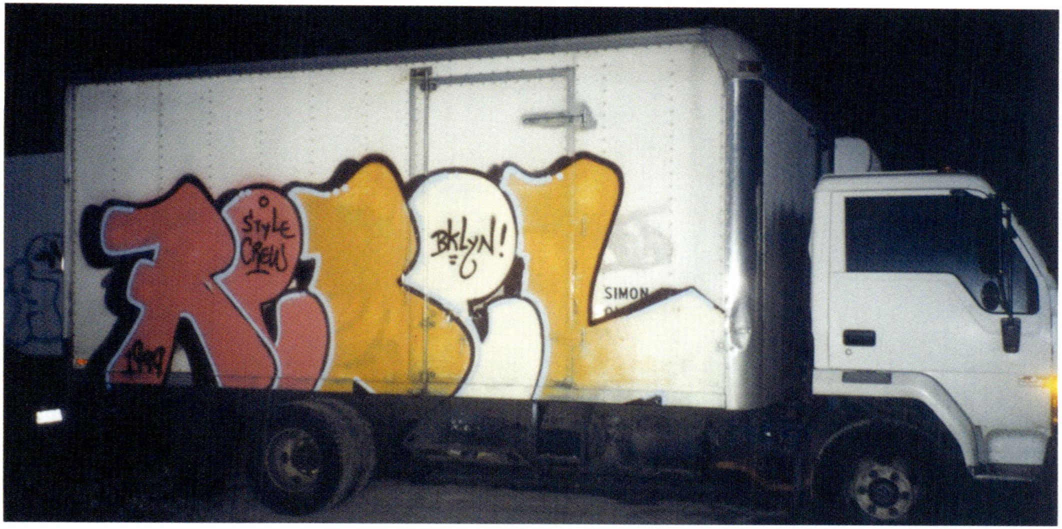

We walked towards the back of the yard and we saw it was pretty full, so as we got back there, we climbed into the first train and started taking marker tags. We noticed an empty bottle of Griffin on the floor, and brand new Casio 182 tags on all the panels. All the trains in there were bombed. They had just taken most of them off the line and out of service. We saw tons of pieces that were the last of the bombed-train era, now sitting desolate and abandoned, getting ready for the scrap heap. We wanted to have our fun while we could. We were tagging the insides, taking old maps, just bugging out. My friend Beware was popping all the seats open, and at the end of the first car, he opened the seat and found a dusty knapsack. As he pulled it out, we noticed there were cans in it! We found a few Nymbco skinny silvers and a few others, so we had a little party. It was such a fun day. I'll never forget the good days we used to have in that yard.

Summer '98 was also a good time. I used to work right across the street from the yard, so I used to check it daily. I became friends with the supervisor of the asbestos abatement program of the yard, Every time they pulled in new trains, we were the first ones in there smashing them. I'd wake up, go to work, check the yard, make the necessary phone calls to let the crew know what time it was, leave work, meet the crew, and head into the yard for an all-night graffiti fiasco! Plenty of nights were spent in there, painting until the sun came up, then going to Ernie's and having breakfast, chipping the paint off our numb fingers, scarfing down a hearty breakfast fit for a king. With a price still stuck in the '80s, who could beat it?

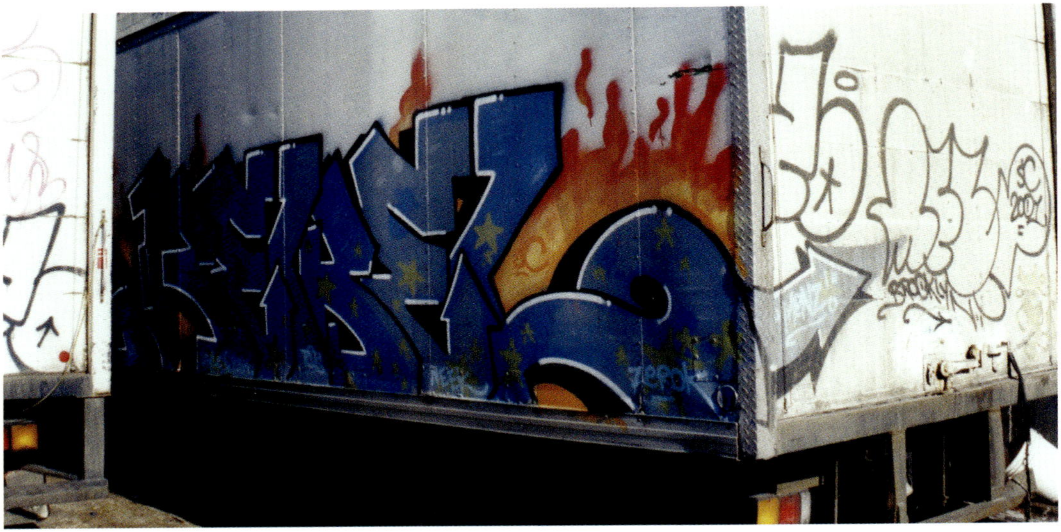

I remember one time in '95, having a picnic in there while doing some whole cars. But one of the best times I remember was summer '98. I got a phone call from Case 2. I was supposed to meet him there and I was running late, so as I get there, I see the gate locked. But I can see them painting, so as I roll up to the fence I see someone coming towards me in a white asbestos suit. When he gets closer, I notice it's Bete TBK. He opens the gate with his key, and I go in. It was like one big party. It was me, Zero, Case 2, Stak, Bete, Krook, Burn, Gump, and Net—everyone piecing the trains. Next thing I know, someone comes to the gate. It was pizza delivery—Bete ordered pizza! Then Krook drives his Chevelle into the yard with the radio blasting and the fuzzy dice hanging in the mirror. Man, those were the days!

After they pulled the trains out of the scrap yard, we moved on to a neighborhood truck yard my partner Zero put me on to. The fun we used to have in there! The place was filled with all these Chinatown delivery trucks from Manhattan. Those trucks would drive around fourteen hours out of the day, and as soon as they would pull in, we would paint them. We would do full sides—huge blockbusters and pieces! We would paint so much that after a while, we were the only ones up on the trucks. Every once in a while, a new truck would park in there, and we'd be all over it. Plenty of nights were spent in there, from sundown to sunrise, pulling all-nighters! We wouldn't leave 'til every can was empty. Every truck in there was pieced up. It was like the parking lot for our rolling gallery.

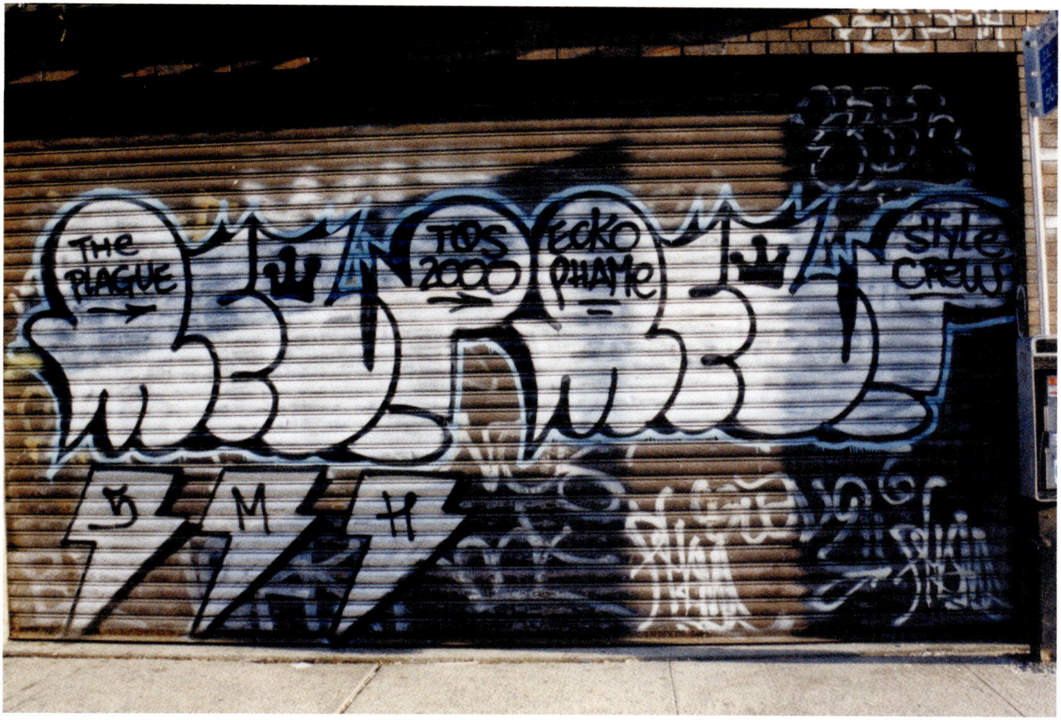

Towards the end of the truck yard bombing, some of my trucks got buffed. I would go back bigger and better, only to come back a week later to find out that my new pieces also met the same fate. They were finally catching up. On one of the last missions to the yard, we ran into some little inexperienced toy in there running around making a mess, so we had to capture him and hold him hostage while we did our pieces. We tried to educate him on some things, but we could see he had no clue, so we did our pieces and left. Recently, I went in there to see what was going on. I only saw a few of my trucks still there—one silver from '98, the fill-in so faded you could see all the tags coming through! It was just a little reminder of all the fun and good times we used to have.

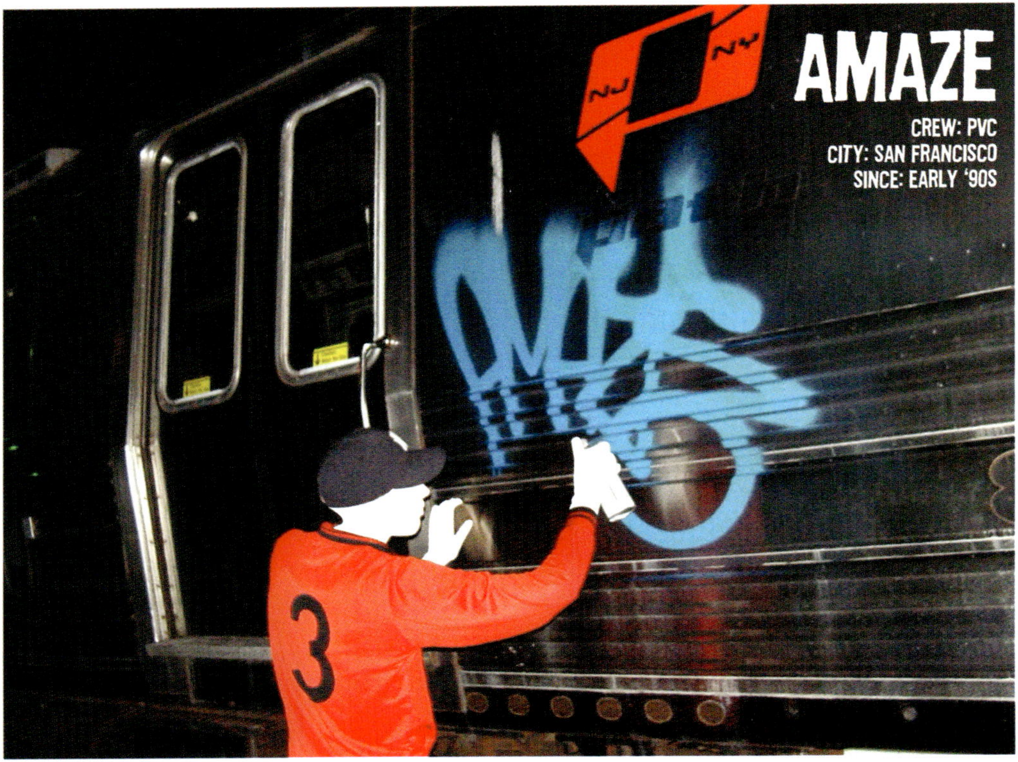

AMAZE

CREW: PVC
CITY: SAN FRANCISCO
SINCE: EARLY '90S

I interviewed Amaze over the phone in late August. He was just getting back from painting the UK.

What names and crews have you written?

Well my first "tag name" ever was Disco (February 1993). I didn't know anything about graff, or even really write, and the word was slang for stupid. My crew [back then] was OPM—just some suburban kids that I skateboarded with. Then, in September of 1993, I changed my tag to Amaze, and I started to try and do graff more seriously. OPM was my main crew until I got into the US crew, another skater graff crew from San Mateo County that did a lot more. They were also pretty much the main crew from the dumb suburbs where I grew up. US was a big deal for me. I thought everyone in the crew was so good. Especially ORFN and REVRS. In hindsight, they were the only two that I would say were real writers in the whole crew. That lasted for a year or so, and then I went back to OPM for a few months. After that, I wrote nothing at all serious for the next five years, except some crews I would hit up when people in the crew would tell me to and I was with them, but again, nothing serious. Then around '98, I started writing AOK. I liked pretty much all of this crew's stuff. I still hit that up on occasion, but the crew really has nothing to do with me. I am the second generation of it, and that's pretty lame. Then there's PVC: primarily me, Geso, and Grey. We have been friends for years, and it just sort of fits. Crews are pretty dumb, though. Graff is all about individual accomplishments, not what people you are "down with" have done.

Who got you into it?

Well, I used to rack tons of stuff. When I was with friends who wrote, I would go with them and rack paint. At first I would just give them the paint, but then I wanted to try it out myself . . . .

What kind of stuff where you racking before? Are we talking Grand Theft Auto, or like, a Snickers bar?

I would rack skateboards, wetsuits, clothes—pretty much anything that I could. If it was fun and I could pull it off, I'd do it. I would steal sets of baseball cards and sell them to kids at school. I had broken into a couple of places and robbed them, but I never really knew what I was doing so I never got anything good.

Do you rack paint now?

I rack my paint. I do it in many ways . . . any way I can. I've had three-hundred-can days and thirty-can days—whatever it takes to get the job done.

One time, Grey rented this van for like a whole summer, because his cousin was a used-car salesman or something, so he got it off him. I met up with Grey in Texas, and we went through the South and up the Eastern seaboard and hit all these cities, like Raleigh, North Carolina, you know, like Houston and New Orleans—places where there's not really graff. You just steal like shopping cart after shopping cart, and just empty it in these towns that had no graff. It's probably like one of the funnest trips I've ever taken.

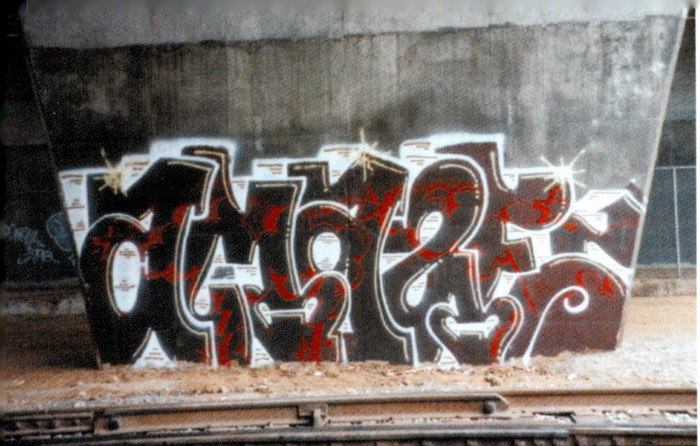

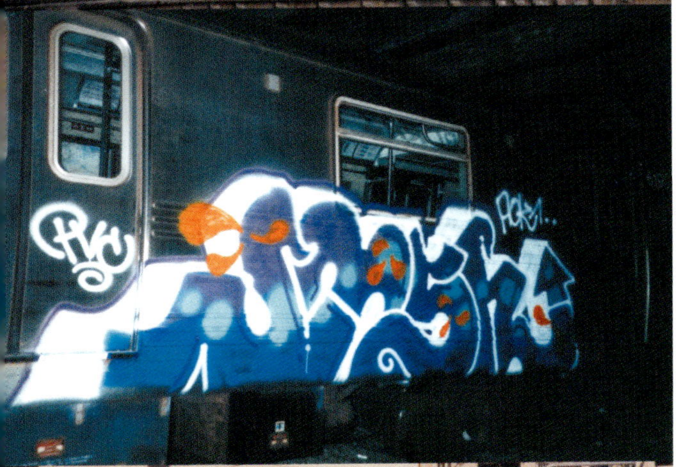

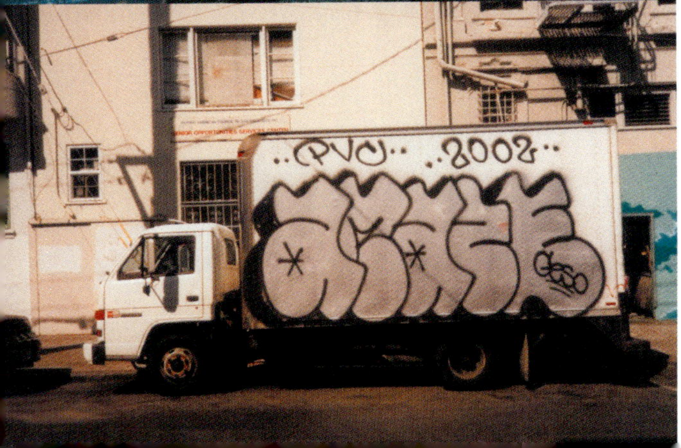

What kind of quantities are we talking?

Each time we'd go into a store, we'd leave with like a hundred and fifty cans of paint. That would last us like four days, three days, I don't know, and then we'd have to do it again.

How many trips into the store is a hundred and fifty cans?

Oh, we'd only go once.

How do you walk out of a store with a hundred and fifty cans?

Just with a shopping cart. I mean, the last week before I went to London, I stole six hundred cans of paint from like four stores.

To bring with you?

No, no, just for here, because I hadn't had any real paint lately, and I was like sick of not having any paint just because I couldn't be bothered to go rack it.

How do you walk out of a store with a shopping cart filled with a hundred and fifty cans without getting noticed?

For me, that's like the easiest way to rack paint—because it's so obvious, nobody's ever going to expect it. It's kinda like how, in New York City, people think it's so hard to rack paint that you just can't, but there are spots in Manhattan that are just the easiest to rack paint, and there are spots in Manhattan that are the easiest to get clothes, or the easiest to get electronics. Just so hot that it's easy, do you understand what I'm saying? The last time I went and racked paint at this place, me and my friend went in, and we each grabbed a shopping cart, and then we brought it to the paint department of Home Depot and told them, "Load all of the aluminum Rust-Oleum, all the flat black Rust-Oleum, and all the flat white Rust-Oleum that you have into these carts." And like three hundred cans later—more than that, I think—they brought [the carts] to where we were. We were like, "Thanks," and they were like, "Okay," and then we just walked out.

So there's no crotching going on with you.

Oh, no way, never. With some things, yes, but with paint? No way. That's like—those days were over when I like turned eighteen.

Have you been caught? How many times?

I have been caught two times that were serious. It pretty much sucked.

You were caught painting or racking?

Painting, but I've been caught racking as well. In every life, a little rain must fall.

What do you think motivates somebody to go out and go all-city? Is it like, "Hey, I'm here," or is it the adrenaline?

What motivates somebody? I really can't say. I think everybody is driven by different things, and I think that's good, because it's like everybody has their own reason for going all-out. I do it, I've done it, just because I think it's fun and I was bored and didn't have anything else to do, so that's what I did. But there's other people that do it strictly for ego. And there's other people that do it purely out of a competitive thing. Everybody has their own reasons, and that's what makes graff so diverse. I don't like to do it now in my home city as much as I used to. I don't like to do graffiti here. I like to do graffiti in other cities. I feel like I have nothing to prove here; there's nobody whose stuff I like, and I'd much rather be in some like European city or in Japan or something, trying to do something that I wouldn't do here.

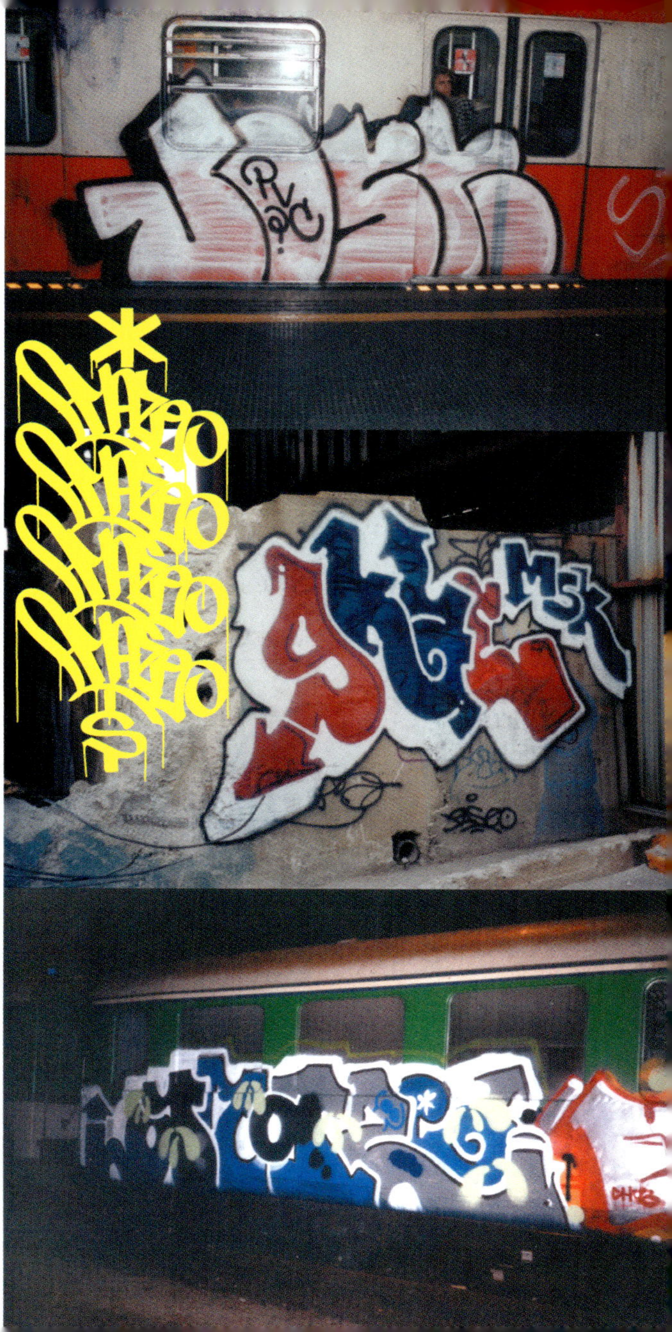

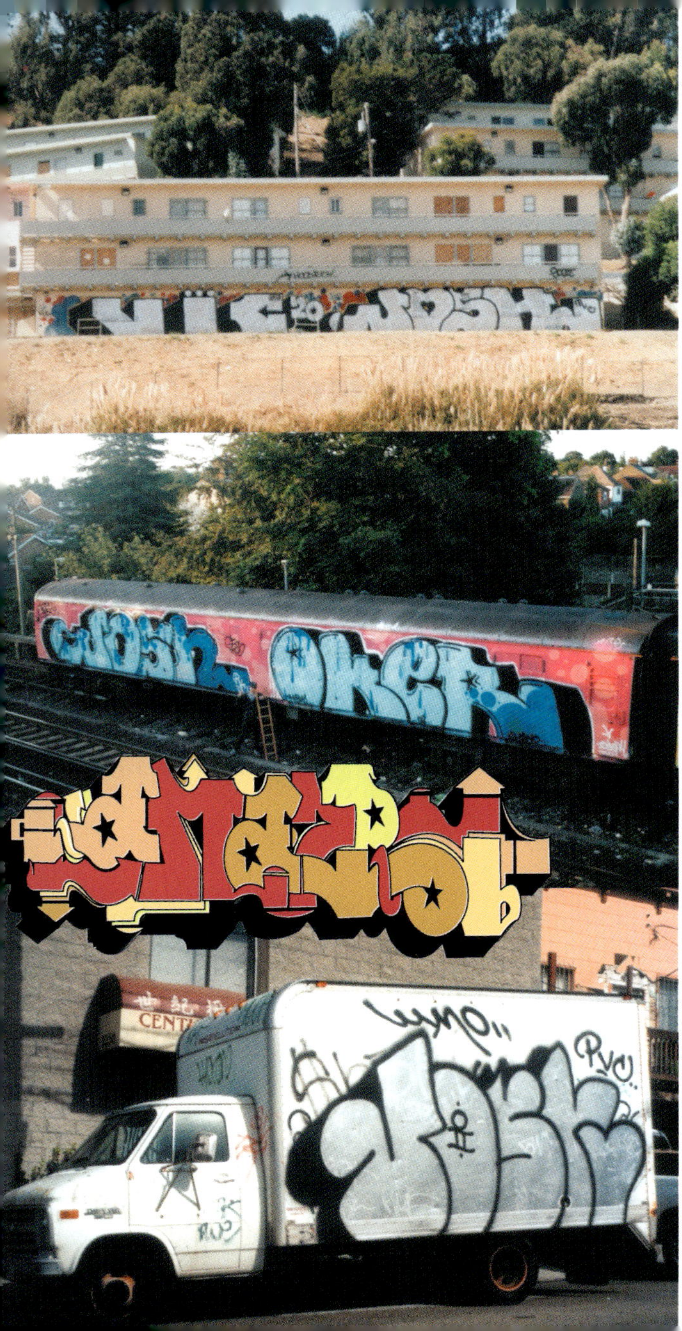

Did you stop writing at home 'cause the police know who you are?

I don't think the police know who I am or anything. There was a time here, one day—I wanna say like six years ago—Saber, Tyke, Revoke, Bless, Some, and Grey and me were someplace. They were all painting, and me and Grey just happened to be there on bikes. They were painting a legal wall in the daytime, and the police came and said something to the effect that, "We're sick of graffiti, and we want to get this Amaze guy. Can any of you tell us who Amaze is?" All this stuff, just like threatening everybody, and saying everybody was going to go to jail if somebody narked, unless they said who I was, and I was right there and it was kind of a nervous moment for me. They said they had like a couple years in jail for me if like I got caught, and all this. They didn't know who I was, and I was sure I was going to get raided, but I never did. I'd say about a year after that, I was riding my bike to hit some spot, and I had paint in my bag. Some policeman just pulls up next to me—and I don't even have a record in my hometown—but these cops pull up next to me and they say, "Hey ________, are you out painting tonight?" And I said, "Yeah, of course," you know, nonchalantly, while I was on my bike right next to them. They just laughed and said, "Well, don't let us see you," and then drove off. You know, they never raided me, and now they have completely different vandal cops, so like the other cops now could probably care less about me.

Is it hard to paint in San Fran?

People always say that it isn't, but they always get caught. A lot of people from LA moved here, and they were saying how easy it is like, "This is the greatest place to paint," but they all got arrested a lot. Most of them have warrants as we speak, so it's kinda funny—people think it's easy, but then they just get caught. I've been to cities that are far easier to paint than San Francisco.

Example?

I think Boston is like the easiest place I've ever painted. But everybody who paints a lot there ends up getting caught because their Vandal Squad is so efficient. They have this lady who like figures out who everybody is, and it's kinda funny—the couple times that I've been there it just seemed really ridiculously easy.

In Montreal, there's no Vandal Squad. The city has set up a program to help kids find walls and space to paint. The mentality is basically that if kids have space to express themselves, they're not gonna fuck shit up.

That's crazy. That's probably better than what happens in most cities. Here, like for a while, they had a gay graffiti vandal cop. It's kind of an odd thing when you have a crime that's primarily youthful male offenders, and like the main cop to deal with it is an openly gay male. It's like, only in San Francisco would that be tolerated. It's kind of comical when you look at it. I hear there are some cities in the States that have it really locked up, like I've never really done too much stuff in New York, and the Vandal Squad—I've never been caught there, but they knew exactly who I was. One day I was just sitting with my girlfriend, on like a bench in SoHo, and they just pulled up in a van and were just like, "________, what are you doing in New York?" And they just arrested me like right then and there.

And said what?

Just like, "We know you did this, we know you did that; you're going to go to Riker's," this and that.

Did you?

No, I didn't. I went through Manhattan, and I plead it out. It got cleared from my record now; I had to hire a delegate.

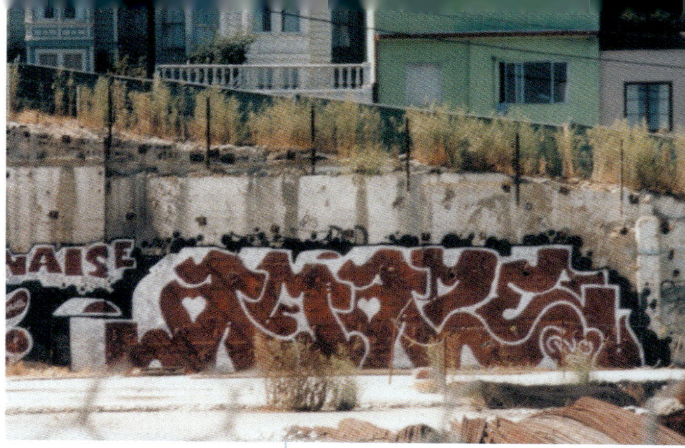

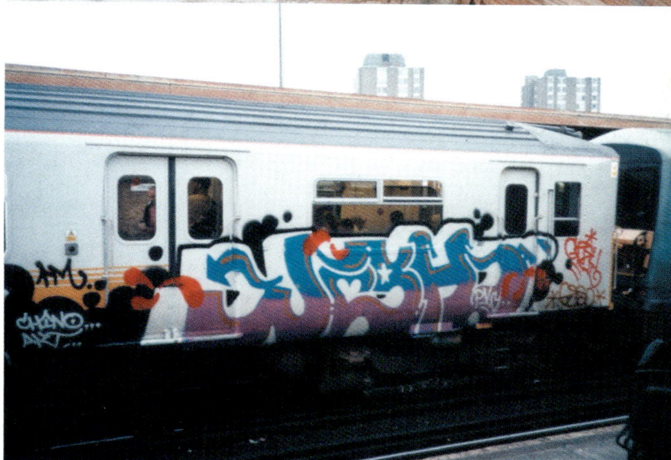

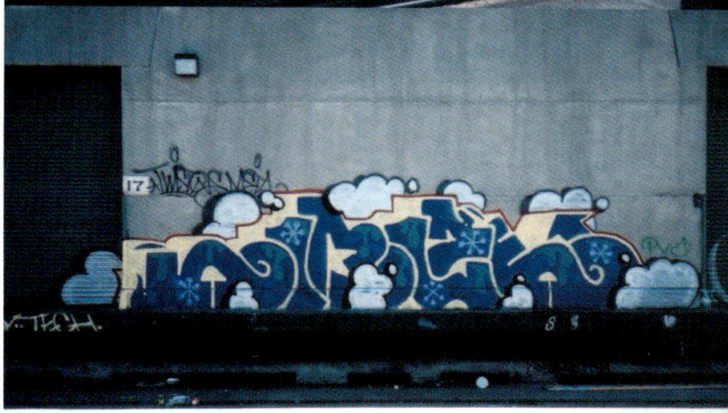

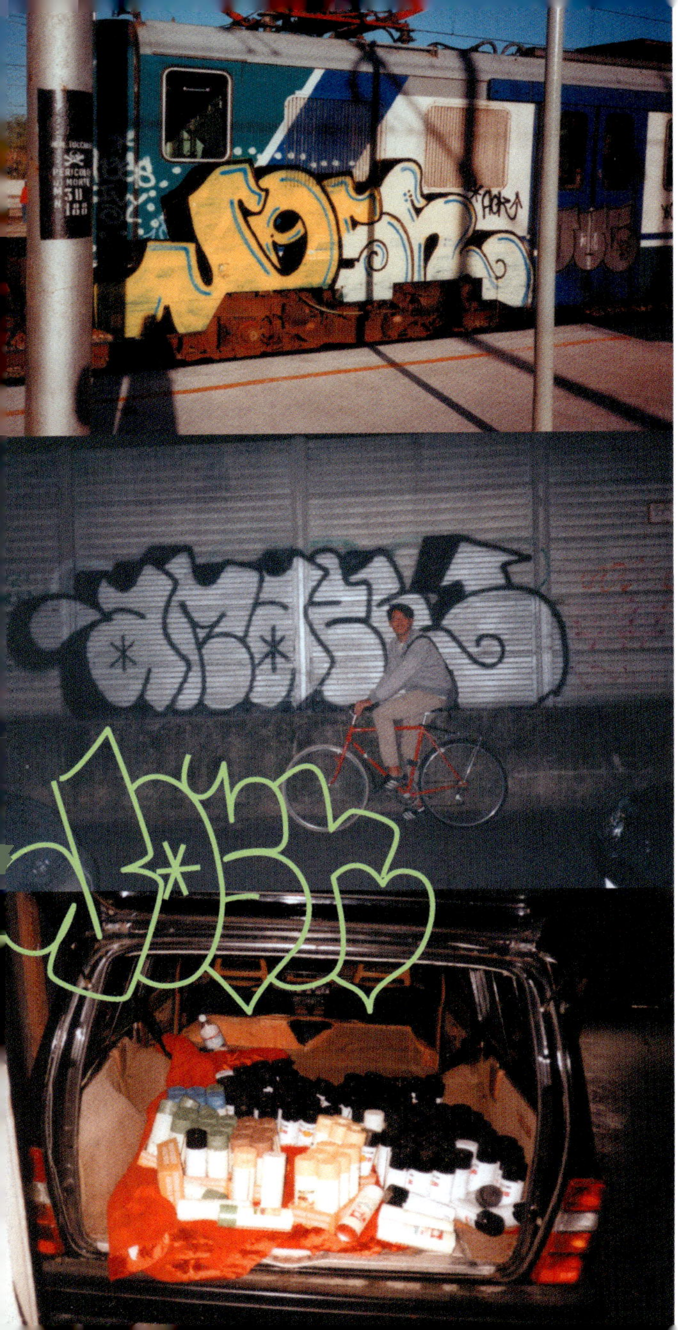

They put you in Central Booking, though?

Yeah, yeah. They didn't have any proof or anything. They claimed to have photos of me, like, doing this spot with Espo, but it was a lie.

That's another thing—how can he function? Did he get arrested?

Espo? Yeah, he got arrested.

How did he put out the book and, like, have his real name in there?

He got busted for it after. He got arrested, and Reas got arrested, and I got arrested. Yeah, Reas got arrested one day, and I got arrested the very next day, in New York.

This is the time you're talking about?

Yeah, this is, like, maybe six months after the book came out. It was pretty wack, because they didn't have any proof, and I had to pay all this money for a lawyer and I had to go back out there for court 'cause [I] don't want some warrant floating above my head out there. But at least my lawyer took care of it.

I've gotten lucky. Like, Twist has an insane amount of connections and whenever shit's going down, he hooks me up. I mean, a lot o the trips I've just taken by myself, but he's hooked me up with a few really good ones. Like I have to do some graphics or something fo somebody, and I get a trip out there. But yeah, traveling is easy. It's really easy to just hook up with graffiti writers. If you're gonna bomb, people are gonna be down to go with you. It doesn't cos much to get a flight anywhere, and you can just rack food wherev er you are. So it's like all these people that don't travel and say it's too hard and all this, I just don't think they care enough about graff or have it in them enough to, like, do it, 'cause it's really not hard The first few times I ever went out to Europe and painted and a this, there was no hook-ups at all. And I just made it happen.

Is graffiti an addiction?

I think it is a full-on addiction. When you kill shit, you feel so good. I can only really compare it to racking, in terms of the excitement, danger, and rewards. It is hard to have a manageable life and do a lot of graff.

Whose shit are you checking for, past or present, that you think is dope?

Well I can go on forever about who I like, but here goes nothing. I love Cliff, early Phase 2, Riff, Worm, Chain 3, Dondi, Fuzz, Skeme, and some others from that generation. I try to replicate their shit and I can't.

After that, I really like Reas, Ven, Ghost, Stak, Noah, Sent, SP One, Cav, Weber, Stryder, Wolf, Relm, Charlie, Tempt, and some others from that generation.

Contemporary people I like are a lot of Euros, and people that do streets. Smart, Dumbo, Skuf, Petro, Hairdo, Diego, Mkue, Adek, Geso, Kraze, Reim, Rens, Yalt, Revs, Grey, Skrew, Revok, and many others.

Do you think that learning about the past is key to a writer's progression?

Not really. I happen to like old graff better than new stuff. For me, I look twenty-five years back to see better ways to do my shit now. There were so many people trying so many different things then. Now a lot of people do the same stuff.

What do you wish you knew before you started?

I wish I knew not to meet certain people; that traveling with graff is everything; what was good, what was wack; that legals don't count for shit; and that fame is overrated.

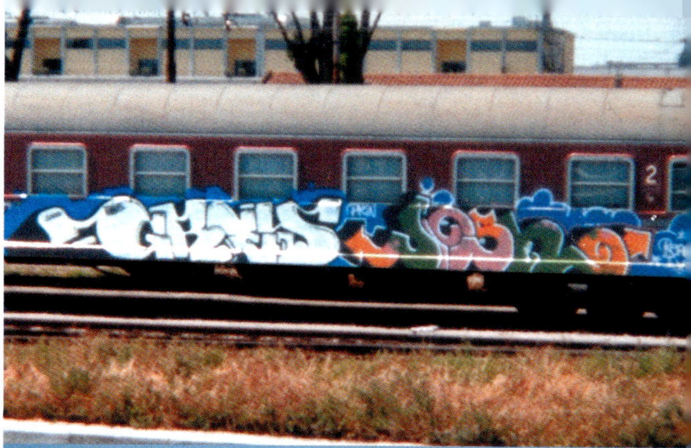

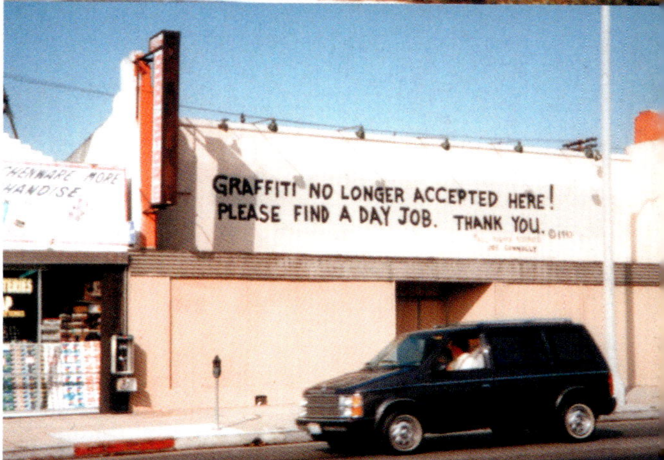

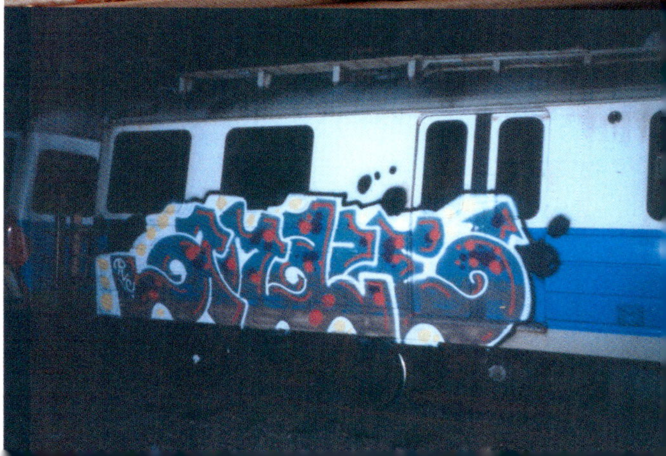

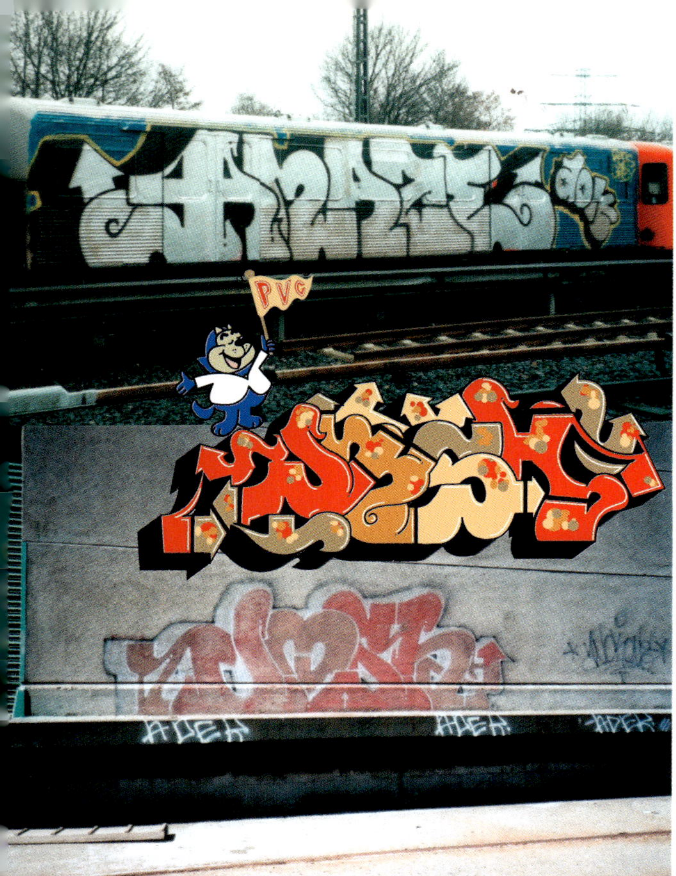

Any regrets?

I regret about eighty percent of the stuff I have done, because most of it sucked. I also regret meeting most writers that I've met. Once you meet someone, the mystery is gone, and they are suddenly marginalized.

How has writing improved your life?

Well, it has given me confidence that I can do what I want. It lets you know that you can go out and cause mayhem without being noticed. If everyone in the world knew what real writers know about what you can get away with, the world would be a different place.

What's your policy on cross outs? Some people don't do it, others take pride in it. What's your stance?

I like it. I've gone over tons of stuff and I've been dissed tons of times. Someone is going to paint over it anyway, so who cares? To go on about it and get your feelings all hurt is dumb. Whenever I paint, I expect it to get dissed quickly. Maybe it's because I'm very negative about everyone else's graff; I don't know.

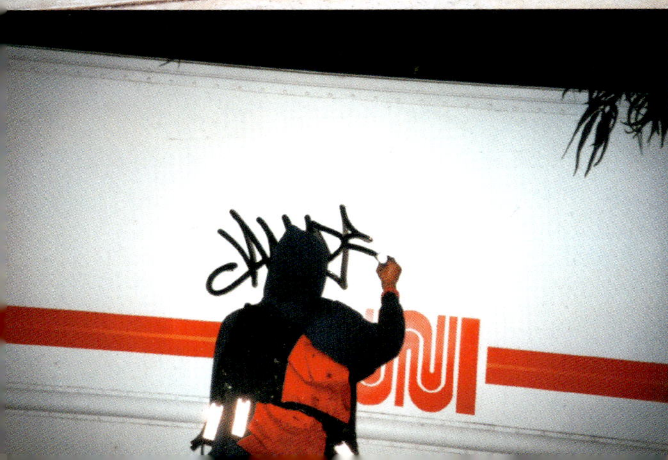

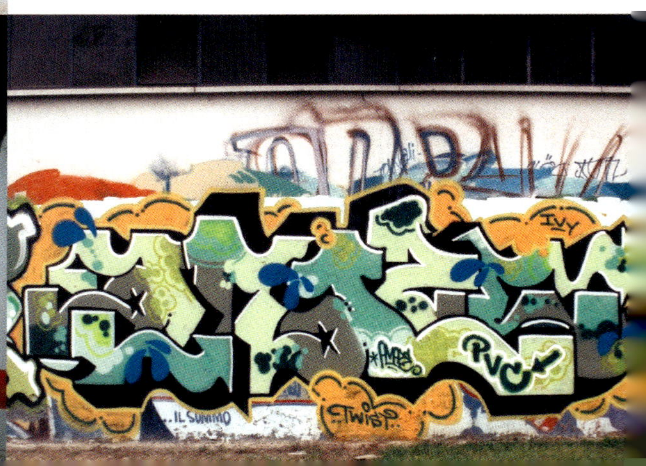

How long will you do this for?

I'll do it for as long as it's fun. I get into other things that are fun, and my graff suffers. Life is too short for me to focus only on graff.

How do you feel about biting? Everyone learns somewhere, right? But if biting's not an option, where should one learn?

I think people should bite. I have bitten, and I still do bite on occasion. People try to get all mad, but who cares? I think at first you bite because you know nothing else, but eventually you find your niche and develop it into something that is your own. You get ideas from everything. The whole act of graffiti is biting, really. Painting trains, roofs, etc. Even painting letters is only because somebody else did it before you.

What's your favorite paint, and why?

I like it all. But Rust-O tends to cover the best. When it comes to cleanliness, I think being clean is lame. If your style sucks, it doesn't matter how clean you are.

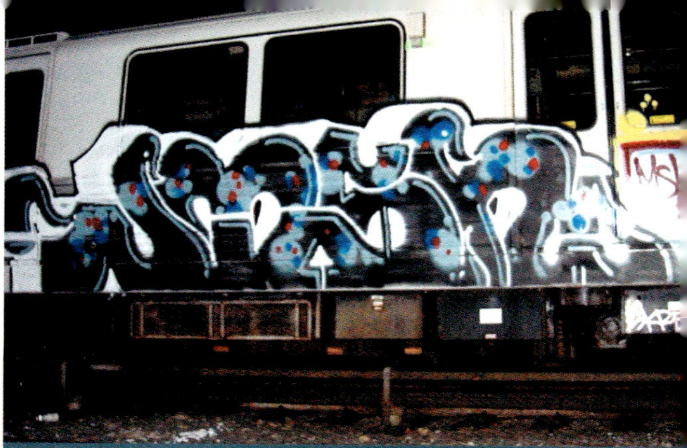

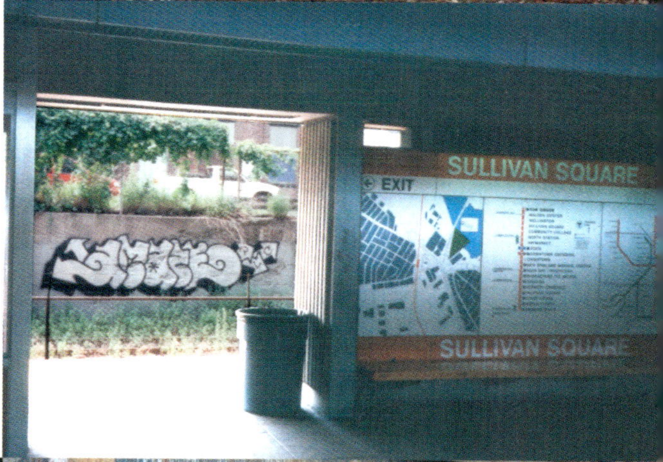

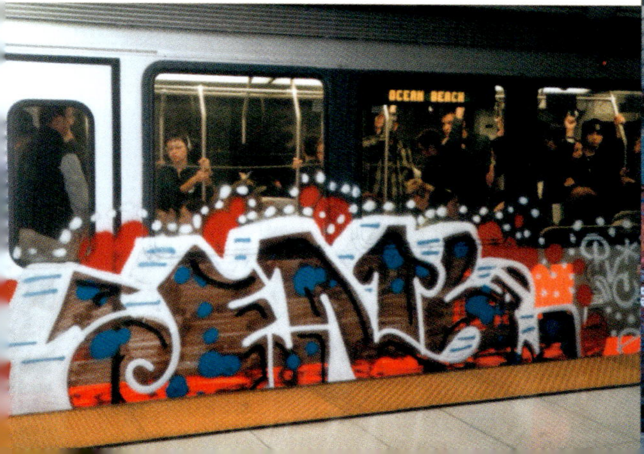

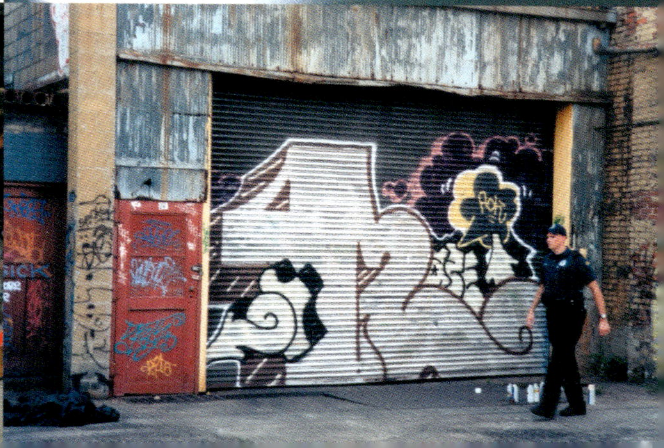

Gimme a chase story to end this off.

This is kind of a weird one: I was painting a roof with this guy Some, who is from AWR. I had finished my piece, and I was waiting for him to finish his. All of a sudden, we hear this noise, and this door opens, and these cops jump out right next to us, on the same roof. And we just—I just drop all my shit and start running full-speed and jumping, like to the next roof, and to the next roof, and they're kind of coming behind us, and there's this little two-by-four on the side of this wall, and Some starts climbing down it and he's going really slow and there's no way for me to get down, and the police are coming closer and closer. So finally I had no choice but to, like—I hung off a little bit and then jumped down. And when I landed I could feel I broke my heel.

How far down?

I think two stories or something. And then I had to run and I had to climb onto this garage and jump off of the top of the garage over a fence, into another driveway, and then climb over another fence. And I got out there, and then Some got out there like, thirty seconds later. In San Francisco, there's a huge gay population, so me and Some held hands like we were a gay couple, and the cops just drove up by us and assumed that it couldn't be us. And then we got around the corner, and I ran to KR's house and he wasn't home, so I had to sit on the corner. I couldn't walk any more after that 'cause I had broken one heel and cracked the other one, and I had to have somebody come and pick me up and take me to the hospital.

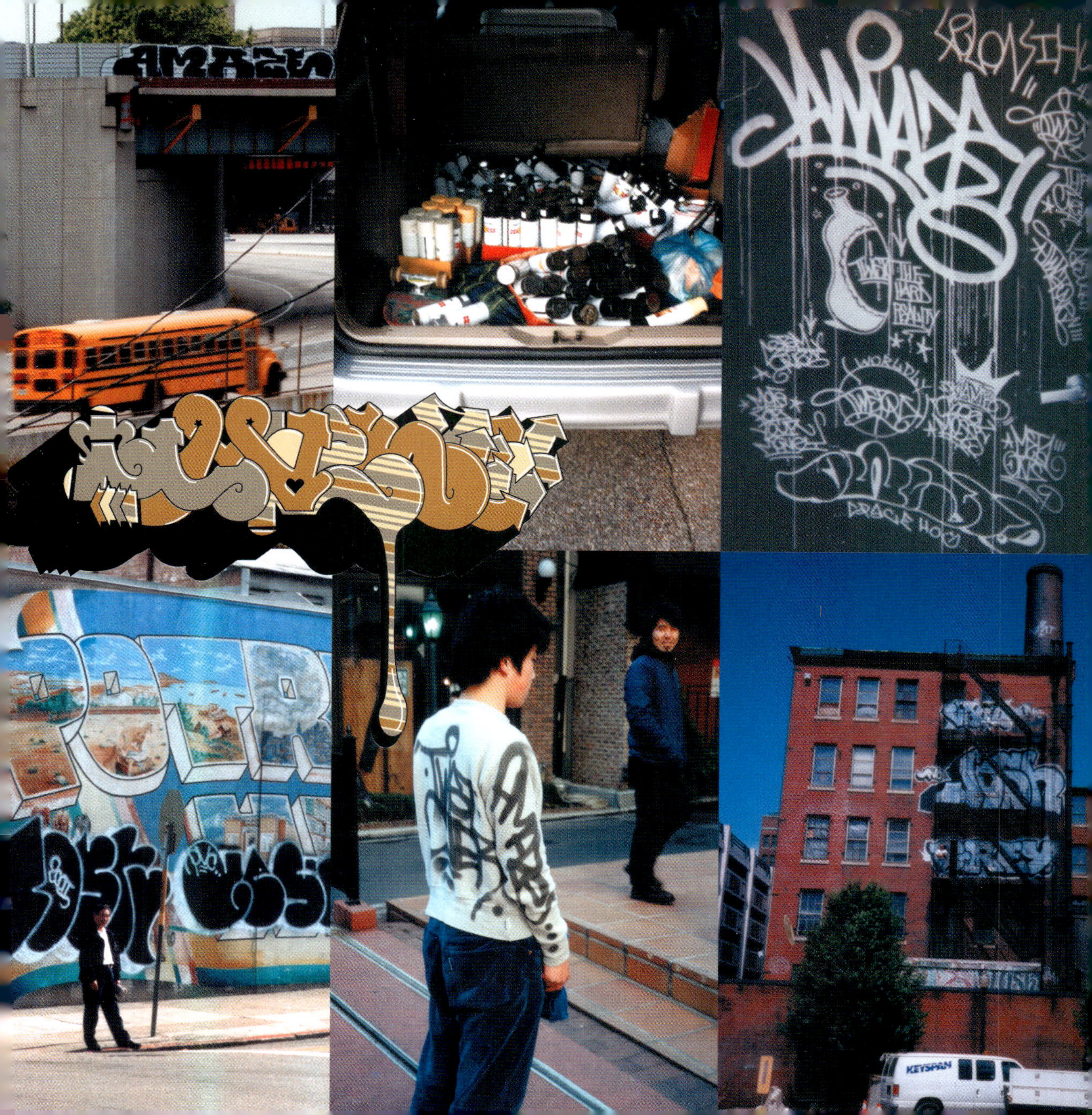
KEYSPAN

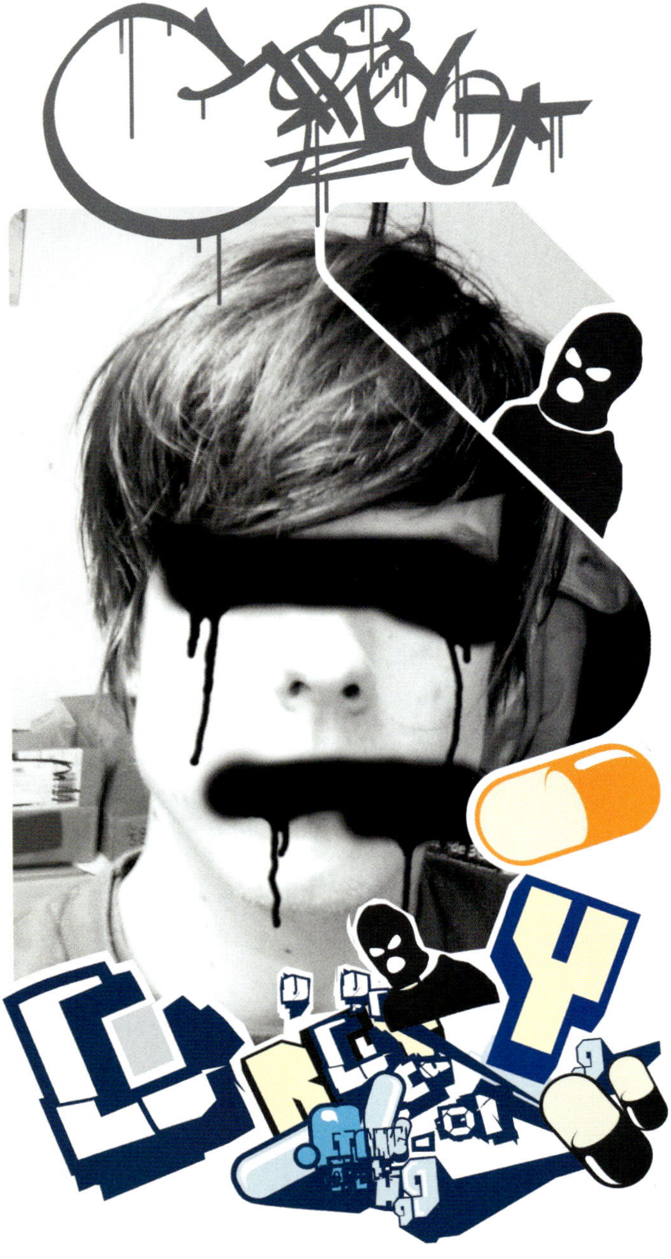

GREY

CREW: PVC
CITY: SAN FRANCISCO
SINCE: EARLY '90S

Grey has called San Francisco home since the early '90s, during the golden years of skating Embarcadero—the prime of SF graffiti and dismissed court cases. After years of crushing alongside PVC crewmembers Amaze and Geso, Grey has taken on the world. His frequent graff-related travels have made him one of the few writers known from Amsterdam to Albuquerque. And now that he's fully dealt with SF's public transit system, MUNI, you can bet this train-obsessed bad boy has the hots for a subway near you.

Ever the purist, Grey will be the first to tell you fuck hip-hop and its four points. He has the strictest reverence for late '70s/early '80s graff, though. At 6' 3," with floppy hair, rocking his signature combo of brown and safety orange, Grey is mod punk to the fullest. Put it this way: he stands out from both the thuggish hip-hop tagger pack and the trucker-hat-sporting graff skate mafia. Practicing his fighting skills on a somewhat regular basis, he defends his right to look like he walked out of *Quadrophenia*.

When he's not hanging out at indie rock shows or playing punk rock hoes to the fullest extent of the law, Grey's perfecting a (life)style based around the classics: aggressive racking, bombing difficult spots, and painting letters that tell the story by themselves, without any corny cartoon shit to get in the way. Mostly a graff purist, he's constantly developing new twists on his signature style. "I work hard because I need to live up to my standard of what a writer should be," says Grey. "For a few years I wrote specifically because I felt I owed it to the faith of graffiti. If I don't live up to my own standards, then I can't expect that ANYONE will."

—Vivian Host

Do you get inspiration from other things outside of graff?

My motivation comes from outside graff, almost one hundred percent. Style-wise, the look of what I'm doing is inspired by other graffiti. To keep me going, I'm more interested in what other people are doing in pop culture. When I see other subcultures where people are making an impact, it makes me want to do the same with my work. Then again, I guess other writers do make me want to go out. If they're really crushing, you want to be the one that's there. If someone comes to a city you've been to, you want them to mention you. I'm working with the world as my focus and there's a lot of people who are focusing on local only. People expect you to compete with them locally and do your thing worldwide as well. It's kind of hard to do both.

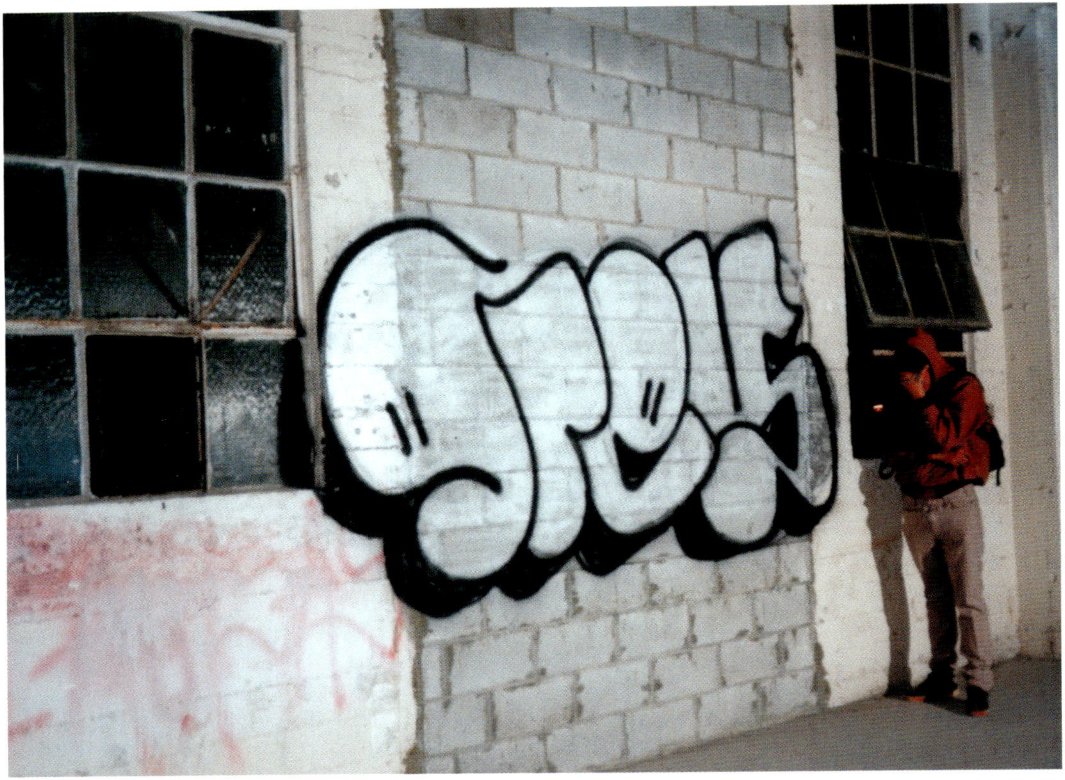

Where are you trying to push the limits the hardest?

For a while, I was trying to do a lot of dangerous spots. When I was doing a lot of dangerous spots, I was pretty much doing the same thing every time because my mind was so focused on the spot. There's some writers that can do both —I'm kind of one-track-minded. I definitely like to do aggressive graffiti. I've never been one to try and find a safe spot to spend hours doing a really complicated piece, although I definitely like to work on letters. These days it's more about me hitting trains. I like to hit as many systems as I can. Now it's being done in America, and I want to hit American train systems. Now, when I travel, I do the street graff when I can't do trains.

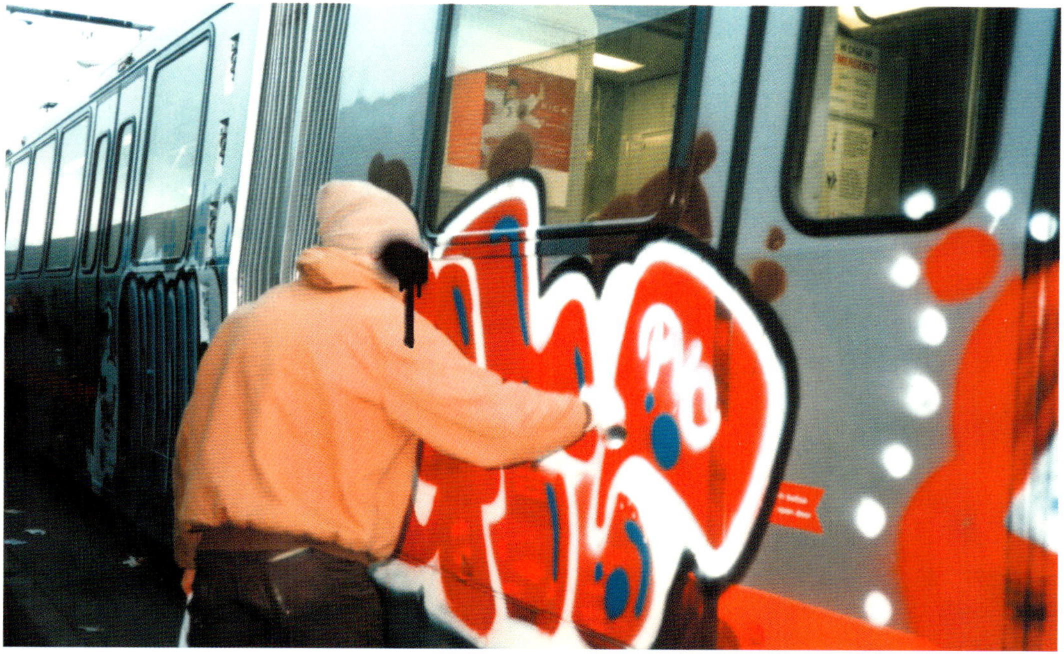

Do you look at it like collecting?

Yeah, for sure. So many cities have kind of [shut down] graffiti and they've secured their systems so [they] can't be hit. Anyplace where the train system is currently vulnerable, I feel like time is running out. Perpetually, transit authority gets more secure, not less secure. So if you see an opportunity, you better take it, because it might not be there later. As far as [San Francisco subway system] MUNI, I caught it when they weren't expecting it. It's not that it was hard or easy, just no one had tried it. I like to take advantage of that.

Bombing trains isn't a new idea. When did you become obsessed with it?

That kind of has to do with when I started. My point of reference was this book, *Subway Art*. I avoid talking about it because it's what every single person says, but that was the graff I got into. To me, that was the best—it looked the most real, it had the best styles. Most of the good styles happened by 1981. Actually, by '79, every style was already done. People think they're doing new stuff now, but with the exception of this technical kind of graff, they're not. All the styles I like were done in the '70s on trains. I just think, "Why not try to do it that way?" Plus, in Europe, trains are a huge deal; they're still happening constantly. If I can be a part of that, then I'm going to.

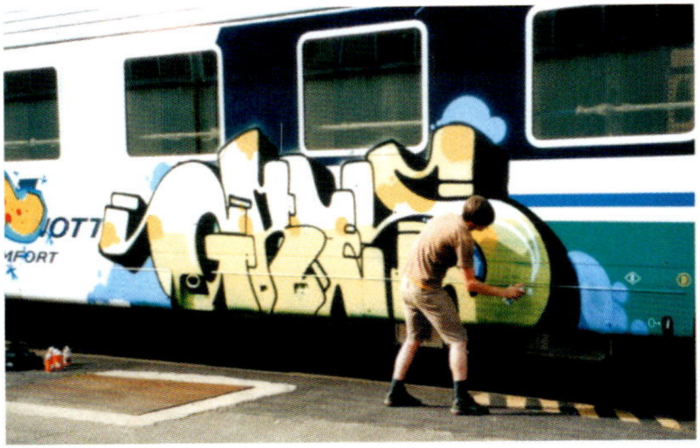

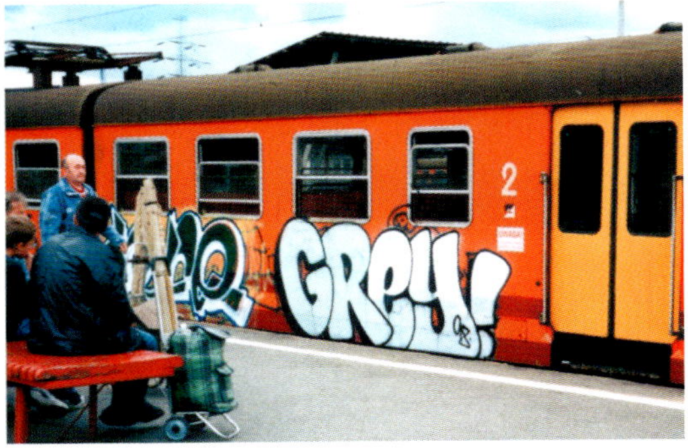

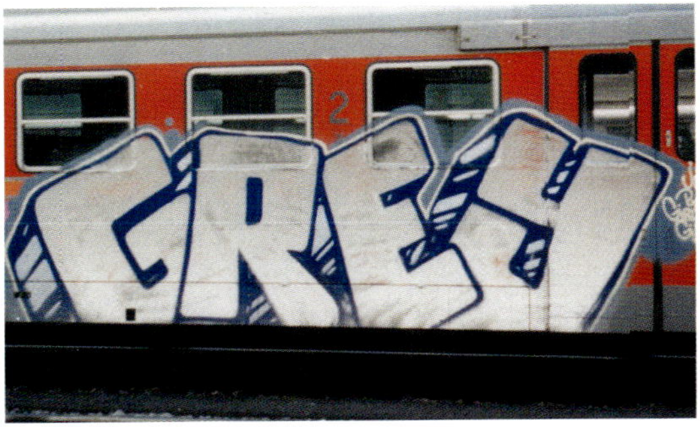

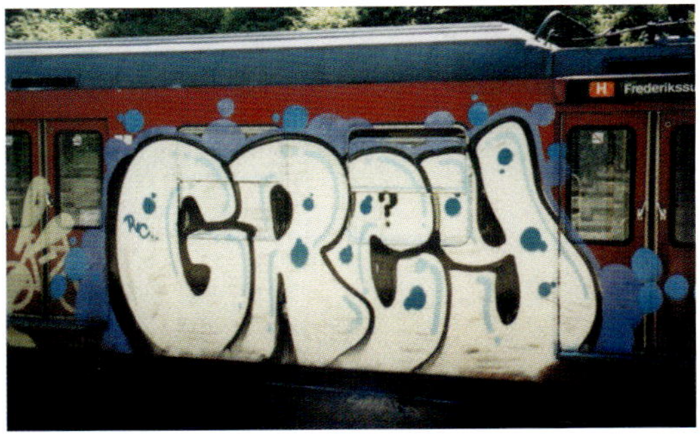

It seems like the '70s and '80s stuff that inspired you has come full circle, and is now popular again.

It's kind of funny how me and Amaze and a few others—there's some guys from Minneapolis—were drawing a lot of inspiration from that era, and some other guys from the '80s, like Ghost, Reas, and other AOK crew members that were really doing vintage stuff. Me and Amaze started getting our influence from that. We've been working on it for a good part of our career, and in the last two years everyone has latched on to what we're doing. It's kind of playing it out for us. Instead of them going to the source and getting their influences from there, they're doing it through us. They started when our style got popular, but we started doing it when everyone hated it. When everyone was doing crazy tech, highly elaborate productions, we were sitting there bombing with simple pieces. And now that's what sells, and all these fuckers are doing the stuff that we popularized.

You're not flattered?

I guess I'm happy that my aesthetic is popular right now, but not when it means that the floodgates open and everyone does it. Then what am I supposed to do, feel played out? Then again, I guess it forces you out of your little comfort zone and makes you step on the gas and get some stuff going to leave them in the dust.

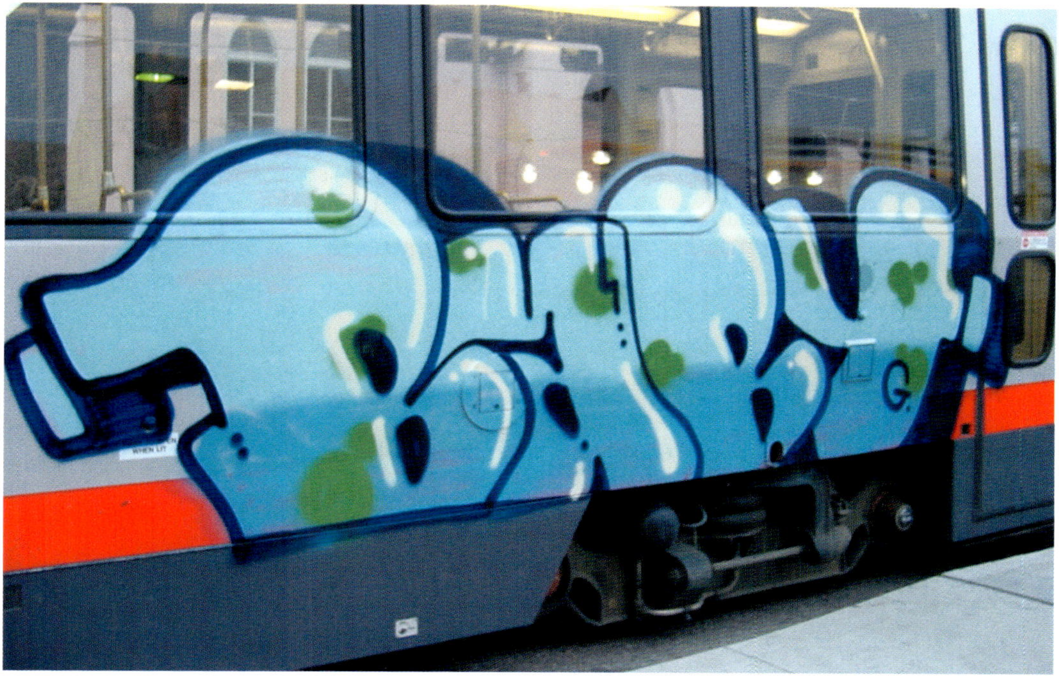

What's the most innovative thing happening in graff right now?

I would have to say that most of the innovations that I really like are more tactical advancements. Like the militant approach that writers have taken. In Denmark, Sweden, etc., the writers have really taken a really forceful and well planned strategy to graffiti, especially on trains. Most of the style innovations are just new takes on existing styles. I am not the least bit into this really intricate type of graffiti that looks like airbrushing; to me, that is regression, not innovative, even though it is new. Cost and Revs were the ones kind of pioneering the campaign approach to graffiti, but that was the early '90s. They were adapting advertising tactics rather than just doing straight graffiti pieces. To be honest, graffiti probably never will gain the attention of the public to the point where the average person differentiates one piece of graffiti from the next. As a whole, it gets attention, but individuals don't. But when you take someone like Cost, or Revs, or Shepard Fairey, they do [get outside attention]. When you deviate enough from classic graffiti, people are forced to look [and] acknowledge it.

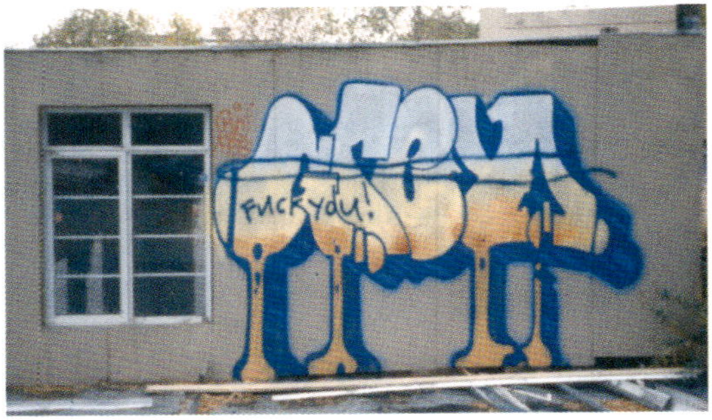

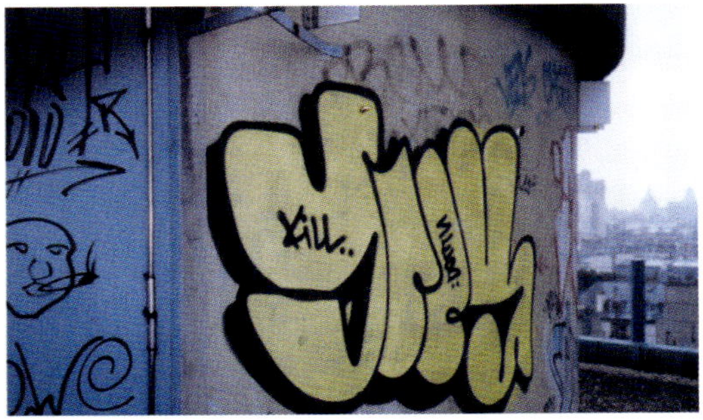

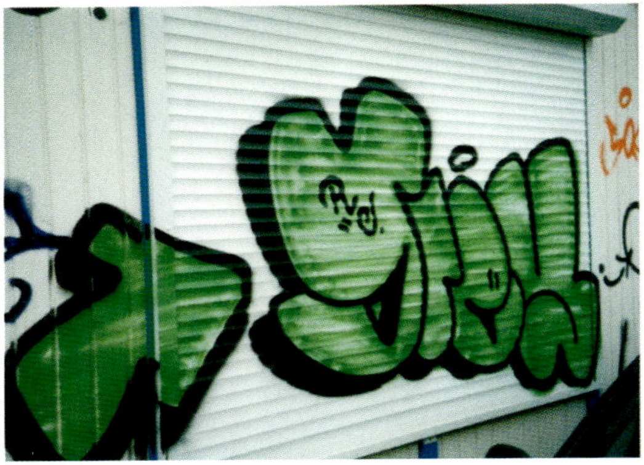

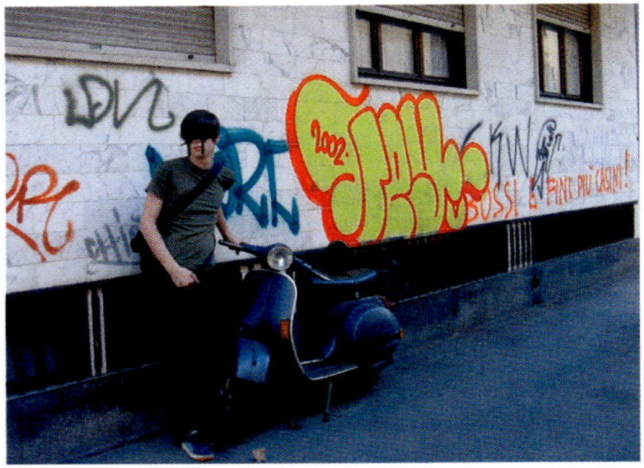

How concerned are you with people outside of graff paying attention to what you do?

I'm not all that concerned, but when I see fraudulent writers being in the spotlight and getting a lot of exposure, that's when it starts to irritate me. When [writers] were out of the media and out of magazines, that wasn't anything I even considered. [The graff culture was] completely self-sufficient; all the credit came from within the scene. When I open up pop culture magazines now and see interviews with writers that ain't doing shit and never done shit, I'm not having it. That makes me think that the real writers should step forward and start getting that kind of attention. That's not the motivation to actually paint, because [the media attention] didn't exist until at least a good seven years into my graff.

Do you think graffiti is renewing the urban space, or destroying it?

It is destructive, but it is an indirect response to the mass public destruction that ads have caused. If you trace graffiti as an urban phenomenon, it really started pretty closely after mass marketing and ad campaigns were introduced. The psychological impact that ads have had on people is largely responsible for the individual's desire for public attention and presence. Graff is really the individual approach to an advertising campaign. It's like advertising, but there's really no product. The person is the product. I don't consider it destructive, because graffiti does not do any structural damage at all. It's just paint.

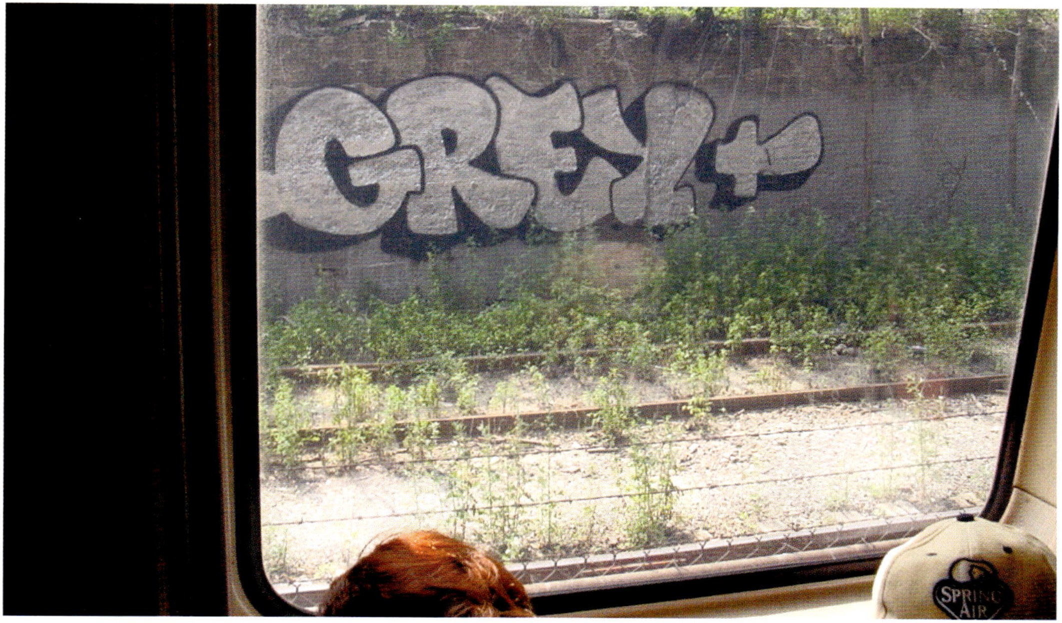

Are you still into the illegal aspects?

That's the whole drive. If it's not illegal, I just don't understand the point of doing it. Something like design is cool because doing it legally, as an occupation, is the nature of the art. With graff, people try to turn it into an occupation, and they end up losing all their integrity as a writer and having very little monetary gain. I don't know too many people that are making any sort of living off graffiti, but I know a lot of people that are trying their hardest. And plus, I am into crime—all kinds, but mainly stealing and graffiti. Without theft, there's no way I could have done so much graff all those years. And at times, shoplifting was more of a lifestyle than the graff.

What's your favorite thing to do that isn't illegal?

Geez. [Long pause.] Well, music is still legal, I think. [Laughs.] Unless it's repetitive dance music, in which case it's illegal. Almost everything I've been naturally drawn to has been illegal. Before I wrote, I skated for ten or twelve years. By the time I had started writing, I had already dealt with police so many times 'cause of skating. I was immune to [the law] before I even started doing something illegal. I really like music and I really like going to shows and clubs. More and more, that gets busted too. When I was more into punk and indie rock, every show would get busted. And then I get into electronic music, and unless it's in a club, it gets busted too. Sometimes it seems like anything fun and modern is criminalized in one way or another.

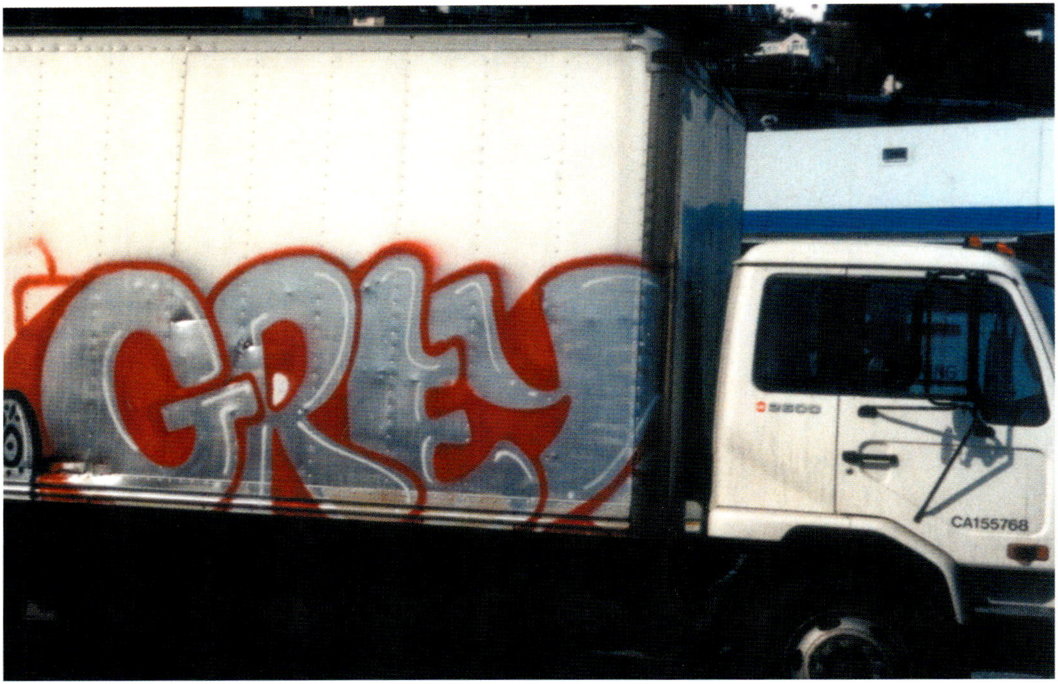

What new tools or mediums do you think are influencing graff right now, or do you particularly like?

That's another thing that keeps people going—the invention of new tools to write with. Stuff like etch and mops created whole new styles. I like how, in Amsterdam, they mix brake fluid with their ink because it penetrates the plastic interior of the subway and stains it for good. I love things where people just adapted and figured out how to outdo the people that were opposing them. There's this one kind of pigment that they use in France that makes your ink really toxic. There's a little tiny gram of it in this bag. It looks like you're buying some kind of drug and it's just for damage. I love it.

Why is travel such an obsession for you?

I just start having a panic. This dates back to high school, when I would just get this urge to go away and I had to do it. It didn't necessarily matter where. I'm not sure exactly what I was looking to find, but I just wanted to keep looking for something. I'm still that way. I've never had too many prescribed intentions with what I'm doing. I just do stuff, and I try not to question it too much. When people start to get too many prescribed motivations for their actions, they're trying too hard, and it doesn't work.

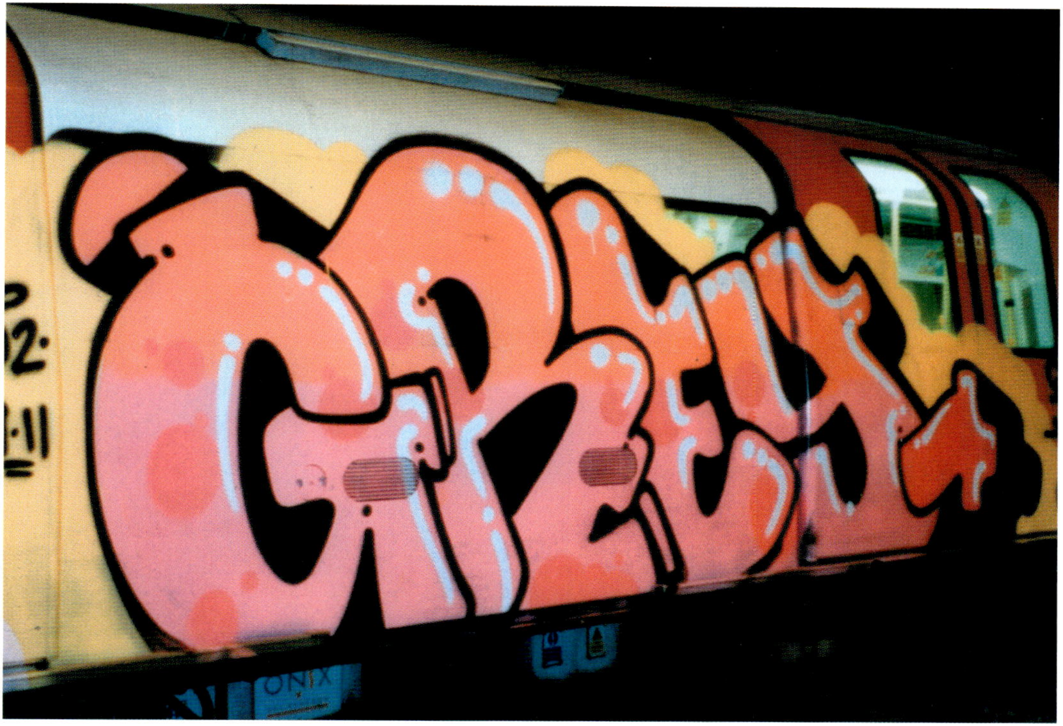

So how do you feel when you look back on your graff career?

I try not to be too nostalgic. I like to live in the present. I've had the opportunity to work with a lot of the world's best writers. I've shared houses with famous writers, just racking all day and having so many crazy times. Every few years, graffiti completely changes for me. I get all-new partners and focus on new missions. I've dealt with very many scary situations; I've seen friends pass away doing this. It all adds up. Graffiti has been so many different things to me by now.

I hope to keep having more experiences and taking my work more places. But, like everything in my life, the process of graffiti has turned out to be the goal. I used to expect a pot of gold at the end of this. I realized about halfway into my career that this doesn't ever end. The only things I will be left with are memories, scars, friends, and enemies. But something has obviously driven me to keep going.

THE MEANING

ALL-CITY: To go all-out; to have saturated the city with your name.

BITE: To copy another writer's style. This is plagiarism, but with different consequences—usually ridicule and a sound thrashing.

BLOCKBUSTER: Huge block letters that take up as much space as possible. Often, the purpose is to cover other writers' throwups and tags.

BOMB: Painting or marking with ink. To cover an area with your tag, throwups, etc.

BOMBING: To go out writing graffiti.

BUBBLE LETTERS: Often used for throwups. They are bubbly, balloonish letters developed in the 1970s.

BURNER: A simple piece that burns whatever else is on the wall. It's more elaborate than a throwup and has a few more colors.

CRACK FILL: A throwup that intentionally hasn't been properly filled in. This is often used as a dis, because what's underneath remains visible.

E TO E: A train painted from one end to the other (end to end).

FILL-IN: A throwup with a filled-in center.

FLICKS: Pictures.

GETTING UP: Getting your name up; also the action of going out and tagging.

GOING OVER: Crossing out someone else's work with your own. The idea is to do something better in order to burn the other person off the wall.

INSIDES: Tags executed inside a subway car.

KING: The highest compliment you can receive in graffiti.

MAD: Crazy; lots.

RACK: To steal.

TAG: A writer's signature.

THROWUP: Your name in big (often bubble) letters, executed in between twenty-five seconds and three minutes, depending on whether it's filled in or not. Originally used to cover space and other writers' work.

TOY: An inexperienced writer. Like a poser in the skateboard world.

UP: A writer who is active and has a noticeable amount of "work" around town.

WINDOW-DOWN: A piece done below the windows of a subway car.

WHOLE CAR: A train car painted end-to-end, top-to-bottom.

WRITER: Someone who does graffiti.

ABOUT US

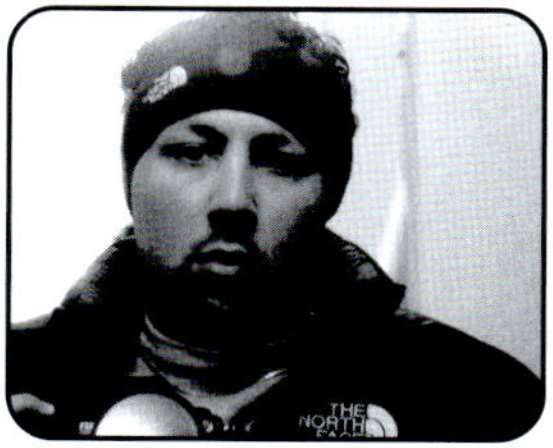

Paul 107 is damage control. A sought-after photographer, he is also the Editor-in-Chief of *Pound* and *Under Pressure* magazines. He manages a record label, Audio Research, and has handled marketing and promotion for world-class DJ equipment companies. He is the founder of Sekondhand Projects, an organization that raises funds and awareness, creates products, and exposes talent. Future plans include making film and another book, then it's off to locksmith school.

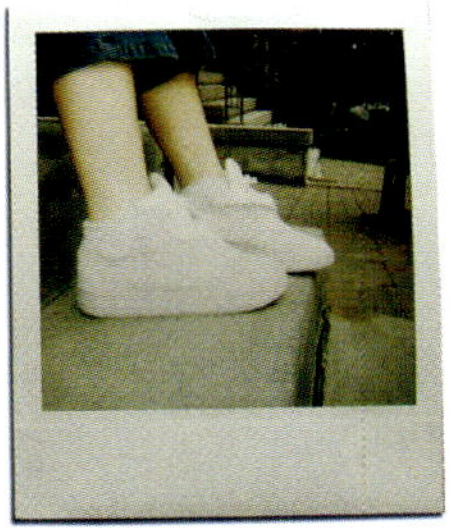

Emma Jane grew up in Vancouver and moved to Montreal to get degreed in letters. She hasn't left yet. Senior Editor at *Under Pressure* magazine, she also edits and writes for some other magazines, and currently works in publishing. She's the Sekondhand Projects starting quaterback. As a kid, she wanted to be the next Shakespeare. She hopes to travel the world one day so she can write all over the place.

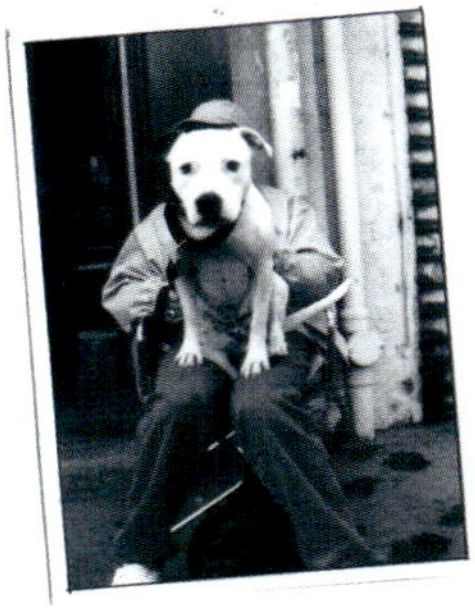

Turf One started doing graffiti in Paris in '88-'89. He now lives in Montreal. He's an illustrator, graphic designer, painter and comic book artist, and he can draw better than you. He has worked for such illustrious clients as Universal Music, *Radikal* magazine, and *Pound* magazine. He's a core member of the Sekondhand Projects gang.

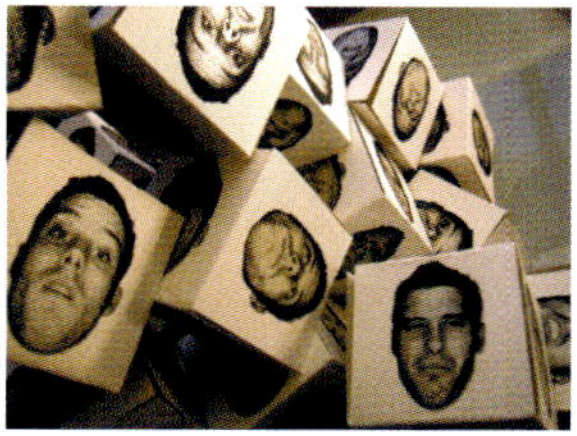

Dyske is a washed-up pro snowboarder, graffiti writer, and designer from Montreal. He's the art director for *Under Pressure* magazine. He likes poutine and draft beer. He also enjoys long walks on the beach at sunset and girls with long mullets.

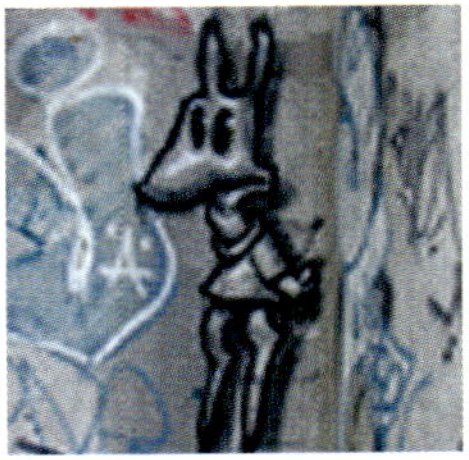
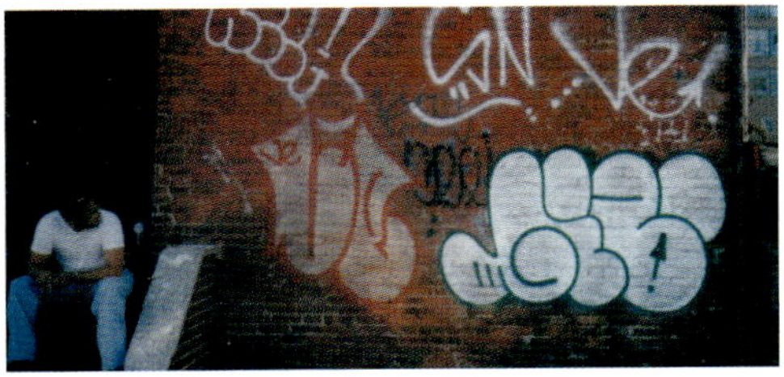
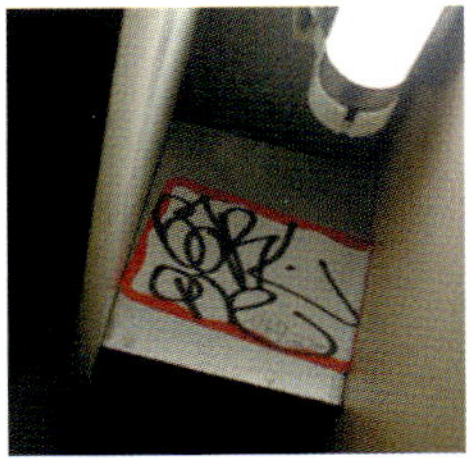
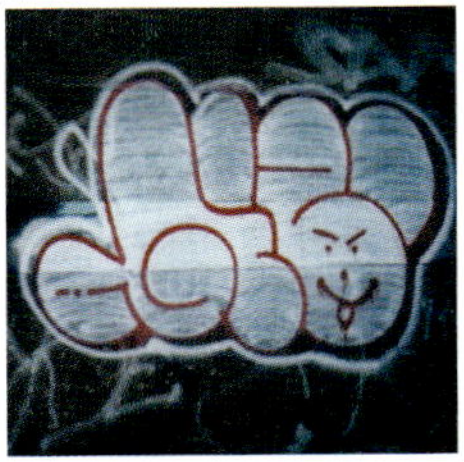
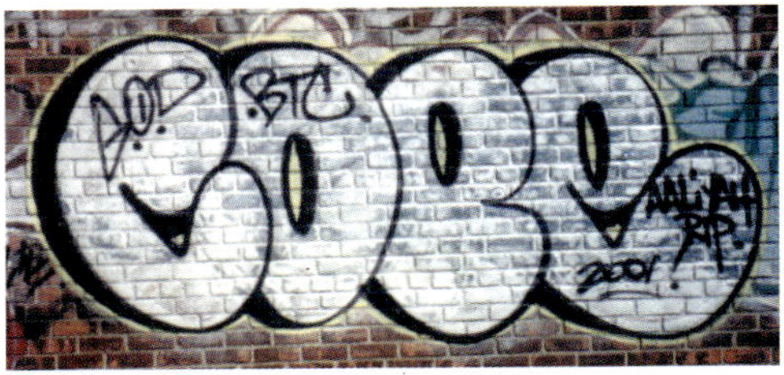
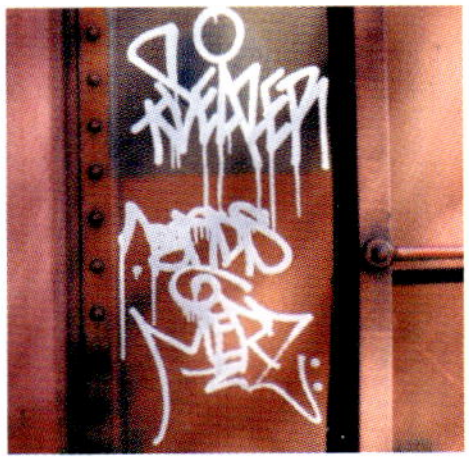
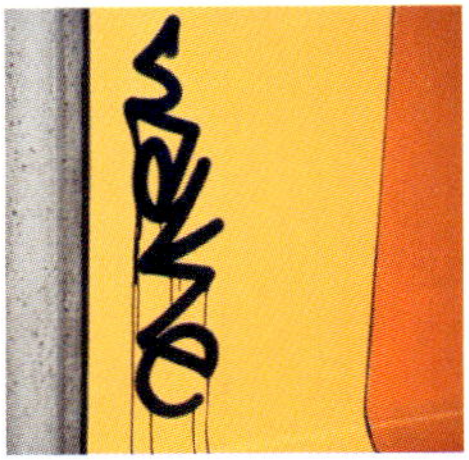
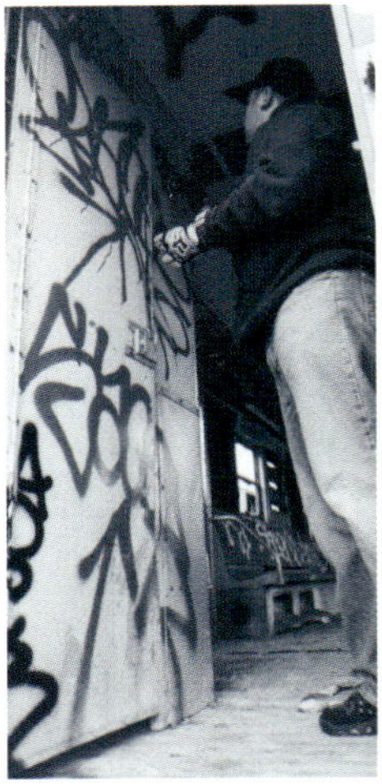
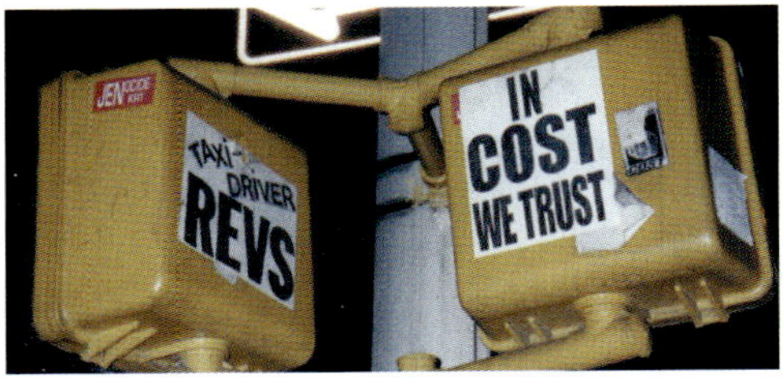
TAXI DRIVER
REVS
IN COST WE TRUST
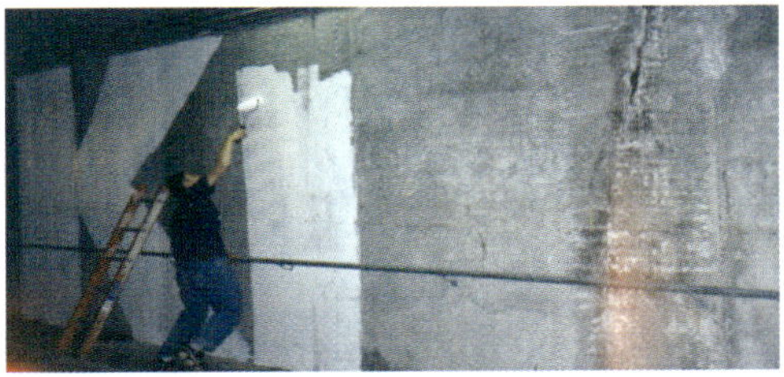
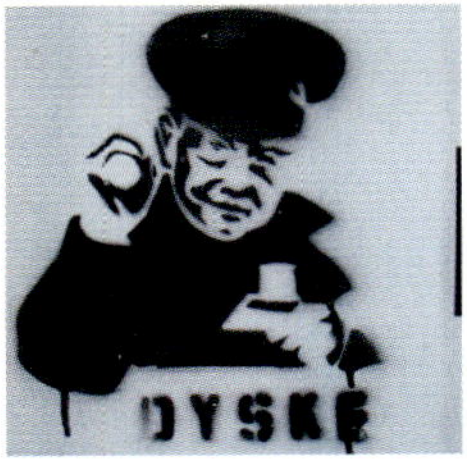
DYSKE
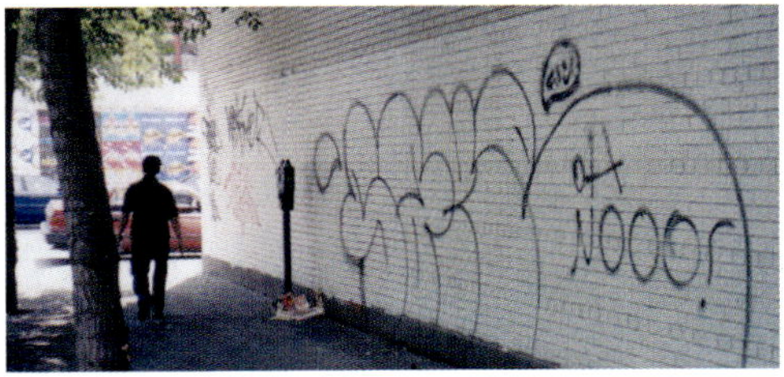
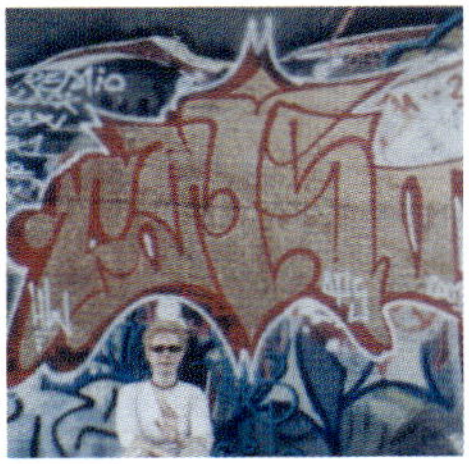
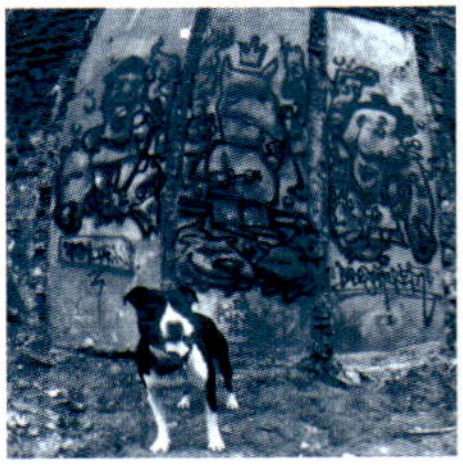
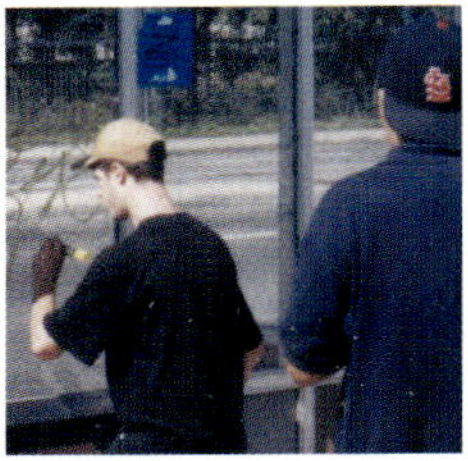
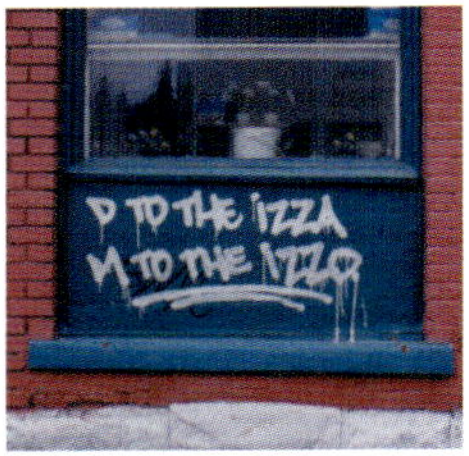
P TO THE IZZA
M TO THE IZZO
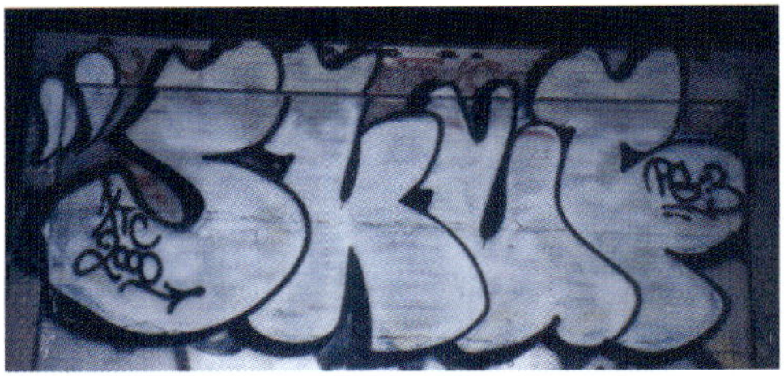
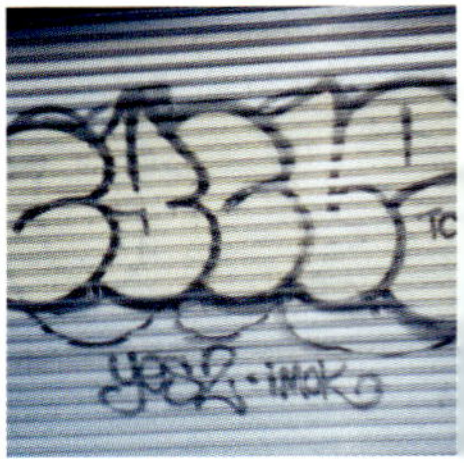